T0346322

Praise for *Fixing American Cybersecurity*

"Economic incentives are one of the most powerful forces. *Fixing American Cybersecurity* brings this often-overlooked economic perspective to the fore to enable better management of cyber threats, risks, and programs. Building starfish-style networks to enhance deterrence and resilience is also covered in the collaboration sections." —**Rod Beckstrom**, first director of the US National Cybersecurity Center; former president and CEO, ICANN; and coauthor of *The Starfish and the Spider*

"Larry Clinton's timely and important book should be required reading for anyone seeking to learn how the United States can modernize its governance structure to favor innovative, risk-based approaches to protecting our data, networks, and devices."—**Matthew J. Eggers**, vice president for cybersecurity policy in the Cyber, Intelligence, and Security Division at the US Chamber of Commerce

"Rethinking cybersecurity requires reframing the cybersecurity challenge as a strategic imperative for both government and business. Larry Clinton and the Internet Security Alliance are the right people to lead that change, balancing opportunity and risk in digital transformation."—**Bob Kolasky**, senior vice president for critical infrastructure, Exiger, and former director, US Cybersecurity and Infrastructure Agency's National Risk Management Center

"Winston Churchill famously observed, 'You can always count on the Americans to do the right thing, after they have exhausted all the other possibilities.' Unfortunately, in cybersecurity we have followed this mantra, exhausting ourselves in a disjointed pursuit of what amounts to 'other possibilities.' This book maps a path for progress to a strategy that unifies industry and government efforts, accentuates and expands our collective capabilities, and leverages weaknesses of our adversaries—which they certainly do have—to enable us 'to do the right thing' and to do it well."—**Thomas Farmer**, assistant vice president of security, Association of American Railroads; former chair, US Critical Infrastructure Cross Sector Council; and chair of the Surface Transportation Security Advisory Committee

FIXING AMERICAN CYBERSECURITY

FIXING

AMERICAN

CYBERSECURITY

Creating a Strategic

Public-Private

Partnership

Larry Clinton, Editor
Foreword by Kiersten Todt

GEORGETOWN UNIVERSITY PRESS / WASHINGTON, DC

Library of Congress Cataloging-in-Publication Data

Names: Clinton, Larry, 1951– editor, author. | Todt, Kiersten, writer of foreword.
Title: Fixing American cybersecurity : creating a strategic public-private partnership / edited by Larry Clinton ; foreword by Kiersten Todt.
Description: Washington, DC : Georgetown University Press, 2023. | Includes index.
Identifiers: LCCN 2021005285 | ISBN 9781647121495 (hardcover) | ISBN 9781647121501 (paperback) | ISBN 9781647121518 (ebook)
Subjects: LCSH: Computer security—Government policy—United States. | Computer security—United States. | Data protection. | Cyberspace—Security measures—United States. | Internet—Security measures—United States. | Hacking—United States—Prevention. | Computer crimes—United States—Prevention. | Cyberinfrastructure—Security measures—United States.
Classification: LCC TK5105.59 .F595 2023 | DDC 005.80973—dc23
LC record available at https://lccn.loc.gov/2021005285

♾ This paper meets the requirements of ANSI/NISO Z39.48-1992 (Permanence of Paper).

24 23   9 8 7 6 5 4 3 2   First printing

Printed in the United States of America

Cover design by Jeremy John Parker
Interior design by BookComp, Inc.

CONTENTS

FOREWORD

Kiersten Todt

According to the 2020 documentary *The Social Dilemma*, data had outpaced oil as the world's most valuable commodity almost two years earlier. This shift poses two pressing questions: If data is our most valuable commodity, why does it sit on an insecure internet? And why is the United States falling behind in cybersecurity on the global stage?

To answer these urgent questions—and more important, to develop solutions that address not only current cyber threats but also the growing and evolving ones we have yet to identify—it is vital to analyze not just the technological and political dimensions of this complex issue but also its economics. In providing that analysis, the Internet Security Alliance (ISA), in *Fixing American Cybersecurity*, fills a critical strategic gap.

The ISA was founded in 2001 with the mission to combine technology, public policy, and economics to shape thinking for a sustainable system of cybersecurity, recognizing that market forces are integral to that sustainability. ISA's pro-market approach proposes economic incentives, based on the increasing interdependencies of our digital economy, that foster the development of a resilient ecosystem, including evolved thinking on how industry and government must collaborate.

Over the years, I have enjoyed many opportunities to brainstorm, debate, and develop forward-thinking policies with ISA's CEO, Larry Clinton, who has authored and coauthored several of this book's chapters. A globally respected voice, Larry comes to the table with economic arguments and approaches for strong and defensible cyber policy, based on years of experience and expertise. His voice has been and remains an important corrective in discussions that have historically been conducted primarily through the lens of technology.

It is held that America's security infrastructure and the tools we are developing rely primarily on technical solutions. This is wrong. Larry, often alone, has reminded stakeholders of the power and impact of economics in developing sound and secure cyber policy. Larry and the other contributors to this book not only identify today's most urgent vulnerabilities and explain the economics of cyberattacks, systemic risk, and the digital economy's increasing interdependencies; they also rightly argue that economics should drive technology policy, not the other way around.

In 2016, I served as executive director of President Barack Obama's independent, bipartisan Commission on Enhancing National Cybersecurity. Its mission was to build a road map for the incoming administration on securing the digital economy. One of the debates in which the commission engaged was between moving security away from the end user (a technology solution) and educating and engaging that end user and the market (an economic solution). Ultimately, the commission agreed on an approach that reconciled the two approaches. Similarly, we argued that neither the private nor the public sector can effectively address cybersecurity on its own. Effective collaboration between government and industry is an absolute must for improving this nation's cybersecurity posture.

The world is dependent on cyber capabilities to run every part of our economy and our infrastructure, and as the interdependencies of our digital economy grow, the attack surface increases. This integration creates an exponential number of vulnerabilities, highlighted by increased exposure that is far too easy to exploit because of the radical asymmetry between playing offense and playing defense.

We cannot eliminate that asymmetry, but we can do much more to address it, to be strong in both cyber offense and defense. Obviously, there is a lower bar for success on offense. Our expansive networks across the public and private sectors are harder to defend than to exploit, and it is much easier to attack adversaries—especially nation-states—than to protect ourselves from them or non-state attackers. In addition, unlike other domains—land, sea, air, and space—the United States does not own the battle space in cyberspace. This reality adds a layer of complexity to the defense of our infrastructure and emphasizes the need and requirement for effective public-private collaboration.

The global competitive dimension of our cyber vulnerability comes into sharp focus in the authors' in-depth discussion of how China is winning the global race to collect data, by any and all means necessary. If data is the world's most valuable commodity, then the country with the most data "wins." One can rightly assume that the data of most Americans has, in some way, been compromised by the Chinese government and that the Chinese are aggregating and accumulating data at unprecedented rates. China is patient, and while we may not know how it is planning to use this data (recent reporting on the pandemic has asserted the Chinese desire to dominate the global healthcare market, in addition to other sectors), we can expect a dominant role for the Chinese government in the global, digital economy in the future. Meanwhile, the United States has failed to create the kinds of market incentives to accompany technological innovation that would ensure that the security of data is prioritized and does not so easily fall victim to China's practices.

A related cause of our diminishing performance on the world stage is that in the United States "first-to-market" almost always trumps "secure-to-market." The authors of this book discuss the lack of economic and market incentives to create secure products. Recently, millions of customers were asking how to protect themselves after the breach of a large commercial company. The challenge is that they were asking the wrong question and inquiring about action at the wrong time. If consumers were incentivized to prioritize security and shop for products and services accordingly, companies would be incentivized to do the same: to prioritize security in the development and distribution of products and services.

The US approach to innovation and capitalism was captured by the Pulitzer Prize–winning author Richard Powers in his novel *The Overstory*: "Money you lose by slowing down is always more important than money you've already made."[1] Or, as Joel Wallenstrom, CEO of the cybersecurity leader Wickr, explains:

> Speed sells, and security may slow down market expansion. Taking a risk-based approach convinces technology companies to invest in legal, incident response and public relations to mitigate the damage of breaches, rather than engineer products that are secure.... It's a well-worn strategy and one that ensures technology is built to perform at the expense of security.... Vulnerable software is inevitable given the current market forces and shifting trust models.[2]

As this book argues, market forces cannot be ignored in building a secure economy, but not all market forces are created equal, and market structure matters. Currently, neither market incentives nor existing legal requirements ensure that cybercriminals will suffer from the consequences of their crimes. Building insecure products to get to market first and reacting when flaws emerge is not a sustainable system. Return on investment at all costs, sacrificing privacy and, most important, security, will only continue to weaken our nation's cybersecurity posture. Ultimately, security needs to be seen not as an impediment to innovation and market success but as a necessary ingredient of a resilient, secure cyber ecosystem. Indeed, appropriate, effective economic incentives will drive technological incentives.

This book effectively uses the experiences of infrastructure sectors to highlight some of the key challenges confronting this growing and evolving systemic risk but also as a means for understanding where solutions lie, including how we define critical infrastructure. The United States must examine this definition and rethink what should be identified as such. For example, social media and cloud service providers, which have an impact on the public and economic security of our nation, should certainly be identified as critical infrastructure. One of the authors' key arguments is the need to engage these technology infrastructure companies in our national cybersecurity strategy and approach. Their impact—and their responsibilities—go far beyond commerce.

Further, the authors discuss the growing challenges of supply chain security and the need among small and medium-sized businesses to have greater cybersecurity support. As long as small businesses are vulnerable, our ecosystem is vulnerable. Throughout our economy, we need to create cultures of cybersecurity, in which all employees—of companies with 20, 200, 2,000, 20,000, or 200,000 employees—understand their responsibility for cybersecurity.

Managing systemic risk is a key priority for our nation. The increasing interdependencies across all sectors—those that are identified as critical and those that are not—mean that solutions must lie in government and industry working together, before an event occurs. This collaboration must go beyond noncontextualized information sharing to sharing actionable intelligence and engaging a whole-of-government approach to prevention, preparation, response, and recovery. We must create economic incentives for investing in security, an area in which the insurance industry can play a positive role.

Both technology and market forces are necessary for a secure and prosperous economy and society, but they are not sufficient. Effectiveness and success are grounded in culture, and creating cultures of cyber readiness depends on human behavior, which is both the chief vulnerability and the strongest potential weapon of enterprise security. In my previous role as managing director of the Cyber Readiness Institute, I saw the positive impact changes in behavior can have on the cybersecurity of any business. An educated and informed workforce can be a force multiplier for security. The government can play a role here, too, by creating incentives, especially for small businesses in global supply chains, to invest in cybersecurity.

Together, business, government, technology, and culture create a healthy and sustainable society. Growth, innovation, adaptation, and security are properties of any enduring complex system. In addition to their thorough and insightful analysis of the key issues affecting the weakened cybersecurity posture of the United States, the authors of this book teach us that the way forward lies in taking a systems-thinking approach—abandoning fantasies of purity and building resilient systems through engagement, trust, and accountability.

As is often the case with the Internet Security Alliance, this book identifies the key issues that have an impact on our nation's ability to succeed in cyber-security and offers a strong, actionable approach to industry-government collaboration. The threats facing the United States and the world are serious, and we have to move beyond merely discussing them. We need bold action to ensure that the United States leads the world in building a resilient, com-plex, and secure ecosystem, grounded in economic incentives and practices, and creating cultures of both innovation and responsible stewardship.

INTRODUCTION

Larry Clinton

Any examination of United States cybersecurity policy must begin with one simple and immutable fact. We are losing the fight to secure cyberspace, and we are losing it badly. Even though the administrations of both US political parties and the vast majority of private sector entities list cybersecurity as one of their top priorities (and billions of dollars have been spent to enhance cybersecurity in the past two decades), our cybersecurity system is weak and getting weaker.[1]

As the authors finished writing this book in early 2022, the United States had recently experienced some of the most extensive and sophisticated cyberattacks in its history. In 2020, multiple, presumably secure, federal agencies, including the Department of Homeland Security (DHS) and the National Security Agency (NSA), as well as thousands of other organizations, were compromised in a sophisticated, nation-state cyberattack that has come to be known as SolarWinds. As of this writing, the full extent of the harm from this attack is still unknown—and may not be known for years. What is known is that the attack was extremely broad and invasive. According to Anne Neuberger, deputy national security adviser for Cyber and Emerging Technology at the White House, the attack affected nine federal agencies and one hundred private sector companies (as of the White House press briefing).[2] We also know that the federal agencies compromised not only were unable to prevent the attack, but were unaware of the attack until a private firm reported it many months after it was initiated.[3] Later that year, a similarly systemic attack was launched from China against Microsoft email servers, which, according to the *New York Times*, "are used by many of the world's largest companies, governments and military contractors."[4] In characterizing that attack, U.S. secretary of state Anthony J. Blinken told the *Times* that the Chinese government has "fostered an eco-system of criminal contract hackers who carry out both state sponsored activities and cybercrime for their own economic benefit."[5]

A somewhat different but similarly troublesome strain of cyberattacks—ransomware, whereby attackers freeze the digital assets of a target entity—has also vastly increased in number and severity. For example, in May 2021 the Colonial Pipeline was hacked in a ransomware attack that led to panic buying of gasoline in the southeastern United States, illustrating not only the vulnerability of our energy infrastructure but also the shared responsibility of the public and private sectors to safeguard the energy systems.[6] Verizon's 2021 "Data Breach Investigations Report" found that ransomware attacks doubled in frequency in 2021.[7] Approximately 37 percent of global organizations were victims of some sort of ransomware attack in 2021, according to the International Data Corporation's (IDC's) 2021 ransomware study,[8] and the FBI reported a 62 percent increase in ransomware complaints in the first half of 2021.[9]

In response to the SolarWinds attack, the Biden administration announced sweeping sanctions against Russia in April 2021.[10] However, the expectation from both industry and government was that, as with similar sanctions in the past, these actions would have little deterrent effect and more strenuous action would be needed. Kevin Mandia, CEO of FireEye (the private company that discovered the breach and informed the federal government) said, "Simply naming the SVR [Russia's foreign intelligence service], as well as the corporations that support it, [is] unlikely to fully deter cyber espionage and we will have to take serious action to better defend ourselves from inevitable future intrusions."[11]

Rep. Jim Himes (D-CT), who sits on the House Permanent Select Committee on Intelligence, was more blunt: "The imposition of sanctions alone in the face of sustained cyberattacks is not enough to deter our foes. We know this because the Obama administration also imposed sanctions on the Russians in 2016 with little effect."[12]

The response to the Microsoft server attack from China was even more muted. Although the Biden administration pulled together a coalition of allies that included the European Union and, for the first time, all the NATO members to jointly condemn the attacks, according to press reports the coalition "stopped short of punishing China highlighting the challenges of confronting a nation with deep economic ties around the world . . . and no sanctions were announced," in contrast to the response to the Russian-based SolarWinds attack.

These sophisticated SolarWinds and Microsoft server attacks did not target a specific entity directly, as was the case in many previous noteworthy attacks, such as the ones on Target, Sony, Equifax, the United States Office of Personnel Management, and the Colonial Pipeline. Rather, these systemic attacks compromised thousands of organizations that used the core software.

The uniqueness of this style of attack, which focused less on specific entities and more on the cyber system itself, is discussed in greater detail in chapter 3 on systemic risk. However, the bottom line is that after decades of cyber awareness programs, thousands of news stories, and billions of dollars spent to increase our cybersecurity, some of our most vital systems can be compromised for months without the government or sophisticated tech industries even knowing it is happening.

The impact of the weak security of the world's cyber systems is difficult to calculate precisely. However, it is undeniable that the impact is dramatic in terms of costs to the global economy, society, and international security. While Americans cannot do much about the cybersecurity of other nations without their cooperation (discussed in later chapters), the United States can do something about fixing its own vulnerable cyber systems. The time has come not merely to update US cybersecurity strategy, but for fundamental reconsideration of what the problem is, what our major adversaries are up to, and what we need to do to begin to address these threats on a sustainable basis. The United States needs to rethink its strategy, its structures, and its policies for the digital age.

In November 2020, the authors of this book, the Internet Security Alliance, created a social media campaign called #RethinkCybersecurity. One of the main themes of this campaign was that the defender community—government and industry—needs to adopt a broader understanding of the cybersecurity issue and forge a new "social contract" to create a sustainably secure cyber system. In addition, the traditional approach, which conceives of cybersecurity primarily as a technical operational issue, needs to be broadened; and cybersecurity needs to be understood as a strategic issue that focuses on the economic causes for the attacks as much as the technical vulnerabilities of the system. This reconsideration would also focus more on the aggressive and sophisticated strategies of our adversaries and the systemic risks we face, in addition to those of specific entities.

As of this writing over twenty-seven thousand cybersecurity operators, academics, thought leaders, and policy makers from around the country have signed up for this campaign. The idea of rethinking the whole approach to cybersecurity seems to have caught on. When President Biden's nominee to head the DHS, Alejandro Mayorkas, first met with the House Homeland Security Committee in March 2021, the new chair of the Subcommittee on Cybersecurity and Infrastructure Protection, Yvette Clarke, told him we need to "rethink" our approach to cybersecurity.[13] The following week the acting director of DHS's lead cyber agency, the Cybersecurity and Infrastructure Security Agency (CISA), Brandon Wales, was called before the Senate Homeland Security Committee to discuss CISA's response to the Solar-Winds attack. He, too, testified that we need to "rethink" cybersecurity.[14]

When the Senate Committee held a hearing in May 2021 on the escalating ransomware cyberattacks, the chair of the committee opened the hearing by saying we need to "rethink" the cyber wars we are now fighting. On May 10, 2021, the cochairs of the Bipartisan Cyberspace Solarium Commission, Sen. Angus King (I-ME) and Rep. Mike Rogers (R-WI), issued a statement calling for the development of a new cybersecurity "social contract."[15]

On May 11, 2021, a bipartisan group of members of Congress comprising the chairs and ranking members of the House Homeland Security Committee, the Committee on Transportation and Infrastructure, the Subcommittee on Cybersecurity, the Subcommittee on Railroads, Pipelines and Hazardous Materials, the Subcommittee on Transportation and Maritime Security, and the Subcommittee on Intelligence and Counter Terrorism wrote a joint letter to the president's national security adviser, Jake Sullivan. The letter stressed "that cybersecurity is no longer just an 'IT' issue but instead an economic and national security challenge that can have real-world impacts on our security."[16]

The following day, President Biden issued his first executive order on cybersecurity. In releasing the order, the administration said, "Today's executive order makes a down-payment towards modernizing our cyber defenses and safeguarding many of the services on which we rely. It reflects a fundamental shift in our mindset from incident response to prevention, from talking about security to doing security."[17]

Rethinking cybersecurity is also gaining traction globally. In April 2021, Europe's most prominent cybersecurity conference, the Munich Cybersecurity Conference, chose as its theme, "Rethinking Cyber (Insecurity)."[18]

While the broad notion of rethinking the approach to cybersecurity has shown some resonance, this must be accompanied by specifics in terms of what a reimagined social contract would look like and what specific policies would emanate from this reconsideration. This book is an attempt to do just that. It attempts to sketch what a freshly conceived US policy for cybersecurity ought to look like. The chapters address questions such as the following:

- Has the United States effectively framed the issues giving rise to its cybersecurity problems to address not only how to fix them but also why they exist and persist?
- How does the US conceptualization of digital security compare with that of its adversaries, and are there lessons to be learned from how these adversaries conduct their own cybersecurity strategies?
- Why are current US tactics to enhance the nation's cybersecurity proving to be inadequate?
- How should the focus of US cybersecurity efforts change?

- Are there new structures needed to implement and institutionalize a more effective approach to cybersecurity?
- Are there models for how such new structures ought to be managed?
- What are the appropriate roles for government and the private sector in this rethought paradigm?
- What cybersecurity challenges do the operators of critical infrastructure face, and how might these be addressed?
- How much will this new approach cost? How will it be financed? And is it worth the expense?

In short, this volume intends to go beyond what cyber practitioners often refer to as "admiring the problem" and move toward defining an approach that will integrate advanced technology with economics and public policy in the hope of creating a sustainable system of cybersecurity.

However, the authors are not so bold as to suggest that we have the ultimate answer to cybersecurity. Indeed, we doubt there is such a thing. Fixing cybersecurity will be an ongoing challenge for the foreseeable future. Although cybersecurity may never be "fixed" once and for all due to the ever-evolving nature of cyberattacks, which are often one step ahead, the ISA does believe that it can be managed far better.

To that end, this volume brings together a unique group of cybersecurity experts, a group of individuals whose day job—and night job—is to defend cyber systems from attacks by criminals and nation-states and others. Over the course of twenty years this group, organized as the board of directors for the Internet Security Alliance, has worked together and in conjunction with a wide range of government and industry partners to develop a different, more coherent, and, we hope, more effective approach to cybersecurity.

This analysis leads to the conclusion that the US government needs to increase the priority it places on cybersecurity. The United States needs to develop a digital transformation strategy like those its adversaries, and many leading businesses, have developed. The government needs to restructure the way it considers digital issues, appreciating the economic and geopolitical aspects of cybersecurity as much as the technical operational aspects. It needs to modernize how it partners with industry. And yes, it needs to spend more money on cybersecurity.

This book covers each of these areas in turn, starting with a broad analysis of the status quo and explaining why the current US posture is proving to be ineffective. Chapter 1 illustrates how US policy makers have heretofore conceived of cybersecurity in an excessively narrow context, as a primarily technical and operational issue. Although there are obviously important technical and operational aspects to the cybersecurity issue, the problem is far broader. The primary causes of the massive and growing cybersecurity problem are not technical vulnerability (although the system is vulnerable) but rather the economics of the digital age, which provide attackers with massive incentives, including low cost of entry, high profit margins, and relative safety from law enforcement.

The United States needs to place a far higher priority, not only on cybersecurity, but also on agility, the ability to react to—and anticipate—the rapid evolution of the digital world. The United States will need to move on from its traditional narrow operational approach to cyber issues and develop fuller strategic thinking about these issues. There will also need to be structural reforms to assure that the digital strategies will be implemented, evaluated, and agile enough to be adjusted in the ever more dynamic digital world.

In assessing if the current US cybersecurity strategy is adequate to the security challenges of the digital age, the benchmark ought not to be previous US policy but rather the efforts of our adversaries. Chapter 2 takes an in-depth look at China, which has taken a far more comprehensive, strategic, and integrated approach to cyber issues, capitalizing on the infirmities of Western digital systems to stimulate its own economy and then building on that digital platform to enhance its military and geopolitical position in the world. To be truly competitive with adversaries like China, the United States will need to develop an approach similar in thoughtfulness and sophistication but based on traditional Western democratic and capitalist principles.

Chapter 3 describes the evolution of the cyber threat analysis, which has moved from its traditional focus on risk to specific entities to now include larger systemic risks exemplified by the Russian SolarWinds attack and China's attack on the Microsoft servers. The chapter illustrates how attacks such as SolarWinds, and its forerunners like WannaCry and Not-Petya, will become increasingly common and dangerous. It also demonstrates that traditional cybersecurity policy is inadequate to address these systemic risks and offers a direction for additional questions that must be answered to address these serious and growing threats.

Chapter 4 provides a detailed analysis of how and why current policies are not adequate to address modern cyber risk. At its core, US policy on cybersecurity has not fundamentally changed for over thirty years. Twentieth-century models like traditional regulation and law enforcement are ill-suited to the dynamism and international dimensions of modern cyberattacks. Even when bolstered with tactical adaptations like information sharing and rudimentary industry partnerships, these methods are not accomplishing the goal of creating a sustainably secure cyber system.

In Chapter 5, the ISA proposes a new collaborative structure, the Office of Digital Security Strategy (ODSS), to guide implementation of a more collaborative and strategically derived digital strategy that includes cybersecurity but is a comprehensive response to the digital world. A principal feature of this approach to government would be to adapt many of the modern managerial models that businesses—and some of our most serious adversaries—have already implemented as part of their own digital transformation. These models reject siloed approaches and require collaboration across business units on cybersecurity and digital issues.

Chapter 6 introduces three directives to integrate the economics of the digital age and guide future policy development.

1. The United States needs to devote far greater resources, including financial investment, to address the digital threat.
2. Systematic and continual reevaluation of programs designed to assess and address cyber threats need to be performed by government agencies and private sector organizations.
3. Americans need to modernize the approach to cyber defense by altering how we approach issues such as law enforcement, regulation, and public-private partnership.

Several specific policy proposals are offered to implement these strategies.

In part 2 of the book, a broad range of cyber experts, typically chief information security officers from six designated critical industry sectors—defense, healthcare, financial services, telecommunications, energy, and retail—explain how to apply the strategic principles to the unique digital issues confronting their respective industries. Each of these critical sectors has a different economic structure. As a result, although the broader policy proposals discussed in part 1 will be applicable, unique sector-specific circumstances also will need attention. These chapters discuss a range of these sector-specific issues and proposed policies.

Chapter 7, on healthcare, illustrates that although the sector is highly regulated for cybersecurity, the impact of this regulation is inadequate. Healthcare institutions' ability to appropriately fund needed cybersecurity is impeded by the regulatory structure. The severe and growing cybersecurity issues in healthcare relate in a major way to the outmoded thinking about cybersecurity as an operational "administrative issue" when the cyber systems are a core element of patient care (as probably anyone who has recently spent time in a hospital can attest). This outdated conception has enormous implications for how medical facilities can finance their needed cybersecurity in the face of vastly increasing threats.

Chapter 8, on cybersecurity in the Defense Industrial Base (DIB), provides a history of how the Department of Defense (DoD) has tried to develop a model that integrates the imperatives of national defense with the realities of the companies that develop and provide the mechanisms through which this is accomplished. There are two different "private sectors" DoD needs to deal with: the prime contractors and the tens of thousands of smaller contractors who do not have the resources to meet the same requirements as the big primes, yet, in terms of national defense, must. The chapter concludes by suggesting a pragmatic pathway to close the security gaps that exist between the smaller and larger providers in a fashion that is economically viable and sustainable.

Financial services, discussed in chapter 9, has a reputation as one of the leading sectors for cybersecurity because of its heavy regulation. However, the statistical realities do not generally bear out this assumption. Indeed, research indicates that the current regulatory system, while expensive, may not only not enhance cybersecurity, but might be counterproductive to it.

Chapter 10 explores the highly regulated energy sector, which, despite a history of warnings of cyber catastrophe, has had an admirable cybersecurity record, the cyberattack on the Colonial Pipeline notwithstanding. However, the drive to create a smart grid, with consumer savings and potential environmental benefits, fundamentally alters the traditional economic model for many utilities while simultaneously enhancing the opportunity for cyberattack. The chapter highlights the need to reassess the economics of public utilities to take into account balancing the benefits of digital technology with the emerging cyber threat.

Chapter 11 discusses the retail sector and the immense cyber threat it lives with while curbed by historically small profit margins, particularly among smaller retailers. How to address the increasing security issues in a vastly changing marketplace accelerated by the COVID-19 pandemic is the prime focus of this chapter.

Chapter 12, on telecommunications, demonstrates the immense societal benefits of the investment in network enhancement, which vastly enhanced society's ability to manage commerce and life through the COVID-19 pandemic. The innovation that helped hundreds of millions of individuals live through the pandemic was spurred by providers' corporate growth. Yet regulatory pressures on these networks may well obstruct their ability to innovate. Complicating the sector's challenges is the fact that China largely dominates the worldwide market for 5G services.

Finally, chapter 13 deals with an entirely new set of issues facing prominent platforms such as Apple, Google, Facebook, and Twitter: information technology (IT). In a digital world defined by and dependent on IT, what roles should be played by the major providers? Are they saviors in a global pandemic? Are they the vehicle to undermine democracy worldwide? What are their responsibilities? Are they modern broadcasters subject to liability for their content? Or are they modern common carriers immune from the impacts of the content they carry?

What this book makes clear is that cybersecurity is a far more complicated and difficult issue than has generally been realized. And, as pointed out above, policy makers are only beginning to reconceptualize the subject and search for new approaches.

The winds of change in cybersecurity policy are clearly blowing swiftly. However, fundamental questions remain; for example: What does the president's "reconceptualization" of cybersecurity entail? What new approaches will the "rethinking" about cybersecurity in the House and Senate and at CISA mean? What are the terms of the new cybersecurity social contract that is going to be developed?

Many of the ideas presented in the following chapters are certain to be major considerations in this ongoing reassessment of the issue. Serious students of cybersecurity policy as well as those interested in how the world's new digital environment will be managed should find substantial information that will inform them as to the nuances of the evolving digital world and enable them to participate in its development.

PART ONE

RETHINKING CYBERSECURITY

CHAPTER 1

THE ECONOMICS OF CYBERSECURITY

Advantage Attackers

Larry Clinton

In addressing the G-20's Digital Security Working Group in February 2020, the World Economic Forum's (WEF) cybersecurity head, Troels Oertling, citing research from Cybersecurity Ventures, reported that economic losses from cyberattacks in 2018 were $2 trillion, and the forum estimated the costs would rise to $6 trillion by 2021.[1] Future projections are even more daunting. A study reported in *Cybercrime Magazine* projects cybercrime will grow at a rate of 15 percent a year over the next five years, reaching $10.5 trillion by 2025.[2] This means that on a revenue basis, the cybercriminal "nation" would be large enough to qualify as a member of the G-20, with an economy about the size of Mexico—the tenth largest economy in the world in 2021—and would constitute the world's third largest economy, after the United States and China, by 2025.[3]

The impact of cyberattacks is more than just financial. In 2013, Director of National Intelligence John Brennan testified before Congress that the prospect of cyberattacks was a bigger threat to national security than international terrorism.[4] And in 2017, Director of National Intelligence Dan C. Coats noted in the US intelligence community's annual threat assessment that "cyber threats are already challenging public trust and confidence in global institutions, governance, and norms, while imposing costs on the US and global economies. Cyber threats also pose an increasing risk to public health, safety, and prosperity as cyber technologies are integrated with critical infrastructure in key sectors."[5]

The US intelligence community has confirmed that the Russian government attempted to disrupt the 2016 US presidential election through cyber means and made another attempt in the 2018 midterm elections.[6] Multiple nations have used cyberattacks to engage in massive theft of both money and intellectual property, including but not limited to stealing the designs for some of our most critical military hardware. Neither our military nor our civilian law enforcement efforts seem to offer any real deterrent.

These facts beg the question: Why are we not making more progress on cybersecurity?

One reason for the relative lack of progress in securing cyberspace is that policy makers have not asked the right questions, and it is axiomatic that if you ask the wrong questions, you get the wrong answers. As a result, US policy has not addressed the cybersecurity issue in a truly comprehensive fashion. A consequence of lacking a truly comprehensive approach is that the efforts to address the issue will fall short, as they have.

What Is the Essence of the Cybersecurity Threat?

The great Roman caesar and philosopher Marcus Aurelius wisely counseled, of all things ask, "What is their essence?"[7]

The overwhelming focus of US cybersecurity policy has been vulnerabilities in the operational technology. However, technical exploitation only explains *how* cyberattacks occur. To appreciate the essence of the cybersecurity problem and to begin to effectively manage it, it is also important to know *why* cyberattacks occur.

The "why" of cyberattacks is almost always economic. Most typically, the economic motive is purely financial, although there are other profit motives as well. The 2021 edition of the "Verizon Data Breach Investigations Report" found that more than three-quarters of all cyber breaches are financially motivated, with organized criminal groups behind a majority of the attacks.[8] As subsequent chapters demonstrate, the economic causation of cyberattacks is fairly common in sectors like financial services, retail, and healthcare, while there is a different, bifurcated economics in a sector like defense and still a different economic calculus in a sector like energy.[9] However, even in non-financial attacks (e.g., Russian attempts to disrupt the US electoral system, nation-state theft of national intelligence data, or hacktivist disruption) there is a profit and loss equation that the attacker uses to decide if and how to launch the attack. For example, the Russian attack on the US electoral system was designed to generate a geopolitical profit for the Russians. Understanding this economic equation is critical to properly confronting the attacker. Approaching cybersecurity from this economic perspective is a crucial piece of developing an effective cybersecurity strategy that needs to be integrated into the traditional operational/vulnerability model that has dominated the field while economic analyses have been all but ignored.

Historically, public policy consideration of digital economics has been largely confined to the economic impacts of cyberattacks. While this metric is clearly significant—for example, suggesting the need for the government to vastly increase its spending on cybercrime—it is far from an adequate one. A fuller appreciation of the multiple textures of the economics of the digital age can yield fresh insights into the causes, as opposed to the operations, of the problem and hence a potentially more comprehensive and effective strategy to secure cyberspace.

For example, over the past quarter of a century the bulk of corporate assets has changed from being primarily physical in nature to digital.[10] The digital nature of these economic assets, combined with the vulnerability of the system, has enabled countries like China, North Korea, and Russia to leapfrog generations of economic development by using cyber means to steal Western intellectual property. This illicit technology transfer, often supplemented by government financial stimulus, facilitated the creation of geopolitical tensions unforeseen in the 1970s and 1980s, at the dawn of the digital age.

Another aspect of how economics and digital technology have altered the public policy terrain is that cybercrime techniques have proven to be far more cost-effective from a business perspective than more traditional criminal activities such as drug trafficking.[11] The magnified cost benefits of cybercrime have created a gap between criminal activity and law enforcement resources. This imbalance has greatly disadvantaged law enforcement and resulted in a stunningly low percentage of successful prosecutions for one of the most common and fastest growing segments of criminal activity.

Another novel texture of the cyber-economic paradigm relates to the unplanned role the private sector may assume with respect to traditional national defense. Both government and industry use essentially the same set of cyber systems: ".com" and ".org" are essentially just different spaces on the same digital platforms as ".mil" and ".gov." These are simply domains on the same set of systems. Although government and industry are using the same digital system, they assess cyber risk—and thus fund security—from markedly, and appropriately, different perspectives. The private sector views security primarily on a commercial basis; it is a cost of doing business. The public sector, naturally, views security in economic terms but has many non-economic concerns, such as national defense, and thus has a lower risk tolerance. Further, the government's funding decisions are not constrained by market economics as are the private sector's.

This creates a conundrum when, for example, critical infrastructure is owned and operated by a private sector entity funding its security on a commercial economic model but is attacked by a nation-state using cyber methods. Even a large utility cannot reasonably be expected to defend against a nation-state attack. This would require security spending at a national defense level. Such spending may be considered necessary from a public policy perspective. However, it would almost certainly be unsustainable in the business models under which the private utilities operate—models that have been affirmed by government via a public or state utility commission. Moreover, if the utility diverted its resources to this national defense security spending, it would likely compromise its ability to carry out the services the community depends on. Such noneconomically justified spending would also likely compromise the utility's ability to generate cash from the market, thus undermining its ability to provide its core services on a sustainable level. This conundrum is made even more complicated when one considers the changing economic stress brought on by digitization, including deployment of the smart grid (see chap. 10).

These complex relationships, discussed in more detail in subsequent chapters, belie the notion that a simple operational strategy, such as the one the United States has historically functioned under, will suffice to achieve a sustainably secure cyber system. The size, frequency, and impact of cyber-attacks clearly indicate that the current model does not work. Addressing the stress of technical vulnerabilities and the misaligned economic incentives of the digital economy will demand a more collaborative, integrated, and economically supported strategy than has been developed previously.

Integrating Digital Technology with Digital Economics and Policy

Attempting to design technology policy without factoring in economics is as misguided as attempting to design economic policy without factoring in technology. This is not to say that most cyber systems are not vulnerable. They are. In fact, the entire system, or more precisely, the system of systems we call the internet, is vulnerable. Indeed, the internet was built as an open system. It was not designed with security in mind. Quite the opposite: security was barely considered at all.

President Barack Obama's chief cybersecurity adviser, Michael Daniel, often remarked that in his position he had the opportunity to meet some of the individuals who wrote the core protocols the internet is based on.[12] One of the things Daniel reported learning in these conversations was that the originators had quite modest intentions when creating the internet. Primarily they were just trying to create a system that would enable scientists to share research data. They were not trying to design a system on which the world would eventually operate and depend. In the twenty-first century, of course, virtually everything is digitally based.

Not only is the internet, at its core, vulnerable, but as the system continues to evolve, we are making it more and more technically vulnerable. No one writes code completely from scratch. The common technique is to build on the (vulnerable) systems already in place. As the systems evolve, the available attack surface grows as new vulnerabilities are added on top of old ones. The number of vulnerabilities added to our cyber systems is extremely large. For example, one major service provider reported to the *Wall Street Journal* that in one year it needed to apply 150 million patches to just one of its systems.[13]

But the fact that a system is vulnerable does not mean that it is going to be attacked. Much of our physical critical infrastructure—water systems, the food system,[14] the ground transport system—is extremely vulnerable, yet it is rarely attacked.

Our cyber systems, on the other hand, are under constant attack. In 2018, one internet service provider reported that it received 80 billion malicious scans a day.[15] The cyber systems of state and local governments are in jeopardy as well. In 2018, the City of Atlanta's municipal networks and computer systems were targeted by a ransomware attack that cost the city $2.6 million for recovery.[16] EY's 2019 cybersecurity survey reported that a single attack had compromised 773 million records, and Microsoft has reported it discovers 77,000 instances of malicious code every month.[17] In 2019, there were 15.1 billion personal records stolen, nearly two for every person on the planet.[18] Ransomware attacks—a malware that infects a computer and restricts access to files, threatening permanent destruction unless a ransom is paid—has become the go-to method for cybercriminals. Current projections indicate that there will be a ransomware attack on a business every 11 seconds in 2021, up from once every 40 seconds in 2016.

These cyberattacks have consequences for individuals. In 2019, the American Medical Collection Agency revealed that numerous patient records were exposed to hackers. Quest Diagnostics was one example of the companies affected, with 12 million of its records compromised. In July 2019, Capital One admitted that the personal information of customers, including social security numbers, bank balances and transactions, addresses, and credit scores, were stolen.[19]

Obviously, there is a technical aspect of cybersecurity. But technical vulnerability is not the only reason, and probably not the primary reason, that cyber systems are under constant attack.

The Economics of Cybersecurity Attacks

The reason cyber infrastructure is attacked so much more frequently than other critical infrastructures is that cybercrime (including attacks from nation-states) is so profitable.

The essence of the cybersecurity problem is that we have an inherently vulnerable system housing incredibly valuable data. Although the system is vulnerable, the real problem is not that the technology is bad but that the technology is under attack. If the economics of the cyber issue remain as they are, we will continue to have attackers that attempt to steal, disrupt, or corrupt this valuable data.

Today many, perhaps most, corporations could not compete in the modern economy without adopting digital innovations to enhance their business models. In fact, the digital transformation of the past thirty years accounts for a great deal of the economic growth and prosperity of the postindustrial era. Viewed from that perspective, organizations have little or no choice but to be part of the digitally transformed world and the risks it carries. Eliminating cyber risk is not an option. However, learning how to manage that risk more effectively is an option that needs to be engaged quickly.

Cyber Risk Management: Balancing Economic Risk against Reward

One of the greatest challenges for the modern economy is to figure out how to balance the economic necessity of digital transformation against the risks of large-scale cyber insecurity and its attendant threats to personal data, intellectual property, and national security. Public policies that fail to address the need to retain the economic viability of private organizations in the digital age will impede socially needed growth and innovation and likely also fail from a security perspective.

This balancing act is made even more challenging because the economics of the digital age are not as aligned as we might think. In fact, in many ways digital economics are upside down. In "The Economics of Information Security," Ross Anderson and Tyler Moore point out that "security failure is caused as least as often by bad economic incentives as by bad technological design. Economists have long known that liability should be assigned to the entity that can manage risk. Yet everywhere we look we see online risk allocated poorly. . . . People who connect their machines to risky places do not bear full consequences of their actions."[20]

If we think about it, we all know this. We all know that if someone uses the same password—say, 123456, the most popular password in the United States—and goes to sketchy websites, their credit card is likely going to be hacked. A hacker may run up $100,000 in false claims on their card, but our sketchy citizen only owes $50.[21] The banks pick up the rest of the cost, then charge it back to all of us in higher fees and interest rates. As a result, we good citizens are subsidizing the sloppy cyber risk takers.

The reason more secure products are not developed is because there is very little market value for them. As a result, secure coding is not valued as a profession—and most universities do not teach it—because consumers do not want to pay more for secure devices. As Anderson and Moore write, "Developers are generally not compensated for creating secure products."[22] Rather than build security into systems on the front end, technological innovators—spurred by broader market economics—focus on getting to market quickly and fixing security problems later with updates and patches.[23]

A different example of how seemingly logical assumptions about digital economics do not turn out as expected in the real world has to do with the impact of serious cyber breaches on investor value. One might imagine that whenever a major company like Target or Sony or Equifax suffers a highly publicized breach, the stock price would tumble, and the investors would pay a heavy price. In reality, that is not always, or even typically, the case.

After a high-profile breach, there is typically a short-term negative impact on stock price, but data shows that in the long term the stock not only rebounds, but very often significantly increases.[24] After the Equifax breach in 2017, the company had already recovered 90 percent of its shares the following year and reported record revenue.[25] This might be attributed to the fact that the market sees the company's fundamentals as good, and the bad publicity from the breach created a "buy" opportunity for stockholders. Also, many breaches often receive little attention and therefore have minimal or no impact on stock prices.

The point is not that cyber breaches are good for stock prices but that many of the assumptions we make about economics in the digital age are simply not borne out by the facts. The digital age has changed many things, including conceptions about privacy, the fundamentals of national defense in an era of asymmetric war, and certainly economics. The role of economics in developing cybersecurity policy needs to be carefully and systematically studied, and policy needs to be based on economic realities, not assumptions.

Enterprises have been quick to build the benefits of the digital age into their business plans whether by expanding markets globally, reducing operating costs, establishing new strategic partnerships, or enhancing the worker experience by enabling business through mobile and remote locations and many other innovations. However, organizations have been far slower to appreciate the downside of the digital revolution: while digital transformation stimulates growth and profitability, it also undermines security, and this insecurity can put personal consumer data, corporate intellectual property, and even critical services and our collective security at risk.

In fact, virtually all the technological innovations and modern tech-based business practices that drive increased growth and profitability also undermine security. Voice-over internet protocol, cloud computing, and Internet of Things all drive economic benefits. Long international supply chains, bring-your-own-device-to-work, and mobile workforces are all modern business practices that can enhance growth and profitability. Although these technologies and business practices enhance competitiveness, growth, and profitability, they simultaneously undermine security.

At the same time that we are digitally transforming our businesses, we are making security more difficult. Moreover, we are helping exacerbate the vulnerability of the entire cyber system because we are all now so interconnected that we suffer from not only our own vulnerabilities but also the vulnerabilities of our customers, our business partners, and our business partners' business partners.

Digital Economics: Advantage to Cybercriminals

As mentioned earlier, the cybercrime "nation" is lucrative enough to qualify as one of the world's twenty most economically powerful countries in the world. However, we need to understand why cybercrime is such a vibrant business. To do this, we need only look at the cost of entry and the profit margins.[26]

Cyberattack methods are comparatively cheap and easy to acquire. There is a robust market for them on the dark web. Some examples of the low cost of entry into the cybercrime world are the following:

- You can outsource a Distributed Denial of Service, or DDoS attack, for about $300.[27]
- You can get false credentials for social media platforms like Twitter and Instagram for about $100.[28]
- You can purchase access to corporate mailboxes for about $500 dollars.[29]

- You can get a tutorial on how to conduct email attacks for $25.[30]
- You can create a "dummy" retail website for $20.43.
- And you can create a dummy banking website for $67.91.[31]

Ironically, while government and industry have, for the most part, not fully grasped the nuances of digital economics, the cybercriminals have proven to be pretty good businesspeople. They regularly take their profits and reinvest in their business, including by integrating the latest technical innovations into their business model. In some cases, their "R&D" departments are discovering entirely new vulnerabilities that we are not even aware of. According to the 2018 McAfee cybercrime report, "Cybercriminals at the high end are as technologically sophisticated as the most advanced IT companies and like them have moved quickly to adopt cloud, computing, artificial intelligence, and encryption."[32]

The digital economic balance between attackers and defenders can be summarized this way. On the attacker side, costs are low and profits high. Attackers also have a great business model: they can use the same methods repeatedly on a worldwide set of targets. And, of course, their capital reserves are very large, since in addition to their massive profit margins many cyberattackers are actual nation-states or state affiliated. On the defender side, the inherently vulnerable system is getting technically weaker all the time. We are almost always playing catch-up, as the attackers have first-mover advantage and there is virtually no law enforcement. We successfully prosecute less than one percent of cybercriminals.[33] As a result, McAfee concludes, "cybercrime is relentless, undiminished, and unlikely to stop. It's just too easy, rewarding and the chances of getting caught are far too low. Cybercrime also leads on a risk to payoff rate. It is a low-risk crime with high profits. A smart cybercriminal can easily make millions without fear of being caught."[34]

The Constantly Evolving Cyber Threat

There is now emerging an overlap in economic cyber espionage and cybercrime as new threat actors enter this market space that has traditionally been undertaken by nation-state adversaries. Cyber threats arise from "independent contractor" actors that are not directly controlled by nation-state governments but are rather suppliers to those governments. As a result of this new dynamic, there has been a significant increase in the number of threat actors that cybersecurity teams must defend against, and it is much more difficult to determine who is attacking and why. These independent contractors acting on behalf of nation-states are leveraging attacks such as ransomware to meet nation-state cyber objectives.

The COVID-19 Pandemic

Perhaps no incident provides a better illustration of society's ubiquitous reliance on the internet—and the intimate tie between economics and technology—than the COVID-19 pandemic, which began in 2020 and in various forms has continued well into 2022. As of April 2021, the virus caused more than 500,000 deaths.[35] In just a few months, the virus completely upended daily routines and the way society works. McKinsey found that COVID-19 has accelerated two broad trends that will reshape work after the pandemic recedes: remote work and virtual meetings are likely to continue, and the adoption of automation and AI will accelerate, especially in work arenas with high physical proximity.[36]

Yet, had this pandemic occurred in the pre-digital era, for example, in 1990, the impacts would likely be far more severe. The presence of the internet and digital services substantially mitigated many of the horrific impacts of the coronavirus outbreak. Almost overnight, the outbreak triggered the largest transformation in how work is done in history. By mid-July 2020, approximately half the workforce was working from home, according to a National Bureau of Economic Research survey—more than double the number of individuals working from home before the pandemic. This transformation would likely have been impossible without digital technology.[37]

Although the economy was staggered by the COVID-19 pandemic, millions and millions of people were able to continue to work; continue to produce; continue to earn paychecks; and continue to provide medical, business, entertainment, and psychological services. All this would have become infinitely more difficult or impossible without the internet.

Yet for all the economic benefits the internet provided during the pandemic, the dramatic transformation significantly undermined security. Unlike the preexisting mobile work programs, which typically were carefully planned and tested, the emergency move to mobile work was largely unplanned and disorganized. As a result, cyber systems, while mostly operational, were not properly secured, and the management structure and necessary training to use these systems remotely had not been implemented. The result was a massive increase in COVID-19-related cyberattacks.[38]

In fact, the COVID-19 pandemic served as a catalyst for both intensified digital transformation and greater cyber risk associated with ever more sophisticated attacks. In one of the first large-scale studies in the pandemic era, the law firm Reed Smith reported:

The coronavirus is hitting hard—on lives, on economies and now even on information security. Scams have increased by 400 percent. . . . Criminals seem to be taking full advantage of a time of crisis, targeting not just individuals and a vulnerable population, but also organizations. They know people are looking for safety information and are more likely to fall prey to malicious links or attachments that are easily clicked or opened. Further, with the wide quarantine policy forcing organisations to make an unprecedented transition to remote working, the pandemic has created an atmosphere in which scammers, hackers and con artists thrive. Security researchers found that hackers were targeting employees doing business from their new, makeshift workplaces, using techniques such as scam emails that pretend to be videoconference invitations but that actually steal network credentials."[39]

As the pandemic progressed and new fears emerged over the shortage of protective equipment and questions about vaccines, cybercriminals tailored social engineering tactics to target this fear and uncertainty by means of phishing scams and fraud schemes.[40] A survey released in September 2020 stated that companies experienced an average of 1,185 attacks every month, with 38 percent of participants noting a coworker was a victim of a cyberattack. Even employees who were confident in their ability to spot a scam were likely to fall victim to the numerous harmful emails.[41]

According to a study from VMware Carbon Black, 91 percent of enterprises reported an increase in cyberattacks with more employees working from home amid the pandemic.[42] CrowdStrike reported that 56 percent of respondents increased teleworking during the pandemic, with 60 percent of those respondents using personal devices (lacking enterprise security controls) for work.[43] On top of that, intrusions were already up in the first quarter of 2020—twice as many as in all of 2019—before the pandemic began having an impact on business operations.[44]

The Cybersecurity "Social Contract"

Cyber risk cannot be eliminated. However, it can be managed. Notwithstanding the overall economic advantages cyberattackers have over defenders, it is possible to create a cyber resilient system within the confines of traditional

Western political and economic principles. This pathway can be understood by following the theoretical model known as the Cybersecurity Social
Contract.

Many of the roots of Western democracy can be traced to the Enlight-
enment philosophers Rousseau, Locke, Hobbes, and others who postulated
that society needed to be based on a social contract between the private
individual and the government.[45] As originally conceived, the social contract suggested that civilized society governance was not preordained but
was based on a form of economic exchange between the individual and the
government. Citizens deferred to government certain allegiance and support
in return for government providing certain services, principal among them
security but extending to economic services such as rules for fair commerce.
Thus, the nation is enhanced by this contract between government and the
private individual.

In the United States, the social contract idea was adopted in the early
twentieth century to help build much of what we now refer to as our critical
infrastructure. In that era, the amazing inventions of the day were distributed
electricity and telephones. Initially, these services were available only where
they made economic sense for the provider—primarily affluent and densely
populated areas. However, policy makers perceived that these essential services needed to be deployed universally. To quickly achieve this public policy goal, an economic deal was struck with the private companies—a "social
contract." In return for providing the shareholders with assurance of solid
returns on their investments, the systems would be aggressively built out
even into otherwise uneconomically justified regions, and service would be
provided at reasonable rates. Thus, the era of rate of return (RoR) regulation
was born.

These companies became the ironically titled "privately owned public
utilities." For decades the utilities were a reliable and attractive stock for
investors. In return, consumers received electricity and telecommunications
services at an accelerated rate. The quality and extent of distributed electricity and telecommunications—the best in the world—were core elements of
the dramatic economic growth across a vastly expanding United States, helping transform the country from a minor regional player around 1900 into a
major world power by World War I and the world's dominant superpower by
the end of World War II.

A similar problem faces the United States as the twenty-first century
matures. The advent of digital technology, while offering great benefit, is insecure. As was the case before the utilities built out their infrastructure, there
are locations receiving electric and telephone services where the economics

made it practical. So too today there are pockets of cybersecurity where the economics permit it.

In their 2019 book, *The Fifth Domain*, Richard Clarke, former top cybersecurity adviser to both Republican president George W. Bush and Democratic president Bill Clinton, and Robert Knake, President Obama's director for cybersecurity policy at the National Security Council and now a Senior Fellow at the Council on Foreign Relations, point out that "hiding in plain sight are many examples of companies with big targets on their backs who have been able to constantly deflect the best nation state offensive teams." Clarke and Knake also point out that these companies all have "massive security teams, budgets of hundreds of millions of dollars," and many innovations "borrowed from the military."[46] These companies are the equivalent of the affluent areas that were able to afford telephones and electricity before the Social Contract model was leveraged to establish these utilities. Unfortunately, the massive financial commitment that Microsoft, Google, and Apple can deploy is not a sustainable model for most of the private sector.

The ability of companies like this to effectively manage their cyber risk offers hope that with visionary policy, such as that at the turn of the twentieth century, we may be able to reform the economics of the digital age system to benefit the whole nation. As in the case of telecommunications and electricity, this will need to be done on an economically sustainable basis for both industry and government as cyberattacks are not likely to diminish. And the terms of the cyber social contract will need to be different from those of the regulatory utility model, which, as we demonstrate in chapter 4, is ill-suited to the digital age.

Taking this approach begins with properly framing the cyber issue as an economic issue rather than a simple technical operational issue. As Clarke and Knake suggest, "Some of the challenges blocking the way to cyber peace are technical but most, at their heart are economic. With the right package of economic incentives, the technical problems can be solved. . . . Most of the solutions will be about how to make markets and government work in the interest of promoting security."[47]

Clarke and Knake's observations are demonstrably correct. They echo a long line of commentators and analysts who have come to similar conclusions. Indeed, the very first ISA white paper arguing for a cybersecurity social contract, which was published in 2008, made virtually the same point: "There are substantial pockets in both the public and private sector that are doing an admirable job of funding and applying strong cybersecurity defense. [However,] because of the interconnection of the system we need a universal solution. Neither companies nor government can, on their own, adequately secure themselves. A new system needs to include not just standards and practices but also economic support for the universal application and continued rapid innovation and adjustment in the face of the ever-evolving cyber threat."[48]

The advent of the digital age has fundamentally changed many aspects of society: how companies do business, how employees do work, how citizens determine what they consider privacy, and how national security is calculated and implemented. The United States needs a far more comprehensive cybersecurity strategy than it has developed to date. It needs a strategy that conscientiously integrates the economics of the digital age into a coherent program that will advance both its economic and its security goals. It needs a strategy that is comparable in thoughtfulness, comprehensiveness, integration, and economic support to what its major adversaries have.

Obviously, there is a need to focus more on the economics of cybersecurity and provide incentives to the digital economy that will promote resilient cyber defenses on a sustainable basis. The key question, which is addressed in subsequent chapters, is how, exactly, we do that.

CHAPTER 2

DANGEROUS AND EFFECTIVE

China's Digital Strategy

Larry Clinton and Carter (Yingzhou) Zheng

"If you know the enemy and know yourself, you need not fear the result of a hundred battles," wrote Sun Tzu in *The Art of War*. "If you know yourself but not the enemy, for every victory gained you will also suffer a defeat. If you know neither the enemy nor yourself, you will succumb in every battle."[1] Sun Tzu's wisdom is as pertinent in the digital age as it was when he wrote two and a half millennia ago. As we consider how to secure ourselves in the digital age, it is as important to know, in Sun Tzu's terminology, who is and who is not the enemy. It is possible we have spent too much time pointing fingers at each other—government pointing at industry, user pointing at vendors, citizens pointing at government—and not enough time analyzing where and why the truly significant cyber threats are coming from.

In this chapter, we discuss how one modern country, China, has consciously and intelligently integrated economics with the unique characteristics of the digital age to enhance its strategic position both internationally and domestically. Specifically, over the past few decades, the Chinese government, ruled by the Chinese Communist Party (CCP), has provided extensive economic support to its private industry[2] in order to then be able to leverage that industry for its strategic geopolitical purposes, including national security, economic growth, and expanding international influence, all to the detriment of the United States.

To be sure, China is not the only adversary of the United States in cyberspace. There are numerous aggressors attacking our cyber systems, including China, and an array of nation-states such as Russia, Iran, North Korea, and others, as well as all manner of cybercriminals—many with weapons equivalent to those of the nation-states. However, China, which ironically is both our adversary and, for the past several decades, our business partner (it owns nearly half of US debt),[3] is worth studying because it has developed an impressively competitive digital strategy. While some have suggested that much of China's current posture is reliant on the personage of Xi Jinping, the digital strategy being implemented has been developed over several years and is designed to be both pervasive and structural. This strategy is designed to have impact beyond the immediacies of current issues or politics.

Introducing "Dual Circulation": A Self-Sufficient Model amid Stiff US-China Relations

China's recently unveiled fourteenth Five-Year Plan, for the period 2021–25 has again set the tone to foster a Chinese-dominated technology supply chain and accelerate the use of antitrust, intellectual property, and standard tools to promote industrial policies through "dual circulation," which comprises an internal and an external channel.

The internal circulation channel aims to boost a self-reliant domestic economy supported by a domestic cycle of production, distribution, and consumption. Already a leader in the digital economy, China seeks to leverage "tens of billions of dollars for its tech industry to borrow," according to a *New York Times* report.[4] One of the major shifts toward technology development is to create technological independence in key areas like artificial intelligence and quantum computing. The fourteenth Five-Year Plan commits to increasing the budget for research and development by 7 percent annually, which is higher than China's 6.8 percent budget growth rate for the military.

China's external circulation channel focuses on securing the supply chain against pressures from the United States. China's Belt and Road Initiative (BRI) and Digital Silk Road (DSR) have been strategically positioned to facilitate secure trade and gain initial global footholds to accomplish its "Made in China 2025" goal. In a speech to the Party's Central Economic and Financial Working Group in April 2020, President Xi called for building "independent, controllable, secure, and reliable supply chains to ensure industrial and national security with access to at least one alternative source for important products." President Xi said the country should "use existing global dependencies on China as a counterweight to pressures to shift manufacturing out of China" and "use the pull of China's market to attract global resources and deepen global dependence on China."

If the United States is to compete with China in the digital age we will need to understand its strategy and develop an equally sophisticated and thoughtful approach in our own digital defense. This begins with knowing our adversaries far better.

The Chinese government quickly perceived that the vulnerabilities in the new digital systems could be used to gain access to Western intellectual property that could help jump-start their own domestic industries.[5] It also understood the international market for advanced digital systems in developing, as well as developed, countries. As a result, the Chinese government has been heavily subsidizing Chinese internet giants, enabling them to provide sweetheart deals and secure the rights to provide internet infrastructure to nations around the world. Winning these contracts has curried favor with these nations, which has attendant benefits in terms of relationship building, along with strategic and military implications.[6] These international partnerships also help loosen nonaligned nations' ties with the United States and the Western world order. In addition, by embedding Chinese infrastructure in networks around the world, the Chinese government could have the ability to access information traveling across these networks for their own national interests whenever they desire.[7] Finally, by virtue of continued investment and international subsidized marketing, China has become a world-class competitor—in fact, leader—in cutting-edge digital technologies such as Artificial Intelligence (AI) and Fifth Generation (5G) wireless communications.[8] This technological proficiency, combined with China's incumbent market status as a worldwide telecommunications provider, places the United States in an extremely difficult position in the immediate and midterm with respect to competing in the digitally dominated new world order.

This chapter focuses primarily on the internet, or cyber, elements of China's digital strategy. It must be understood, however, that the cyber elements are just one integrated aspect in a much larger and ambitious strategy, the BRI, which is examined in depth in an article by Hong Shen.[9]

The Chinese Approach to Digitalization versus the American Approach

China's state capitalism strategy is, perhaps ironically, consistent with several fundamental elements of Western social contract theory, but its roots lie in traditional Chinese philosophy. It is in fact a modernized integration of elements of both Eastern and Western culture. Moreover, this integrated approach has been—and continues to be—quite successful. In chapter 4, we discuss how the US government has been unsuccessful in developing a similarly comprehensive and effective cyber strategy, which has contributed to its massive cybersecurity problem. An important reason for this failure is that the US government has not wisely integrated its economic and technical assets as well as China has. We argue that a US version of the cyber social contract may be a better road for it to follow in the twenty-first-century competition with China.

However, we do not argue that the US government should mimic the CCP's strategy. For the United States to do so would be largely illegal, arguably unethical (at least by Western standards), and most likely unsuccessful. Instead, we argue that the United States needs to develop its own creative cybersecurity strategy that leverages its strategic goals with economics and public policy to create a sustainably secure cyber system consistent with Western ethical standards, our free market philosophy, and our democratic traditions.

The Chinese government's strategy is best analyzed on a value-neutral basis. A number of germane concepts, such as the value of private intellectual property, vary greatly from culture to culture. For the sake of clarity, this analysis views the Chinese government strategy pragmatically, demonstrating that the process of integrating digitalization, economics, and national security has been successful in achieving many of its strategic goals. The point is not that the Chinese approach is better from an ethical perspective but that there are pragmatic lessons that can be learned from the Chinese approach that can be adapted and applied to create a more successful US digital policy.

It can be argued that the CCP-led Chinese government has a number of inherent advantages in creating the integrated digital policy we describe. It has a one-party political structure, which makes implementing decisions easier. It has a centralized economy, which affords a number of efficiencies. It is generally not burdened by legacy regulations and procedures that can make modernization more cumbersome, and, by Western standards, it gives strikingly low priority to individual freedoms. All these attributes, it can be argued, make it easier for China to develop the sort of unified approach to digital policy we describe.

However, the United States and the other Western democracies have advantages too. To begin with, the United States has a far larger economy than China and an even greater advantage if Western Europe is included. The West also has at least a century of historic alliances, interwoven economies, and trading regimes, while the Chinese are comparative newcomers to international trade. The free-market system also enabled a greater capacity for innovative thought and commerce—assets that if properly incentivized should be especially powerful in the rapidly changing and competitive digital world. The United States cannot and should not match the Chinese government–controlled economy; indeed, increased government control over US industry under the guise of creating greater security would be counterproductive. Instead, the United States will need to use the innovative aspects of the free market to compete on this international playing field. As discussed in chapters 5 and 6, a key pathway for the United States to develop a more effective posture in the digital age is to adapt a number of the innovative concepts, structures, and tools that the free market has developed in the drive toward digital transformation and managing the cyber risks that accompany it.

Even if one considers China to be in an advantageous position based on its centralization, there is no reason that the United States cannot have a comparably well-thought-out, strategic, conceptually integrated and supported set of policies. One might argue it is ironic that on these executive function characteristics, the United States is behind China since presumably it is these traits that helped make the United States a world power.

China's Disadvantages

Aging Population

In the next ten years, approximately 120 million Chinese will be fifty-five or older. Its aging population coupled with its lowest birthrate rate in seven decades means that China will likely face workforce shortages. Because over time China's one-child policy has limited the human resources available to support its dependent population, the nation will lose much of its ability to invest for future growth. According to United Nations (UN) data, China's workforce has already begun to shrink absolutely even as the country's dependent elderly population has continued to grow rapidly. Of course, labor power shortage can be offset by technological advancement and productivity. But the demographic situation will nonetheless limit Beijing's options, especially huge development projects such as the BRI and China's military buildup.

Environmental Issues

Rapid economic growth in China over the past forty years has been inseparable from high resource consumption and pollution. According to a report released by Greenpeace and CREA, in 2018 dirty air cost 6.6 percent of China's GDP, compared to 5.4 percent for India and 3 percent for the United States. Pollution also reduces grain yield by severely impeding photosynthesis.[10] A Chinese agriculture expert has suggested that if smog persists at high levels, China's agriculture sector would suffer conditions "somewhat similar to a nuclear winter."[11] As food security concerns mount, China faces growing pressure to import more grain from the world market. Pollution is also threatening China's political stability. According to a Harvard survey conducted in 2016, one-third of respondents in China said they would petition or protest against air pollution if it negatively affected their own health or the health of their family members.

The Rural-Urban Divide

China's urbanization process excluded hundreds of millions of migrant workers and their families from accessing education, healthcare, and social security. The household registration, or *hukou*, system prevented people who were born in the countryside from migrating to the cities. Although today people in the countryside are permitted to migrate, in most cases they cannot gain access to social welfare benefits—healthcare, education, pensions—in the cities even when they live there. They have to pay for medical care at private clinics in the cities or travel back to the countryside for healthcare.

Strained Relations with US Allies

The first face-to-face summit meeting between Japanese prime minister Suga Yoshihide and President Joe Biden during the pandemic in April 2021 focused a lot on China, including China's violations of human rights in Hong Kong, its genocide and crimes against humanity in Xinjiang, and the prospect of a Chinese attack on Taiwan. The agenda also included enhancing the Quadrilateral Security Dialogue with Australia and India.

China's Conscious Integration of Digitalization in Economic Development

Before the "opening" of China just over forty years ago, its economy can be fairly described as centrally controlled, isolated, stagnant, inefficient, and extremely poor.[12] Since then China has had one of the world's fastest growing economies. On average, since 1979 China has had a real average gross domestic product (GDP) growth of 9.5 percent through 2018. The World Bank has called China's growth "the fastest sustained expansion by a major economy in history."[13] Among the significant impacts of this economic expansion has been that China has raised an estimated 800 million people out of poverty during this time.

The turn toward a conscious industrial policy, which led to the coordinated use of economic levers and digital technology to achieve strategic national security goals, started in the mid-1980s.[14] The first CCP document to explicitly use the term "industrial policy" was the seventh Five-Year Plan (1986–90). In 1989, the State Council released the document "Decisions on the Important Issues of Current Industrial Policies," which stated that industrial policies would enhance industrialization and macro controls.[15] This idea was made concrete in the subsequent eighth Five-Year Plan (1991–95). The State Council, in the document titled "Outline of National Industrial Policy," published in 1994, stated that industrial policies would promote the development of the "pillar industries" of the economy.[16]

Starting with the tenth Five-Year Plan period, 2001–5, government-led industrial policies in the spirit of selective intervention were put into practice on a systematic scale. The Sixteenth National Congress of the Communist Party in 2002 put forward the notion of pursuing "a new path of industrialization," with emphasis on the development of science and technology capabilities, environmentally friendly and resources-saving technology, and information engineering and related industries. The culmination of these emphases was in the speech by President Hu Jintao in 2006, "Medium- to Long-Term Plan for the Development of Science and Technology."[17] It set out the target of transforming China into an "innovation society" by 2020. Since President Xi came to power, large-scale government-led technology initiatives, including "Internet Plus," "One Belt One Road—Digital Silk Road," and "21st Century Cyberpower," have been launched. The central government of China has repeatedly stressed the importance of internet security, cross-sector information, and digitization of the economy as part of the national strategy.[18]

Concurrently, China has adopted the Belt and Road Initiative as a core component of its foreign policy. This has led to a growing and complex alliance between the state and its homegrown internet companies to build the Digital Silk Road. A major objective of this and the other initiatives has been facilitating corporate China's global expansion. It is estimated that fully implemented BRI investments will total more than $1 trillion and affect more than sixty countries.[19]

Using the Vulnerabilities of the Internet as a Catalyst for Economic Growth

While substantial investment is clearly a major part of the Chinese strategy, it is not the only tactic China has used. China also cleverly accessed the vulnerabilities in the networks the West was using to fuel its own growth. In short,

Chinese intellectual property theft and cyber espionage became a large part of China's industrial strategy. "Illicit acquisition of foreign technology has long been promoted by the Chinese government," according to James Lewis of the Center for Strategic and International Studies (CSIS). "Since the early 1980s China has engaged in an energetic espionage campaign and moved into cyberspace two decades ago. The Chinese discovered that the Internet gave them unparalleled access to poorly secured Western networks. Cyber espionage is accompanied by human collection efforts[,] . . . but the most rewarding collection of programs have shifted from human agents to cyber espionage."[20]

It is perhaps not surprising that the Chinese government would use weak cybersecurity as an avenue to stimulate economic development given the significant economic incentives and clear technical opportunity outlined in chapter 1.

The Chinese View of Intellectual Property

It is noteworthy that the Chinese do not feel constrained by traditional Western philosophy and law when it comes to gaining an advantage in business competition.[21] Wu Handong, former president of Zhongnan University of Economics and Law and an expert in Chinese property law, has argued that the main stumbling block of Chinese intellectual property legal systems is the historical inertia of China's traditional culture and value system.[22]

Wu has suggested that individualism is the cultural foundation of modern private law. In essence, the development of private law culture, including intellectual property culture, is the development of identity in private law. However, China's traditional culture, especially Confucianism, prioritizes the group over the individual, whereby individual rights and values cannot exist without family, group, or country. Conceptually, liberalism is the ideology that underpins modern private law: freedom of thought and economic freedom have been fundamental in the West and have empowered innovation and technology advancement.

Comparatively, Chinese society has not yet embraced the free flow of ideas and the freedom to exercise human rights; these rights and values are essentially nonexistent in Chinese history and tradition. According to Wu, Western intellectual property laws based on individualism and liberalism will require a long time to transplant to the traditional Chinese cultural soil of Confucianism and authoritarianism.

Theft of Intellectual Property

The issues the Obama and Trump administrations agreed on are few, but the impact of Chinese intellectual property (IP) theft via the internet stands out as a major area of agreement. In 2016, the US Trade Representative (USTR) report issued by the Obama administration stated, "Actors affiliated with the Chinese government have infiltrated computer systems in the U.S. and stolen terabytes of data including firms' intellectual property for the purposes of providing commercial advantage to Chinese firms."[23] Under the Trump administration, the findings were nearly identical. In 2018, the Trump USTR reported that "cyber intrusions give Chinese actors access to commercially valuable business information including trade secrets, technical data, negotiating positions, sensitive and proprietary internal communications."[24]

The impacts of this strategy have been difficult to fully and precisely measure, but they are widely understood to be massive. In 2018, the USTR estimated that the theft of trade secrets alone has a cost of between $180 and $540 billion annually.[25] And even earlier, in 2013, the former head of the National Security Agency (NSA), General Keith Alexander, told Congress that the cyber intellectual property theft constituted the largest transfer of wealth in human history.[26]

The negative impact of intellectual property (IP) theft goes well beyond a dollar-and-cents calculus. A 2016 report by the Institute for Defense Analyses concluded that "large scale theft of intellectual property and trade secrets from U.S. businesses undermines our international competitiveness and erodes high-skill jobs for US workers. . . . If the U.S. cannot protect our IP, our technology leadership will be eclipsed, our economic potential eroded, and our future growth stolen."[27]

The Multiplier Effect

The value China received from their internet attacks was not limited to direct financial gains. The cyber espionage program gave China an invaluable intelligence resource useful from a broad economic as well as military perspective. China has realized that acquiring the know-how from IP theft combined with forced technology transfers was, in the end, more important than just acquiring the IP. By adding a coordinated economic stimulus, China can maximize the value of IP theft. "Stolen IP does not guarantee success for the acquirer, but in China this new competitor may have access to government subsidies or may benefit from a protected domestic market built with non-tariff barriers to hobble competition," according to Lewis. "Subsidized Chinese companies have an immense advantage operating from a closed domestic market and selling into an open international market. If nothing else, this distorts the global market by creating overcapacity and putting unsubsidized foreign firms at a disadvantage."[28]

The multiplier effect Lewis notes highlights the integrated nature of the Chinese digital economic strategy. The role of the internet, both as a source for knowledge, stolen or leveraged, and as a basis for additional strategic value should not be underestimated. As Hong Shen has noted in the *International Journal of Communication*:

> Relatively little attention has been granted to the role of the Internet in the promulgation of BRI. Often overlooked in the current discussion are the massive digital infrastructures (e.g., fiber-optic cables and data centers) that have been laid alongside transport and energy projects. . . . Speaking at the first BRI forum in Beijing President Xi reiterated the critical role of the Digital Silk Road in the overall initiative. He called for further integration into BRI of next generation network technologies—including artificial intelligence, nano-technology, quantum computing, big data cloud and smart cities—to enable innovation driven development.[29]

Military-Civil Fusion

Speaking at the second annual Multilateral Action on Sensitive Technologies (MAST) Conference in 2019, US assistant secretary of state Christopher Ashley Ford said:

> The Chinese system of military-civil fusion (MCF) presents an additional layer of problems. Military-civil fusion is a national level Chinese effort led by Xi Jinping himself that seeks to systematically take down barriers between China's civilian and military sectors. . . . [F]irms such as Huawei, Tencent, ZTE, Alibaba, and Baidu have no meaningful ability to tell the Chinese Communist Party "no" if officials decide to ask for assistance—e.g., in the form of access to foreign technologies, access to foreign networks, useful information about the foreign commercial counterparts, insights into patterns of foreign commerce, or specific information about activities or locations of users of Chinese hosted or facilitated social media computer or smartphone applications or telecommunications.[30]

The Synergistic Nature of China's Digital Strategy: Huawei Technologies

A primary example of the synergistic nature of the Chinese digital strategy is Huawei. A *Wall Street Journal* (*WSJ*) analysis concluded:

Tens of billions of dollars in financial assistance from the Chinese government helped fuel Huawei Technologies' rise to the top of global telecommunications, a scale of support that in key measures dwarfed what its closest rivals got from their governments. Huawei had access to as much as $75 billion in state support as it grew from a little-known vendor of phone switches to the world's largest telecom equipment company. Besides the subsidies, since 1998, Huawei received an estimated $16 billion in loans export credits and other forms of financing from Chinese banks for itself and its customers.[31]

The *WSJ*'s review excluded other forms of financial support available to Huawei such as salary, tax benefits, property tax abatements, and subsidized raw materials. It estimates that such benefits netted Huawei the equivalent of another $25 billion in revenue.

Although not directly included in the basic calculations of benefits there seems ample examples of how such indirect subsidies were provided to Huawei. For example, state records show that in the southern city of Dongguan, Huawei bought more than a dozen state owned parcels in largely uncontested bids between 2014 and 2018. The company paid prices that were 10 to 50 percent less than the average rate for similarly zoned parcels in Dongguan.[32]

Strategic Implications

For the Chinese government simply building the world's largest telecommunication equipment company is just a tactic in a broad national strategy. In its 2013 assessment of China's three wars strategy, the US Department of Defense identified China's goals as regaining global status as the premier power by weakening US alliances and defeating the United States through non-kinetic deceptive warfare.[33]

The Chinese Communist Party's strategy to achieve these goals is not by invoking the communist revolutionary zeal of old, but instead through a multifaceted effort to entice states to buy into a Sinocentric world order. This global insurgency incorporates two sub strategies with the BRI functioning primarily as an economic and diplomatic tool fostering goodwill through massive infusions of investment to US allies and non-aligned states.[34] This strategy is fully consistent with the traditions of Sun Tzu and Mao by appearing non-threatening while engaging the United States asymmetrically and attacking its vulnerabilities. Although this is not a military conflict, it has deep implications for American security and for the future of an international system based on the rule of law and democratic norms.[35]

A central element of the BRI is to offer needed infrastructure investment to cash-strapped states throughout Asia, Europe, and Latin America—and even to rural areas in the United States. By virtue of its massive government support, Huawei was in an excellent position to compete for contracts. The *WSJ* analysis indicated that Huawei's subsidies were 17 times larger than subsidies reported by Nokia of Finland, the world's second largest telecom equipment maker, while Sweden's Ericsson, the third largest, posted none for that period.[36]

As a result, Huawei was able to make nations around the world offers that they literally could not refuse. The potential economic development benefits from installing the high-quality Huawei equipment on extremely favorable terms made security issues an insufficient reason to pass on working with the Chinese supplier, who often offered the telecom equipment as a package deal, according to a Eurasia Group report published in 2020.

> In many cases . . . security and data privacy issues are considered less important than the need for telecommunications infrastructure and the difficulties of paying for more expensive Western equipment. Many countries continue to see Chinese technology investments as key to economic modernization plans and China is excellent at linking its Belt and Road to national plans. . . . Developing economies prioritize cost considerations over security risks related to Chinese equipment. Many African countries that rely heavily on Huawei and ZTE equipment appear to have a similarly relaxed view on security concerns. In 2018, Western media reported that the African Union (AU)—for which Huawei had supplied telecommunications equipment—had its servers compromised which resulted in information leaking back to China for five years. Nonetheless, the AU president joined Huawei in decrying the allegations of espionage and in 2018 signed a renewed agreement with Huawei.[37]

Acting in concert with the Chinese telecoms, Beijing has shown remarkable flexibility with respect to financing these projects, including easing debt burdens and complying with on-sourcing requirements.[38] According to the *WSJ*'s analysis, the mega-lenders China Development Bank and Export-Import Bank of China made available more than $30 billion in credit lines for Huawei's customers. World Bank official data indicates their banks were lending to the company's clients in developing economies at 3 percent— around half of China's five-year benchmark rate since 2004.

The *WSJ* quoted Fred Hochberg, former chair of the US Export-Import Bank: "If you are going to buy a home and you can say you have a half-million-dollar line of credit it's going to make you a much stronger bidder. What Huawei did, cleverly, is to make sure that when they made a bid it came with financing terms that surpassed those of competitors."[39]

These infrastructure investments are part of the Chinese government's broader strategic aim to replace the United States as the global underwriter of economic development, thus decreasing the perceived necessity of participating in the US-led international order.[40] Aid and investment from established donors in the West tend to involve political and economic conditions that may make it unattractive. However, Chinese aid or investment has not historically been tied to demanding reform programs.[41] This seemingly conditionless aid attracts states that are unable or unwilling to meet the demands of Western benefactors.[42] By replacing the West as the incubator for growth, China could alter global perspectives among developing states to favor it rather than the United States and the West.

The implications of China's success in implementing this strategy could be dire. A report issued by the chair of the Senate Foreign Policy Committee, Robert Menendez (D-NJ), in July 2020 stated, "The United States is now on the precipice of losing the future of the cyber domain to China. If China continues to perfect the tools for digital authoritarianism and is able to effectively implement them both domestically and abroad then China, not the United States and its allies, will shape the digital environment."[43]

While as a whole the BRI projects are primarily designed for economic and diplomatic benefits, certain projects have particularly significant geostrategic implications. The Port of Gwadar is an example. The port will connect the Persian Gulf to China through the China-Pakistan Economic Corridor currently being built, which will allow energy supplies to reach China without passing through the strategic choke point at the Strait of Malacca.[44] In addition, the port is deep enough to accommodate Chinese submarines and aircraft carriers, which provides further utility as a base from which China could balance and contain US naval activity in Asia.[45] Similar investment in the Maldives and elsewhere may likewise allow the People's Liberation Army navy to operate further from China and exclude the US Navy from Asia.[46] While BRI projects are designed to build goodwill toward China and develop Chinese and partner states' economies, there exists an undercurrent of utility provided to the Chinese military.

The strategy is also extending to the western hemisphere. In November 2020, the *New York Times* (*NYT*) reported that the US ambassador to Jamacia, Donald Tapia, was cautioning that government not to install 5G mobile networks made by Huawei and ZTE due to the companies' history of spying and stealing. The newspaper reported further that "the initiatives were part of a quiet but assertive push by China in recent years to expand its footprint and influence in the region through government grants and loans. . . . China's growing interest has come in the form of much-needed help for Caribbean nations that have serious infrastructure needs but whose status as middle-income countries complicates their access to finance and development." In addition, the Chinese government was donating security equipment to military and police forces in the region.[47]

In 2021, a *NYT* article analyzed how China's COVID-19 vaccine diplomacy has been leveraged in Brazil to reengage Huawei's 5G deal.

> With Covid-19 deaths rising to their highest levels yet, and a dangerous new virus variant stalking Brazil, the nation's communications minister went to Beijing in February (2021), met with Huawei executives at their headquarters and made a very unusual request of a telecommunication company [which allowed Huawei to participate again in the 5G auction]. The precise connection between the vaccine request and Huawei's inclusion in the 5G auction is unclear, but the timing is striking, and it is part of a stark change in Brazil's stance toward China. The president, his son and the foreign minister abruptly stopped criticizing China, while cabinet officials with inroads to the Chinese, like [communications minister] Mr. Faria, worked furiously to get new vaccine shipments approved. Millions of doses have arrived in recent weeks.[48]

A recent study has shown that alignment with US–Latin American voting patterns are negatively correlated with increasing Chinese trade and investment.[49] In 2016 Greece, a recipient of substantial Chinese investment, sold a controlling share of the Port of Piraeus to COSCO, a Chinese state-owned enterprise.

As in Latin America, Greek voting patterns have changed. In 2017, Greece was the sole vote blocking an EU statement at the UN criticizing China's human rights violations.[50] The degree to which these actions can be considered voluntary is debatable considering the position of power that China occupies compared to the states in which it invests.

While it may be easy (if unwise) to shrug off China's ability to seduce a smaller, poorer nation-state, the combination of economics and technical enhancement has proven enticing even for nuclear power–level nations. The *WSJ* provides a telling example in Pakistan in 2009.[51] According to the report, Huawei pitched a surveillance system to Pakistan that was approved by the prime minister. However, the country's procurement rules required competitive bidding. In order to sidestep that issue, the Export-Import Bank of China offered to lend Pakistan the $124.7 million price and waive the 3 percent interest fee on the twenty-year loan. The only condition was that Huawei would get the contract. The competitive bidding process was circumvented, and Huawei installed the Pakistani prime minister's surveillance system. At the inauguration ceremony Pakistan's interior minister told the assembled proudly, "The Chinese government funded it and Huawei built it."[52]

Growth and Sustainability

The notion that Huawei is building the surveillance systems for a purported US ally with nuclear capabilities is chilling on its face. The opportunities for the Chinese company to embed backdoor into highly complex IT networks that only it knows about and can access provides obvious and substantial problems.

Thanks to years of intellectual property theft, massive government support, including substantial government investments in STEM education (far outstripping US and other Western investments), and hard innovative work, Huawei is not only the world's largest telecom equipment provider, but one of if not the best.[53] So not only are they able to provide systems around the world at low cross-subsidized prices; they can provide technically superior systems. Only they really know what is in these systems.

By May 2020 the US government finally pulled the plug on Huawei activities in the United States and placed the company on the Department of Commerce's "Entity List," which imposes restrictions on US commercial engagement. Huawei was placed on this list after it was indicted by the US Justice Department for theft of trade secrets, attempted theft of trade secrets, conspiracy, wire fraud, and obstruction of justice, as well as bank fraud, conspiracy to commit bank fraud, conspiracy to commit money laundering, and violations of the international Emergency Powers Act in illegally assisting Iran with evasion of sanctions.

Consistent with the sanctions, Washington moved to cut Huawei off from key semiconductor supplies.[54] However, because of its size and diversity, "Huawei is doubling down on pivoting to a software/cloud and services company," Neil Shah, research director at Counterpoint Research, told CNBC. "Huawei with this effort is becoming like Google."[55] According to Shah, the tech giant is also working on in-car software, potentially giving it a huge mobile platform to compete with Google's Android mobile operating system for smartphones.

Meanwhile, the concern about securing internet networks from Chinese access may already be a closed issue. In midsummer 2020, US secretary of state Mike Pompeo announced a series of agreements with Eastern European countries to "rip and replace" Huawei technology from their networks. This is similar to agreements reached with several rural US-based telecom companies.

While "ripping and replacing" may be a short-term solution to a limited number of the digital threats China poses, it can scarcely be considered a cost-effective solution. Moreover, while the recognition of the potentially significant impact of Chinese control of Western telecommunications in the digital era is welcome, the US response has been limited, incremental, reactive, and largely unsuccessful.

For example, in 2018 the United States announced a multiyear Digital Connectivity and Cybersecurity Partnership focused on the Indo-Pacific. However, the US financial commitment paled in comparison to that of China.. In another example, the United States scrambled to provide a competitive bid to build fiber-optic cables to Papua New Guinea (PNG) and the Solomon Islands to compete with a proposal from Huawei's joint venture Huawei-Marine. Notwithstanding the US-led effort and the serious security issues the United States raised, the PNG decided to continue with Huawei-Marine to build its domestic infrastructure, with a key minister noting he was not worried about US security concerns.[56]

The breadth of China's influence in Asia may well be underestimated in the West, but even close US allies in the region attest to the degree of China's current influence. Kunihiko Miyake, a former diplomat who served Japan in both Beijing and Washington, DC, and now heads the Tokyo-based Foreign Policy Institute attempted to put China's status in terms Americans can understand: "Chinese influence in Asia is actually much larger than Soviet influence was in Eastern Europe."

Although the United States has banned Huawei products from its networks and pressured other allies to restrict use of Huawei equipment they have integrated into their systems, that may already be impractical if not impossible due to the economics. The United Kingdom is arguably the most reliable ally of the United States. Vodafone, based in the United Kingdom is the world's second largest telecommunications system (after China Telecom) and has used Huawei products for years.

In an April 2020 essay for *Lawfare*, Vodafone executive, Joachim Reiter, argued that the US position—that Huawei products need to be eliminated from Western networks that are part of the international security supply chain for security purposes—is simply impractical for economic reasons.[57]

European carriers and governments are working hard to figure out how to best reconcile market conditions and the EUs ambitions for implementing 5G with Washington's perspective on supply chain security. The decision to continue to utilize Huawei is born of practicality, given Europe's past use of Huawei and the lack of options when it comes to vendors and the prevailing market environment. . . . Unlike the U.S., European carriers long ago installed Huawei products throughout 3G and 4G networks. . . . Removing them from 5G means removing [them] from 4G, etc.[58]

In July 2020, at least one European nation, the United Kingdom—no longer a member of the EU—agreed to a compromise position: it would stop purchasing Huawei equipment by the end of the year and clear Huawei equipment from its network in seven years (traditionally the typical length of time telephone companies swap out their technologies). While there may be some follow-through by other major European countries, however, as of this writing they have not followed the UK lead and to do so in the post-pandemic environment may be extremely difficult.

The Impact of the COVID-19 Pandemic on China's Digital Silk Road

If the prevailing market structure made replacing Huawei products impractical, the existence of the COVID-19 pandemic exacerbated the environment dramatically. In nations around the world, the vast majority of the workforce has moved from offices to homes to continue to earn their livelihoods. This has put new pressures on carriers like Vodafone to reconfigure and upgrade service while its own workers are struggling to survive. At the same time, the pandemic stretched government resources for needed medical care. The pandemic, the relocation of vast numbers of workers, and the security threats from use of the Chinese systems caused a perfect storm for European carriers.

Insistence that friendly governments implement measures that match the U.S. stance on Huawei was always going to be difficult—bordering on impossible—to implement. After COVID-19 it will grow even harder to sell. Such a plan would impose an unacceptable financial, economic, and social calculus on Europeans who will already be financially squeezed, economically weakened, and exhausted from weathering the crisis. Revamping the EU 5G network would cost billions of euros for taxpayers—money that after COVID-19 will be devoted to urgent health expenditures.[59]

The potentially synergistic impact of COVID-19 and the largess of China's Digital Silk Road—for both the United States and China—was highlighted by the Eurasia Group's 2020 Report: "The ultimate impact of the pandemic on the DSR will also depend on the extent of any global economic downturn and the success or failure of U.S. efforts to further restrict access to Huawei and other important Chinese technology."[60]

The reach of China's influence includes even some of the US government's closest allies. James Curran, a former Australian official and expert on US-Australia relations at the University of Sydney, told the *Washington Post* that "the Australian government knows, even if it will not say it publicly, that China is crucial to its post-pandemic recovery."[61]

Beijing promoted its early success at containing the virus (after several missteps) to provide medical assistance and medical supplies to a growing list of countries in Europe, Asia, Africa, and Latin America.[62] The *New York Times* reported that "the pandemic allowed China to strengthen its relationships further by donating or selling personal protective equipment in what has come to be called 'Mask Diplomacy.' The Chinese foreign minister, Wang Yi, pledged in July that China would extend $1 billion in loans for vaccinations to Latin America and Caribbean countries."[63]

Although Huawei has garnered the lion's share of attention in the Western press, it is simply the tip of the spear in China's DSR program. The Eurasia Group's 2020 Report on Expanding China's Digital Footprint found that

> a key thrust of the DSR is to ensure that leading Chinese platform players such as Alibaba, Tencent, and Baidu—as well as Huawei—and state-backed telecom carriers such as China Mobile, China Telecom, and China Unicom can take advantage of the DSR umbrella and market access provided by BRI projects to compete in emerging markets with leading U.S. companies in so-called over-the-top services[,] . . . including smart cities, cloud services, mobile payments and social media applications, and [will] eventually include technologies such as AI, autonomous vehicles, and Internet of Things technologies and services.[64]

These Chinese-based commercial digital companies generally follow the paradigm detailed in the Huawei example. Assistant Secretary Ford noted:

> The Global Chinese firms do not always make decisions for com-
> mercial and economic reasons. . . . All such firms are subject to a
> deep and pervasive system of Chinese Communist Party control
> which uses them as instruments not only for making money but
> also for pursuing the Party-State's agenda. . . . Such firms are sub-
> sidized by the government with massive lines of credit and long-
> duration loans with generous grace periods from state-owned banks
> in order to undercut competition and penetrate foreign markets
> more deeply.[65]

Moreover, as is the case with Huawei, there are a wide range of Chinese
laws that require these companies to cooperate "unconditionally" with the
Chinese Communist Party's security apparatus. For example, the National
Intelligence Law requires entities in China to cooperate with its intelligence
services and covers both privately owned and state-owned enterprises. Anal-
ogous provisions are also included in China's National Security Law, Counter
Terrorism Law, and Cybersecurity Law.[66]

This integrated model provides substantial advantages to these companies competing in the international free market for digital services. Chinese
success in these markets creates enormous leverage and strategic importance as Chinese companies expand their foothold in the digital ecosystems
around the world, including those of Western allies.

Even if the US government is successful in motivating governments to
stop using Huawei in their core telecommunications networks, the range
of other Chinese technology giants each presents its own, possibly larger,
issues. Three such firms, Baidu, Alibaba, and Tencent (BAT), already have a
combined value of over a trillion dollars and, with China state support and
allegiance, are making remarkable inroads into all manner of world commerce and culture.

Alibaba is leading the world in FinTech disruption, already controls the
world's largest money market fund, and handles more payments than MasterCard. It operates in over two hundred countries and is launching a $15
billion initiative in AI, quantum computing, and emerging new tech-driven
markets.

Baidu is the first such company to apply deep learning and is extending
into multiple markets, such as brain-inspired neural chips and intelligent
robotics—all under the Chinese government's umbrella. And regarding
Tencent, the analyst Peter Diamandis states, "When it comes to Chinese
tech giants with absolutely no analog in the West, Tencent takes the cake,
hands down."[67] Tencent combines the functionality of Facebook, iMessage,

PayPal, Uber Eats, Instagram, Expedia, Skype, WebMD, GroupMe, and many others into a single ecosystem with its WeChat system. It is aggressively entering markets as varied as high-end healthcare and mobile gaming (its League of Legends game is played by over a hundred million people every month).

China is aggressively using this vast and growing technology base to expand its reach to both influence and, when needed, spy on the rest of the world. Beijing's 2019 Digital Economy Event announced cooperation agreements with twenty-two countries for DSR sectors and projects. The list of new Chinese partners included Japan, New Zealand, Israel, Austria, Chile, Brazil, Indonesia, and Kenya. Argentina signed a $28 million deal with ZTE to build a fiber optic cable system. The China Export Import Bank signed an agreement with the International Telecommunications Union to address digital access and promote the sustainable Development Agenda.

Chinese Digital Currency: Blockchain

"Blockchain" is mentioned for the first time in China's fourteenth Five-Year Plan.[68] The already mature Chinese digital currency, or DCEP, aims to influence global finance and e-commerce and to depart from US dollar dominance in the global financial system. Pilot programs have been launched in cities like Shenzhen and Hainan since 2020 to test cross-border digital trade based on DCEP.

Internationally, DCEP has the potential to empower as many as two billion people along the Digital Silk Road trading corridors with high-speed, convenient, and person-to-person transfers, not in US dollars or their native currency, but in China's renminbi (RMB).[69] This will help China achieve its strategic goal to avoid the "dollar trap" through RMB internationalization. China's thirteenth Five-Year Plan (2016–20) stated that China "will take systematic steps to realize Renminbi capital account convertibility, making the Renminbi more convertible and freely usable, so as to steadily promote Renminbi."[70] A study indicates that the Digital Silk Road will substantially increase renminbi demand through expansive foreign investments and economic engagements with Europe and Asia.[71] The formation of an RMB trading bloc over time will conceivably quicken the systematic integration to DCEP. A report projects that the annual trade value between China and Digital Silk Road participating nations will surpass $2.5 trillion, and many deals will be settled in RMB instead of the US dollar.[72]

Digital Authoritarianism

China has aimed to continually promote the "use of ICT [information and communications technology] products and services to surveil, repress, and manipulate domestic and foreign population" in DSR partner countries like Pakistan, Kyrgyzstan, and Turkey as part of a program Robert Menendez describes as "digital authoritarianism."[73] The CCP has developed this sophisticated digital authoritarianism model through a combination of technologies, regulations, and policies in four areas: surveilling and tracking Chinese citizens, exploiting and blocking data and content stored or transmitted on the digital domain, implementing authoritarian cyber laws, and directing massive investment in new technologies to secure the Party's future. Replicating, internationalizing, and institutionalizing this digital authoritarianism model is far more profound than 5G and AI standard setting via the International Telecommunication Union (ITU) and the International Standards Organization (ISO) as it poses a direct threat to the democratic countries that is as significant as the domino effect created by the Soviet Union during the Cold War.

The Soft Power of Standards

At this point it should be obvious that the Chinese's digital strategy is strategic, sophisticated, integrated, and comprehensive. The extent of its breadth is illustrated by China's efforts to go beyond frontal tactics like stealing intellectual property all the way to the ultimate nuts-and-bolts operation of creating technical standards. For years Chinese government officials have campaigned for their ICT companies to become more engaged in the technical standards setting processes, and this campaign has been successful.

China's stated goal is to move from being a standards taker to being a standards maker.[74] Operating through companies such as Huawei, ZTE, and China Mobile, in conjunction with DSR allies and partners, China is demonstrating growing influence in bodies such as the ITU and ISO, as well as industry bodies such as the Institute for Electrical Engineers, on issues ranging from 5G through AI and patent royalties.

The United States has urged domestic companies to have greater participation in the standards process, but, again, the effort has been more reactive to the Chinese and less aggressive in intensity. While the Chinese are a long way from dominating the standards setting processes in telecommunications,

China and its DSR partners have signed nearly a hundred standards setting agreements with fifty countries—notably leaving out the previous emphasis on integrating with the United States and the European Union.[75]

Unlike the brute force methods of cross-subsidizing networks around the world with a legal mandate to share information with the Chinese government on demand, the standards setting process represents an element of soft power that can be used to increasingly and quietly bend the international digital community to technical processes in which China has preeminent access and control.

Conclusion: Competing in the Economic and Geopolitical Digital World

China has cleverly integrated the realities of the digital age with its economic levers in a supportive partnership with its version of the private sector in order to advance its national interests, enhance its security, and undermine its major world rival, the United States. The United States has not done the same.

Maya Wang, senior China researcher at Human Rights Watch, has noted, "While it is legitimate for other governments to be very worried about the Chinese government, the U.S. approach has been insufficient and amounts to a 'whack-a-mole' approach. Some policies appear to be rooted in an anti-China approach rather that a holistic approach on how to deal with privacy and security issues. The U.S. government needs to rally the international community around a common goal of offering an alternative to the Chinese digital model."[76] The Senate Foreign Policy Committee Report commissioned by Menendez is even more blunt: "China will write the rules of the Internet unless the United States and its allies counter Beijing's efforts."[77]

Chapter 3 illustrates that the risks associated with our current efforts in cybersecurity need to more aggressively account for emerging systemic threats. Chapter 4 analyzes the tactics the United States employs to enhance cybersecurity and shows they are largely out of date and ineffective. Chapters 5 and 6 define a different structural and policy approach that will, one hopes, be more effective at safeguarding US cybersecurity in both the public and private sectors.

CHAPTER 3

THE SOLAR WINDS OF CHANGE

The Threat of Systemic Cyber Risk

Anthony Shapella

Between March and June 2020, an estimated 18,000 entities downloaded malicious code via standard software updates to the widely used SolarWinds Orion network monitoring tools. The downloads would provide a door for attackers to access thousands of systems and terabytes of sensitive data and enact significant future damage.[1] SolarWinds has a customer base of 300,000 entities, including 425 of the US *Fortune* 500, the top 10 telecommunications companies, all 5 branches of the US military, the top 5 US accounting firms, hundreds of colleges and universities, and many US government agencies.[2] Not three months later, Microsoft announced that a malware campaign was affecting 30,000 customers of its Exchange email platform. The malware allowed threat actors to exfiltrate sensitive emails from government contractors and thousands of organizations globally.[3] These events, perhaps more than any other, demonstrate the truly systemic nature of cyber risk.

At the same time, the world is fighting a powerful network of ransomware attackers that are exploiting vulnerabilities in commonly used software and imposing annual economic losses of up to $20 billion.[4] Recent attacks have directed crippling ransomware at hospitals treating COVID-19 patients,[5] technology companies supplying aviation navigation information,[6] and energy companies supplying natural gas.[7] As our critical infrastructure and service providers become increasingly interconnected and leverage common hardware, software, and vendors, the nation's cyber risk level is dramatically increasing.

Today, more focus and attention are needed to manage systemic cyber risk. Although more attention has been paid to managing systemic risk in the wake of the SolarWinds and Exchange server attacks, most cyber risk management efforts still focus on codifying firm-specific best practices and incentivizing individual companies to adopt them. For example, the leading cyber risk management frameworks—provided by the National Institute of Standards and Technology (NIST), ISO/IEC 27000 series, and the Center for Internet Security (CIS)—focus largely on protecting a company's own networks and assets.[8] However, numerous examples demonstrate that risk manifests not only at the individual company level, but at the systems level, cascading across suppliers, vendors, business partners, and customers. Cyber risk management needs to advance materially and marry company- and systems-level views of cyber risk.

This chapter aims to frame the dynamics of systemic cyber risk. First, we provide definitions of firm-specific and systemic cyber risk to establish clarity and level set. Next, we briefly describe a few recent systemic cyber risks to provide better context and review the current framework for assessing cyber risks to National Critical Functions (NCFs) and recommend enhancements. Last, we provide recommendations for work that can be done by the federal government, in collaboration with industry, to better defend the nation's critical infrastructure from systemic technology failure.

Defining Systemic Cyber Risk

We begin with a definition of risk, as the concept is often misconstrued and loosely defined. Simply put, risk exists because *many things can happen, but only one thing does.*[9] The range of possible outcomes, each with an associated probability, represents *risk*. As individuals, and societies, we form *expectations* about what will happen, and when the world deviates from our expectations, we say we have been impacted by "risk." A good example is the outbreak of COVID-19. We certainly expected a wave of seasonal influenza infections in 2020. We knew that rarer and more impactful infectious diseases could happen based on recent experience with acquired immunodeficiency syndrome (AIDS), severe acute respiratory syndrome (SARS), swine flu, Middle East respiratory syndrome (MERS), and Ebola. But COVID-19 took most people by *surprise*—widely infecting individuals, disrupting global travel, overwhelming medical infrastructure, and reshaping our economies and work environments. Future expectations and risk models will be forever changed by it.

We can apply the general risk definition to cyberspace. It is a common expectation that information captured, stored, and transmitted electronically will remain confidential, its integrity preserved and available (known as the CIA triad).[10] When this does not happen, individuals, companies, or governments say they have been impacted by *cyber risk*, for example, when malicious thieves steal sensitive data, encrypt it in ransomware attacks, or launch denial-of-service attacks on critical systems. These events may surprise us and cause unexpected strategic, financial, operational, and reputational outcomes.

In the worst cases, these adverse outcomes extend beyond the four walls of a single company to a set of connected counterparties. Systemic cyber risk is the potential for the failure of the CIA triad at one entity or product to result in cascading damage across many entities, or to critical systems such as financial payments, transportation, healthcare, or internet services. This phenomenon has also been referred to as "digital supply chain risk," or cyber-induced "ripple events."[11] The attack on the SolarWinds network management software illustrates the scale and depth that systemic cyberattacks can have on the United States.[12]

Fortunately, there is a process and method to sharpen our expectations and understanding of risk *before bad things happen*. We call this the risk management process. It aims to identify, prioritize, measure, and manage the catalog of events that could drive deviation from what we expect and therefore *minimize surprises*. Much work has been done to apply this methodology to risks in cyberspace; however, the historical focus was very firm-specific, addressing the potential for single company failures to safeguard information or maintaining the integrity or availability of data and systems. A single company view aims to answer the questions: How likely is it that Company X will have a critical failure of cybersecurity? And how damaging will that failure be to the company?

This firm-specific risk management is valuable to ensure that we minimize the potential for large *single-company losses*. However, it does not address the problem of *multicompany, cascading impacts* and the breakdown of systems that underlie the country's economic health and well-being. The truth of the matter is that we have built a network of *highly interconnected and tightly coupled* counterparties that rely on common technology products and services. Failures at a single critical point can lead to cascading effects across the entire system.

Technology Product / Service Market Structure

Systemic cyber risk is not solely a technology problem. It is also an economic problem. Systemic cyber risk emanates from highly concentrated markets for technology products and services. Table 3.1 shows a sample of important technologies that US businesses rely on to run their operations. Here we

Table 3.1. Critical Technology Product / Service Market Share

Top Three Companies/Providers	Market Share (Percent)
Desk/Laptop Operating Systems	100
Mobile Operating Systems	100
Web Server Software	92
Web Server Operating Systems	74
Electronic Medical Records (EMR)	70
Transport Layer Security (TLS)	67
Point of Sale Transaction Software	62
Cloud Services	56
Domain Name System (DNS)	47
Firewall/Security Appliances	40

Note: Market share statistics are very rough estimates based on many sources, including company financial reports, SEC disclosures, and industry reports. They are not meant to be precise but rather to demonstrate roughly how much concentration exists in each critical service.

show the market share of the top 3 companies in each segment; if a product or service in these areas is flawed or fails, it could result in widespread impact to the US economy and citizenry.

Much of the recent ransomware activity exploits this market phenomenon. Ransomware attackers focus on vulnerabilities in widely used operating systems and software. For example, recent ransomware attacks have focused on companies with misconfigured Remote Desktop Protocol (RDP)—a Windows feature that allows systems to be managed remotely. Attackers are also targeting vulnerabilities in commonly used Virtual Private Networks (CVE-2019-11510), Application Delivery Controllers (CVE-2019-19781, CVE-2020-5902) and Firewalls (CVE-2020-2021). Attackers know that exploiting commonality maximizes opportunities to achieve their goals—financial, competitive, or geopolitical.

As a society our expectations, and hence risk models, have not caught up with this reality. The key systemic risk questions that must be answered include the following:

- Which companies and technology products represent critical nodes of aggregation (NoAs) based on the number of counterparties that rely on them?
- How vulnerable are the NoAs to material failures of cybersecurity? How secure are the products supplied to the network?
- Which NoAs are being actively targeted by attackers? What is the attackers' motivation and intent? How likely are they to succeed?

- How well prepared are NoAs to handle the significant costs and demands in the event of a security failure in their technology products or services?
- What policies will incentivize strong security at NoAs, make protecting the system a top priority, and minimize negative externalities?

Great progress has been made exploring these questions in some sectors—for example, in financial services, via the risk register and scenario work being done by the Financial Systemic Analysis and Resilience Center (FSARC).[13] NIST has also published information recently that guides companies in identifying and addressing digital supply chain risk.[14] This work will be foundational to expand practices to other critical sectors and functions and ensure that the country is not surprised by, and unprepared for, future systemic technology failures.

Past Examples of Systemic Cyber Risk

Companies rely on many critical technology products and services to support their businesses. Some of these are well known, such as operating systems, email, internet service providers, and cloud computing platforms. Others are more obscure and less well known outside of information technology circles. One of those services, the Domain Name System (DNS), exists to translate text-based web addresses, or URLs, into numeric Internet Protocol (IP) addresses. Without the DNS translation service, users of web browsers would face significant challenges traversing the internet and reaching their desired destinations.

On October 21, 2016, a major US-based DNS provider was disabled by a targeted distributed denial-of-service attack. The attack compromised ~100,000 insecure, connected Internet of Things (IoT) devices, such as web cameras and digital video recorders (DVRs), and used their computing power to overwhelm the DNS provider. As a result, many large businesses faced business disruption simultaneously, with customers unable to access thousands of websites or services.[15]

Seven months later, on May 12, 2017, many companies were significantly impacted by a ransomware attack, which has been attributed to North Korean state actors.[16] "WannaCry" exploited a common vulnerability in unpatched and unsupported versions of a widely used operating system. It spread globally to 200,000 computers in a period of four days before it was stopped by a security researcher who discovered a "kill switch." Impacted companies had data encrypted and were asked to pay a ransom in Bitcoin to recover it. The result was significant business disruption, data, and income loss; some estimates suggest that the WannaCry attack resulted in $4 to $8 billion of economic loss.[17]

A month later, a more damaging attack called "NotPetya" was launched. Numerous governments have concluded that this attack was launched by the Russian military with the intent to destabilize Ukraine. Companies operating in Ukraine, using a dominant accounting software called "MeDoc," with unpatched operating system vulnerabilities, were most heavily impacted. The attack resulted in major business and industrial manufacturing disruption and other financial impacts. Some estimates suggest that NotPetya resulted in over $10 billion in global economic damage.[18]

In a highly targeted August 2018 attack, a malicious actor gained access to the systems of the American Medical Collection Agency (AMCA), a large provider of medical collection services for the healthcare industry. The breach was discovered eight months later; sensitive healthcare and personal information for over 25 million patients treated at more than twenty medical facilities was stolen.[19] AMCA declared bankruptcy as a result of the breach, citing a "cascade of events" that led to "enormous expenses that were beyond the ability of the debtor to bear."[20] This pushed many of the costs back to AMCA's customers, demonstrating how failure of a common vendor can result in material negative externalities. Direct financial costs included mandated breach notification and personal credit monitoring; indirect costs included loss of brand equity and customer trust. Most troubling, patients face the prospect of future identity theft, financial fraud, and other potentially harmful impacts.

These "outsourced" business processes are becoming bigger sources of systemic cyber losses. In August 2019, an attacker launched a ransomware attack on twenty-two Texas municipalities, blocking access to data and demanding ransom payments.[21] An investigation after the attack suggested that the attackers infiltrated a Managed Service Provider (MSP)—an entity hired by the towns to manage their IT systems and infrastructure. In a similar event, attackers targeted another MSP to block four hundred dental practices from accessing their medical records and interrupted medical care.[22]

SolarWinds and Microsoft Exchange Server Attacks

Two recent cyberattacks on SolarWinds' Orion management software and Microsoft Exchange servers around the world have garnered far more attention on systemic cyber risk, in large part due to their scope and scale. Government response efforts, while welcome, have been insufficient or misplaced, but some progress is being made to confront systemic risk.

In December 2020, the threat intelligence firm FireEye uncovered a computer network exploitation affecting private and public sector networks around the world.[23] For nine months before FireEye's revelation, threat actors engaged, without restraint, in a highly targeted intelligence gathering effort to exfiltrate sensitive data from victim servers, which included at least one hundred companies and at least nine federal agencies, including the Departments of Defense, State, and Energy.[24] The threat actors, which American intelligence has assessed were Russian, gained access to these servers by entering malicious code into a software update of the SolarWinds Orion IT management program, enabling them to move laterally across victim networks, escalate administrative privileges, and impersonate users.

The SolarWinds attack is notable not only for its technical complexity, but, more important, for its scope, scale, and impact. The infected Orion software was downloaded by over eighteen thousand customers, and although the number of entities that were deliberately targeted is likely far fewer than this, an investigation into the attack's full scope will take years. In fact, we may never know the full extent of the SolarWinds campaign. The financial impacts are also jarring. Recent reports estimate that government agencies and private organizations will spend $100 billion over the next few years investigating the incident and remediating the damage.[25]

Three months after FireEye's revelation of the SolarWinds attack, reports surfaced that another attack was exploiting four zero-day vulnerabilities in the Microsoft Exchange email platform globally.[26] Microsoft attributed the attack to Hafnium, a Chinese espionage unit that targets email communications across a range of industry sectors, including infectious disease research, defense, and think tanks, all of which work closely with federal agencies.[27] Microsoft released a patch for the vulnerabilities in March 2021 but not before at least thirty thousand organizations were compromised. Just like the SolarWinds campaign, the Hafnium exploitation is notable for its scope and scale, and it will likely require millions of dollars to remediate.

The SolarWinds and Hafnium attacks have ushered in a renewed focus by the public and private sectors on the need to manage and allay systemic cyber risk. For example, President Joe Biden signed an executive order in spring 2021 bolstering federal network security by requiring third party suppliers to comply with a set of specific standards. As has been discussed elsewhere in this book, compliance and regulatory schemes do not address the crux of the nation's cybersecurity problem, which is that companies lack the resources and guidance to improve their own cyber hygiene. An incentive structure is more suitable to confronting these issues. Moreover, the administration's focus on improving federal cybersecurity only partially addresses systemic cyber risk, as most of the US network infrastructure is owned and operated by the private sector. To really address cyber risk at the *systems* level, the government's response should build bridges between the public and private sectors. The Cybersecurity and Infrastructure Security Agency (CISA), described below, is well positioned to begin this process

These incidents illustrate the potential for a number of companies to be simultaneously affected by failures of cybersecurity. The common element across all of them is the *reliance on a widely used software product or vendor*. Failure of the central product or counterparty leads to widespread losses and cascading impacts. The number of these multiparty ripple events is growing. Cyentia Institute and RiskRecon report that such incidents are increasing at an average annual growth rate of 20 percent. Over the past ten years, more than 800 multiparty events have occurred, resulting in downstream damages to nearly 5,500 entities. Cyentia estimates that the median financial cost of ripple events is 13 times larger than single-party incidents.[28] This is a significant challenge to national security that requires collaborative action across industry and government.

Department of Homeland Security, CISA, and National Critical Function

The US Department of Homeland Security (DHS), under the leadership of CISA, has a comprehensive program to

- collect cyber incident data;
- issue alerts, bulletins, frameworks, tips and tools; and
- work with the private sector to assess and address critical cybersecurity risks.

In January 2021, in the wake of the SolarWinds Orion campaign, CISA launched the Systemic Cyber Risk Reduction Venture, which centralizes systemic risk management by attempting to improve cross-sector information sharing, collecting and collating cyber risk data from multiple sources, and attempting to understand shared risks holistically.[29] Housed within CISA's National Risk Management Center, the Venture seeks to apply a common risk analysis architecture to a list of National Critical Functions. The

April 2019

National Critical Functions Set

CONNECT	DISTRIBUTE	MANAGE	SUPPLY
• Operate Core Network • Provide Cable Access Network Services • Provide Internet Based Content, Information, and Communication Services • Provide Internet Routing, Access, and Connection Services • Provide Positioning, Navigation, and Timing Services • Provide Radio Broadcast Access Network Services • Provide Satellite Access Network Services • Provide Wireless Access Network Services • Provide Wireline Access Network Services	• Distribute Electricity • Maintain Supply Chains • Transmit Electricity • Transport Cargo and Passengers by Air • Transport Cargo and Passengers by Rail • Transport Cargo and Passengers by Road • Transport Cargo and Passengers by Vessel • Transport Materials by Pipeline • Transport Passengers by Mass Transit	• Conduct Elections • Develop and Maintain Public Works and Services • Educate and Train • Enforce Law • Maintain Access to Medical Records • Manage Hazardous Materials • Manage Wastewater • Operate Government • Perform Cyber Incident Management Capabilities • Prepare for and Manage Emergencies • Preserve Constitutional Rights • Protect Sensitive Information • Provide and Maintain Infrastructure • Provide Capital Markets and Investment Activities • Provide Consumer and Commercial Banking Services • Provide Funding and Liquidity Services • Provide Identity Management and Associated Trust Support Services • Provide Insurance Services • Provide Medical Care • Provide Payment, Clearing, and Settlement Services • Provide Public Safety • Provide Wholesale Funding • Store Fuel and Maintain Reserves • Support Community Health	• Exploration and Extraction Of Fuels • Fuel Refining and Processing Fuels • Generate Electricity • Manufacture Equipment • Produce and Provide Agricultural Products and Services • Produce and Provide Human and Animal Food Products and Services • Produce Chemicals • Provide Metals and Materials • Provide Housing • Provide Information Technology Products and Services • Provide Materiel and Operational Support to Defense • Research and Development • Supply Water

National Critical Functions: The functions of government and the private sector so vital to the United States that their disruption, corruption, or dysfunction would have a debilitating effect on security, national economic security, national public health or safety, or any combination thereof.

CISA.gov

Figure 3.1. CISA National Critical Functions Set. CISA 2019.

functions represent services provided by "government and the private sector [that are] so vital to the United States that their disruption, corruption, or dysfunction would have a debilitating effect on security, national economic security, national public health or safety, or any combination thereof."[30] The NCFs are listed in figure 3.1.

President Biden's proposed fiscal year 2022 budget calls for a $110 million increase in CISA's budget, on top of a $650 million allocation in the

American Rescue Plan. The funding would "allow CISA to enhance its cyber-security tools, hire highly qualified experts, and obtain support services to protect and defend Federal information technology systems."[31] This funding boost and the establishment of the Systemic Cyber Risk Reduction Venture are welcome steps toward increasing CISA's ability to address systemic risk.

Fortunately, the number of historical cyber events causing systemic property damage or loss of life has been limited. Unfortunately, this may change as we transition to fifth-generation (5G) cellular wireless and rely more on connected devices in critical applications such as transportation (e.g., autonomous vehicles), healthcare (e.g., robo-surgery), and energy (e.g., smart grids), among others. While 5G connectivity will improve access, efficiency, and quality, *it will likely concentrate risk in a small number of critical manufacturers, software providers, and telecommunications firms.* As an example, prior to the advent of robo-surgery, the risk of medical errors was widely distributed across many doctor and hospital groups. Correlation between accidents was weak, driven by factors such as hospital-specific governance and protocols or medical education. Robo-surgery could completely change the risk landscape, with a critical software vulnerability, widespread data integrity issue, or inadequate bandwidth serving as the nexus of medical errors across the system.

While few "physical" cyber catastrophe examples exist, we can view the "nonphysical" examples above as canaries in the coal mine, early warnings about what we might experience in physical systems. NCFs will invariably rely on common operating systems, widely used hardware and software, and continuous high-fidelity bandwidth. NCFs will connect themselves—upstream and downstream—with counterparties that also rely on operating systems, hardware, software, and bandwidth. There is a significant likelihood that one or more nodes in NCF networks will fail, possibly leading to property damage or loss of life. We need to work swiftly and aggressively using the risk management process to assess

- the common components, that is, technology products—hardware, software, sensors, and so on—that support delivery of the NCFs;
- how the components fit together and interconnect into systems at company, industry, national, and international levels;
- the common vendors that supply the NCFs and facilitate delivery of services to the US population;
- the corporate governance, hardware, and software development standards employed by NCFs and their vendors; and
- the "gray space" and interconnections between the nodes where risk often accumulates unknowingly and creates "blind spot" surprises.

On this last point, it is important to stress the danger of artificial boundaries or overcategorizing when evaluating systemic risk. The biologist Robert Sapolsky puts it best: "If you pay lots of attention to where boundaries are, you pay less attention to complete pictures."[32] Donella Meadows, a pioneer of systems thinking, notes, "The greatest complexities arise exactly at the boundaries."[33] She continues, "There is no single, legitimate boundary to draw around a system. We have to invent boundaries for clarity and sanity; and boundaries can produce problems when we forget that we've artificially created them."[34] Nassim Taleb goes further, noting, "Categorizing always produces reduction in true complexity. . . . [I]t drives us to a misunderstanding of the fabric of the world."[35]

Moving from Functions to Fabric

To achieve a full understanding of the "fabric of the world," it will be necessary to evolve the National Critical Functions to a set of end-to-end "maps" of critical systems. To illustrate, let's look at one example, the availability of fuel at gas stations across the United States. Many different actors are involved from the point of finding crude oil in the ground to pushing the button on the gas pump at the corner gas station. The American Petroleum Industry's map of the oil supply chain includes many points of transportation and storage, each with its own technology infrastructure and ecosystem, including hardware, software, and vendors.[36] To properly assess the risk of disruption at the gas pump, we must *work backward*, map the strands in the fabric and zoom in on each thread. Some threads will be steel braid, having more secure systems and software. Others will be weaker, relying on outdated operating systems, vulnerable software, or unstable vendors. *All will be at risk* because the fabric is woven together—or as is commonly said, the system is only as strong as the weakest link.

Recognizing the industry interplay, DHS recently moved the NCF model from an industry-based to a function-based framework. An industry-based view is incomplete as multiple industries interact to deliver the same critical service. For example, the delivery of fuel requires activity across the energy, industrial manufacturing, technology, telecommunications, transportation, and warehousing sectors. Taking a functional view widens the lens to move closer to this interconnected, multi-industry reality. The next step will be focusing on the "connective tissue"—the links that join each subfunction together to arrive at a macro function. Then analysis can be performed on weak points in the system and prioritized for risk management action.

Addressing the Systemic Cyber Risk Problem

Continued work is needed to accelerate understanding of and action on systemic cyber risk. The federal government is in a central position to organize this effort in collaboration with private industry and academia. It is well within the federal remit of protecting the nation's critical infrastructure and keeping citizens safe from the economic, physical, and health impacts of systemic cyber events.

Proactive Identification of Nodes of Aggregation and Cross-Sector Scenarios

More research is needed to comprehensively identify systemically used systems and software across NCF ecosystems and develop plans to address attacks *before they happen*. This was the crux of the global NotPetya attack: a software update was pushed to users of the MeDoc tax and accounting software, which has 90 percent market share in Ukraine. NotPetya also leveraged the EternalBlue vulnerability in Windows, an operating system with over 90 percent market share of desktop operating systems.[37] Vectors of attack that are characterized by this level of market dominance should be a major area of attention. Scenario analysis is very effective for understanding how the system may respond if these products or services are exploited or fail. Plans can then be designed to proactively manage risk and engage stakeholders in the risk management process.

Uniting Public and Private Parties to Address Systemic Cyber Risk

One of the most important roles of the federal government is to bring together actors across public, private, and nonprofit sectors and academia to work on systemic cyber risk. We applaud the government's active participation in the Information Sharing and Analysis Centers (ISAC). To achieve success in addressing systemic risk, it is necessary to *build bridges across the ISACs* to construct the maps and risk assessments for NCFs. We suggest an expansion of workshops that bring together cross-functional experts to design, build, execute, and annually rerun scenarios. In the fuel example above, a workshop devoted to preventing pandemonium at the pump would convene energy, industrial manufacturing, telecommunications, transportation, and warehousing companies, *along with* technology companies that supply critical hardware, software, and technology services. This level of cross-industry collaboration is essential to properly understand and address the risk. It will also broaden each company's view and understanding of its position in the broader network and contribution to system-level risk. The Office of Digital

Strategy and Security proposed in chapter 5 would be well suited to assist in these programs.

Incentivizing Companies to Proactively Manage Systemic Cyber Risk

Companies need to dramatically improve their cyber hygiene. Patching practices are not nearly aggressive enough to address the risk that exists in the system. Software vendors issue critical patches, CISA sends automated and special alerts, and many companies seemingly still do not patch.[38] Others fail to configure technology assets properly, leaving them exposed to the internet via open ports or accessible without proper access controls.[39]

More action is needed to prompt strong cyber hygiene at the company level, which will ultimately reduce risk at the systems level. This is best achieved via positive incentives that nudge companies toward sound practices. Greater momentum is needed to advance voluntary actions such as tax incentives for cybersecurity spending and liability limitations for demonstrable adherence to standard frameworks and continued rigor in security as a prerequisite to government contracts.[40]

Engaging with the Global Insurance Industry

The global insurance industry is well versed in assessing the risk to complex systems. Insurers regularly underwrite the risks of their clients related to failures in critical infrastructure such as energy, aviation, marine, manufacturing, healthcare, and transportation. The methods used to model such failures are well-established and can support the efforts to model systemic cyber risk. Some of the scenarios that are most concerning have already been modeled by insurers, including cyberattacks on the US power grid, aviation software and navigation systems, and medical devices. Insurers can not only lend technical expertise, but also guidance on how to build scenarios, set and calibrate assumptions, test models, and apply them to risk management problems. An added benefit of insurance industry engagement is a focus on best practice and risk controls that will permeate underwriting and be applied broadly to companies across the country. This will help improve the overall cyber posture and practices across industries which purchase cyber insurance.

Facilitating Threat Intelligence Data and Information Sharing

Great risk models and scenarios require great data and intelligence. CISA is doing an impressive job tracking and issuing alerts for critical hardware and software vulnerabilities, as well as bulletins on attack campaigns. This work can be expanded by linking the alerts to the NCF "maps" described above. Companies that sit within an NCF can be alerted when a certain type of attack or exploit is observed in the wild that could affect the NCF. This intelligence may emanate from any federal agency including the Federal Bureau of Investigation (FBI), the Department of Defense (DoD), and the National Security Agency (NSA), among others. It may also emanate directly from companies within an NCF chain via DHS's Cyber Incident Report platform. DHS might consider asking in the reporting questionnaire whether the reported incident has the potential to impact other companies in one of DHS's defined NCF chains. The NCFs can be listed, and the user can check those that apply. Then new scenarios can be built to assess the impact of failure, or existing scenarios can be updated to reflect observed activity.

Promoting Standards for Hardware and Software That Supports NCFs

The Mirai botnet that crippled a major US-based DNS provider in 2016 was built on a foundation of over one hundred thousand insecure connected devices.[41] To mitigate the growing risk of such IoT-based attacks, it has to be the norm that connected devices are shipped secure *by default*. The security expectations and standards for device manufacturers and software providers need to rise given the very real risk of putting human life or property in danger. Expectations for hardware production and software development need to be clear, well documented, and codified, and adherence to standards needs to be independently validated for the most critical applications. While it is best to allow flexibility in how companies choose to meet such standards (no one-size-fits-all), we suggest a nonprofit, similar to Underwriters Laboratories, that coordinates efforts and promulgates standards. Standards can be developed jointly and collaboratively with industry to ensure that they balance the government's interest in safety with industry's interest in fostering innovation, speed, and cost-effective product management.

Zero Trust Architecture and Its Applicability to Systemic Risk Management

The SolarWinds and Microsoft Exchange server attacks have sparked a renewed focus on a risk management concept called zero trust (ZT). ZT is a security strategy that assumes that an enterprise's software and devices—and those using them—cannot be trusted *by default*.[42] An enterprise employing a ZT architecture consistently verifies its users and devices through assessments of default access controls, multifactor authentication, and least-privilege access. ZT is not so much a specific tool as a model to be integrated into a broader security strategy. For this reason, it requires *real-time insight* into third-party relationships, enterprise network activity, and user attributes such as identity, operating system versions, patch levels, and more. Because of this holistic focus on enterprise-level cyber-security, ZT can be a comprehensive risk management framework. Guidance on how to implement zero trust can be found in the National Institute for Standards and Technologies' Special Publication 800-207.[43]

Educating Companies, Government Entities, and Individuals on Systemic Cyber Risk

Systemic risk is notoriously difficult to visualize and understand, and companies lack clear guidance on how best to manage the risk associated with third-party relationships. They also generally have a narrow view that focuses on their market space. The view becomes even narrower as activities—such as management of IT infrastructure—are outsourced. The list of vendors for a single company can grow to hundreds, thousands, or even tens of thousands for the largest companies. As the list grows, exposure to ripple events grows exponentially and visibility becomes more and more challenging.

DHS has made this a high priority recently via the External Dependencies Management (EDM) Assessment. The EDM is an interview-based assessment tool that allows an organization to assess its dependence on external counterparties.[44] NIST has also boosted efforts to help companies understand their exposure to cyber risk. For instance, it updated its framework (Version 1.1) in April 2018 to incorporate more specific maturity levels related to understanding cyber supply chain risk and critical dependencies. It is also working to update its 2015 Supply Chain Risk Management Practices for Systems and Organizations to "better help organizations identify, assess, and respond to cyber supply chain risks while still aligning with other fundamental NIST cybersecurity risk management guidance."[45] The updated version is expected to be released in April 2022. Incentivizing companies to complete an EDM, update their NIST maturity level for third-party vendor risk, and understand their overall supply chain risk is the first step in achieving better understanding of standard cybersecurity practices.[46]

Beyond the EDM and NIST cybersecurity frameworks, it would be helpful for DHS to publish educational materials that explain and illustrate systemic cyber risk. Publishing NCF maps with supporting technology infrastructure like the fuel example above will increase transparency and understanding. Such DHS publications might also include case studies and scenario analysis that further build out narratives on how and where system failures can occur. We recognize the balancing act of being transparent and forthcoming with information and maintaining safety and security by not disclosing too much information. Disclosure can be tiered, with companies in an NCF flow receiving more detailed reports and less detailed reports being shared with the general public.

Funding Pragmatic Research on Cyber Systemic Risk Management

The book on methods for applying the risk management process to systemic cyber risk has not been written yet. This is a promising area of research that will only grow in importance as 5G connectivity and new technologies emerge. The federal government should continue to support promising private, non-profit, and academic research that explicitly aims to improve the country's understanding of and ability to manage systemic cyber risk. Research should be highly interdisciplinary as the problem is multifaceted: it is not simply a technology problem; it is economic, social, psychological, and mathematical. Applying creative problem-solving approaches from other domains such as epidemiology (i.e., the spread of disease through vulnerable populations) and economics (i.e., game theory in decision making) should be encouraged.

Conclusion

Systemic cyber risk represents a major threat to national security and safety. Numerous nonphysical examples demonstrate the damaging and growing impact of multiparty cyber events. These nonphysical examples portend more concerning physical events given common system components and 5G-enabled connected technology advances. Risk management efforts have not caught up with our highly connected reality; they are focused too much on firm-specific cyber risk management and too little on the connections between firms and the ubiquitous technology that underlies delivery of critical services.

NIST and DHS have established strong programs to address cyber risk. A good next step is to bring industries together across boundaries with the goal of mapping National Critical Functions, developing scenarios, and proactively addressing sources of systemic risk. Some risk will stem from common vendors, others from common hardware and software. Actions to address these risks include the following:

- Proactive identification of Nodes of Aggregation (NoAs);
- Strong standards for NoAs that are integral to NCFs;

- Clear and codified standards for hardware and software product security;
- Attention to NoA market structure and economics;
- Incentives for companies to invest in cybersecurity;
- Links between threat intelligence collection and NCFs maps; and
- Research and education on the topic of systemic risk.

We end with our earlier definition of risk: many things can happen, but only one thing does.[47] We are surprised and underprepared only when we focus too little or misperceive the range of possible outcomes, that is, the true fabric of risk. There is an opportunity to apply the risk management process, avoid major future surprises and unwanted systemic failures, and in the process protect human life and property. The ISA stands ready to partner with the federal government in this noble endeavor.

CHAPTER 4

OUTDATED AND INEFFECTIVE

Why Our Current Cybersecurity Programs Fail to Keep Us Safe

Larry Clinton and Alexander T. Green

In chapter 1, the authors documented that the United States is failing to secure cyberspace largely because it has focused too narrowly on the operational and technical aspects of cybersecurity and not enough on the economic causes of the attacks. Conversely, as discussed in chapter 2, one of our major adversaries, China, has developed a sophisticated digital policy that integrates technical vulnerabilities with economics in a broad geopolitical context that has been extremely successful in achieving China's strategic goals. And in chapter 3, it was pointed out that not only are the number of attacks and attackers growing, but the very nature of cyberattacks is evolving, potentially leading to even more catastrophic systemwide risks. This chapter is an analysis of the current and long-standing US approach to cybersecurity and an explanation of why these tactics are proving insufficient to the task of providing the nation with a sustainably secure cyber system.

Richard Clarke and Robert Knake are two of the most experienced and well-respected experts in the field of cybersecurity. We use their description of the state of US cybersecurity policy as a baseline for our analysis. In their 2019 book, *The Fifth Domain*, Clarke and Knake wrote:

Since the Clinton Administration our cybersecurity strategy has changed very little.... We return to the basic idea that companies that own and operate the internet and the things they connect to it ... will be responsible for protecting themselves. Government's role will be limited to support the private victims of cyber-attacks with law enforcement, information sharing, diplomacy and in the rare cases where it is both feasible and in the national security interest, military force. Government will also play a role of helping industry help itself through nudges to encourage investment and cooperation in cyber-security through research training convening and ultimately through regulation.[1]

It is worth noting that nowhere in the authors' description of US cyber strategy do the words *economic, partnership,* and *leadership* appear. We argue that all three concepts need to be centrally located in a competitively effective cybersecurity policy.

Based on the analysis provided in chapter 1, it would be hard to argue that the current approach has been even remotely successful. Analyzing our current tactics demonstrates why they are, as currently practiced, insufficient.

Traditional Regulation: Ineffective in Cyberspace

Perhaps the most common response for those becoming aware of the cyber-security issue, and the ultimate tactic suggested by Clarke and Knake, is to suggest that what is needed is a standard regulatory model. Presumably, in such a system the federal government would prescribe a set of effective standards that industry would have to comply with, subject to independent audit and enforcement for lack of compliance, including stiff penalties.

Unfortunately, this suggestion demonstrates a fundamental lack of understanding of the nature of the cybersecurity problem. It also highlights lack of awareness of the extent to which regulation has already been attempted, where it found little success. More important, it demonstrates the failure to realize that the traditional regulatory frameworks are fundamentally ill-suited to the digital age—a conclusion that has been reached even by those who have been put in charge of implementing such frameworks.[2]

Much of our traditional regulatory processes and judicial enforcement is designed to address malfeasance. However, the core problem with cybersecurity is not that the technology or the users are incompetent, uncaring, or evil. The core problem is technology is under attack. The attacks are not *because* the system is inherently vulnerable, although it is. As discussed in chapter 1, most of our infrastructure is extremely vulnerable but rarely attacked. The primary cause of cyberattacks is overwhelming economic incentives. Certainly, technical modifications and operational enhancements, which are the focus of most cyber regulations, may improve security on the margins, but the evidence is now clear that these regulatory models are not up to the task and only pile on more requirements to overtasked security teams without demonstrating corresponding security gains.

Cybersecurity is a unique twenty-first-century problem. Traditional regulation is based on the independent agency model, which was initiated with the Interstate Commerce Commission (ICC) to deal with the hot technology of the 1800s: railroads. This model essentially calls for elected officials, such as Congress, to set broad policy parameters. An expert agency would then implement these policies by adopting specific standards or compliance requirements. This model has been copied for the past two centuries to deal with issues as divergent as consumer products (Consumer Product Safety Commission [CPSC]), telecommunications (Federal Communications Commission [FCC]), and financial management (Securities and Exchange Commission [SEC]). It assumes that the independent agents have adequate expertise to set the standards or compliance requirements and that, when followed, the requirements achieve the goal, whether safety, transparency, or fairness. It also usually assumes that there is a stable set of standards or requirements that the agency can determine have been followed, consistent with the broad policy parameters. Typically, regulated entities are audited to assess compliance with these standards.

The reasons these industrial age methods are proving ineffective is largely because they were designed to address fundamentally different types of problems from those we face today in cybersecurity. The model essentially attempts to locate a static standard that, for example, assures consumer safety wherever producers are in compliance. The key factor is that the subject being regulated is fairly stable. However, cybersecurity is not like consumer product safety. If a regulator were to set standards for automobile brake pads, scientific analysis would be done to determine the appropriate amount of friction required to stop a vehicle of x size and y weight traveling at z speed. Over time, the size of the vehicles and the speeds at which they travel may vary, but the math doesn't change. So a standard in this sense can be developed and reliably applied with penalties for noncompliance.

However, in cyber, the technology is constantly changing, as are the attack methods, and new vulnerabilities are continuously being introduced or resurfacing. In other words, the target state for security is always moving. Clear standards, such as those needed for auto safety, become outdated quickly. The typical notice and comment rule-making process used for regulation by most agencies and government institutions is not equipped to handle the ever-changing cyber landscape. Transforming a proposal into an enforceable final rule can take several years, and by the time it is finalized, the initial risk or vulnerability of concern has evolved into something completely different. While there may be best practices, sometimes referred to as "process standards," these operate at a higher level of abstraction than traditional standards, such as in the consumer product safety model, and hence are difficult to precisely audit or confirm as to their actual impact.

The Coast Guard published its Cybersecurity Strategy concerning cyber risks at facilities regulated by the Maritime Transportation Security Act in 2015. The strategy went through Notice and Comment in 2017, and rules were made final in 2020. Five years is too long to develop rules for cybersecurity.

While the traditional regulatory model proved effective during the industrial age and may even be helpful in isolated areas of cybersecurity, as we discuss below, generally speaking, it is inappropriate for the digital age.

Cybersecurity Regulation

It is a common misconception that cybersecurity regulation has not been tried. As Clarke and Knake point out, "There is a mountain of cybersecurity regulation created by federal agencies. Banks, nuclear power plants, self-driving cars, hospitals, insurance companies, defense contractors, passenger aircraft, chemical plants, and dozens of other private sector entities are all subject to cybersecurity regulation by a nearly indecipherable stream of agencies including FTC, FAA, DHS, FERC, DOE, HHS, OCC, and so on."[3]

Clarke and Knake examine certain cases of cybersecurity regulation that demonstrate the faulty nature of the model in this space. For example, healthcare institutions were among the first entities regulated for cybersecurity, under the Health Insurance Portability and Accountability Act of 1996 (HIPAA). Yet they are one of the sectors that fares the worst when it comes to cybersecurity. In fact, data breaches are the number one regulatory challenge facing the healthcare sector.[4] Just because an entity is HIPAA compliant does not mean it is properly protected from cyberattacks, which increased at an alarming rate during the COVID-19 pandemic.[5] In fact, a recent industry analysis showed that the number of confirmed healthcare-related data breaches had increased 71 percent since 2019.[6] As John Schneider, chief technology officer at Apixio, noted, "We shouldn't look to HIPAA to provide guidance. . . . Expecting regulations to fix data security problems is unrealistic."[7]

One of the deficiencies of the regulatory model is that its goal is compliance, which is generally a minimal accepted practice, and there is little incentive for entities to go beyond the compliance standard, even if more is required to provide actual security effectiveness. Put another way, compliance is helpful but not sufficient to combat today's cybersecurity challenges. In a post-COVID comprehensive study, ESI ThoughtLab found healthcare institutions ranked 11 of 13 critical sectors in terms of average loss compared to revenue.[8] Healthcare also ranked 11 of 13 sectors in terms of understanding cyber risk using state-of-the art quantitative methods and 13 of 13 sectors in terms of plans to increase spending. The study also found that on average healthcare institutions vastly underestimated the probability of a cyber breach and that less than half of the healthcare institutions had disaster recovery plans or cyber incident recovery plans or did regular cyber risk assessments or stress tests.

The heavily regulated financial services industry did better than healthcare but was empirically not the consensus industry leader, as might have been expected. In fact, among the 13 industry sectors analyzed, financial services led only in terms of plans to boost spending (followed closely in second place by the largely unregulated technology sector). This is consistent with the general understanding within the industry that regulations spur increased spending but not necessarily increased security. Financial services came out in the middle of the road in terms of losses compared to revenues: it was equivalent to healthcare in terms of vastly underestimating the likelihood of a cyber breach and was only slightly better than the healthcare sector in terms of cybersecurity effectiveness, with just over 50 percent of financial institutions having disaster recovery plans and cyber incident and recovery plans and conducting regular risk assessments and stress tests.

Overall, the ESI study found that heavily regulated sectors like finance and healthcare regularly ranked below generally unregulated sectors like the tech, general automotive, and manufacturing sectors in several critical cybersecurity measures.

Even government officials charged with implementing cyber requirements in heavily regulated sectors like telecommunications have come to the conclusion that traditional regulatory efforts have proven to be inadequate, not because they have not been tried, but because they are the wrong tool for this particular problem.

The former chair of the FCC under President Obama, Thomas Wheeler, and Rear Adm. (Ret.) David Simpson both worked in heavily regulated industries, telecommunications and defense, respectively, and are experienced regulators themselves. In 2019, they wrote for the Brookings Institution:

Current procedural rules for government agencies were developed in an industrial environment in which innovation and change—let alone security threats—developed more slowly. The fast pace of digital innovation and threats requires a new approach to the government business relationship. As presently structured, government is not in a good position to get ahead of the threat and determine standards and compliance measures where the technology and adversary's activities change so rapidly. A new cybersecurity regulatory paradigm should be developed that seeks to deescalate the adversarial relationship that can develop between regulators and the companies they oversee. This would replace the detailed compliance instructions left over from the industrial era.[9]

Cybersecurity and Sustainability

Virtually any proposed solution to the cybersecurity problem that begins with the phrase, "All you have to do is . . . ," is almost certainly wrong. Despite what some marketers may claim, cybersecurity is a difficult problem to address sustainably. To address cyber risk, you need to deal with extremely complicated technical systems that interface with even more complicated technical systems that are under constant attack by extremely clever, well-resourced, and motivated actors who have little or no fear of substantial risk to themselves.

For nearly a decade the US government has touted the use of the NIST Cybersecurity Framework (NIST CSF) as the answer to most cybersecurity problems and made it the core of most government cyber regulatory structures.[10] "It's easy; just follow NIST," is the implicit, sometimes explicit, message. However, the government has resolutely refused calls to test the NIST CSF for effectiveness and cost-effectiveness, as called for in Presidential Executive Order 13636, which gave rise to the development of the NIST CSF.[11]

Meanwhile, independent studies have found little basis for government claims regarding NIST CSF effectiveness. ESI ThoughtLab's 2020 study found that a minority (42 percent) of companies found to be leaders in terms of NIST CSF compliance were also leaders in terms of cybersecurity effectiveness.[12] "ESI's statistical finding confirms what many CISO's know: Firms need to go beyond NIST and other frameworks to secure their enterprises from escalating cyber-attacks."[13]

Similarly, a 2020 MIT report notes that standards such as the Center for Internet Security controls (CIS 2020) and the National Institute of Standards and Technology framework (NIST 2018) provide limited protection capabilities against sophisticated threat actors like nation-states. The report quotes a former official from one government agency: "Compliance [with standards] does not mean security. Certified compliance is a joke. We were constantly violating systems that were supposedly compliant." Further, the report states that government and private sector experts worry these standards are well below the existing capabilities of the largest firms in key sectors. So codifying these standards as a regulation or conducting audits based on those standards would not enhance security at the companies whose failure presents the greatest systemic risk.[14]

The cybersecurity problem is not the result of lack of awareness. There is hardly anyone who does not know there is a cybersecurity problem. The bigger issue is not understanding how complicated the issue is.

It is a completely unproven assertion that better cybersecurity will make an enterprise more profitable. If that were really the case, the world's business community would have discovered it by now and responded by making their systems secure. The truth is, as detailed in chapter 1, that much of digital economics is upside down. We need to reorder the economic incentives of the digital age, not issue more technical standards via regulation.

The Regulatory Compliance Model and Cybersecurity

Traditional compliance is essentially a pass-fail issue. You have either filed the forms or not. You have fulfilled the requirement or not. You can check the box or not. You are in compliance, or you are out of compliance.

Cybersecurity is not pass-fail. You are not secure or insecure. Security is a continuum with gradations of security. Moreover, not all entities, even within an industry sector, have the same security needs or the same threats to their security. As a result, a traditional check-the-box compliance system is inappropriate for the cybersecurity domain.

Traditional compliance is a backward-looking system. Did you do *x* or not? Cybersecurity is not a backward-looking exercise. Good cyber risk management is future oriented. A critical step is to anticipate what sorts of threats you are likely to be subjected to and appropriately allocating your (usually meager) security resources accordingly. In today's compliance world, you can be compliant and not operationally effective. For example, every security compliance standard says an organization needs to have antivirus on the endpoint. However, there is no differentiation in the operational effectiveness of that solution. An organization can deploy the cheapest, simplest rule-based antivirus solution and get the "check" for having met the requirement. However, those that deploy a more sophisticated (and expensive) anti-malware, behavior-based" solution get no additional credit. So if compliance is the only goal, it can be met without gaining the necessary operational effectiveness needed in today's cyber threat environment. For a truly effective cybersecurity paradigm, security itself—properly measured—not check list compliance, must be the goal. That is not currently the case with most government regulation.

In addition, the measurement systems that are the basis of most regulatory models is similarly inappropriate. In his excellent book, *How to Measure Anything in Cyber Risk*, Douglas Hubbard provides an extensive review of the statistical literature on the ordinal scales that are the standard measurement technique for much of the existing cybersecurity regulation. He determined that "there is not a single study indicating that the use of such methods actually helps reduce risk."[15]

A Waste of Resources

In addition to undermining security by setting a low minimal compliance bar, regulations may siphon valuable resources. As noted above, most regulations are not built around procedures that have been empirically shown to be effective in enhancing security, or in doing so, in a cost-effective fashion. In their 2020 report, MIT researchers Sean Atkins and Chappell Lawson note, "Because the value of specific cybersecurity investments is uncertain, government mandates tend to be both ineffective and economically inefficient. Firms may even cannibalize useful investments in order to comply with ill-conceived or inappropriate mandates."[16]

Numerous studies have indicated that we do not have enough cybersecurity professionals. It is estimated that as many as 3.5 million cybersecurity jobs will be unfilled by 2021.[17] As a result, the few professionals we do have are already stretched thin. Complying with regulations that have not been shown empirically to enhance security takes away precious time and resources that security practitioners could instead use to focus on their actual security mission. In addition, as discussed in the following chapters, the uncoordinated regulatory structure results in duplication of effort that wastes between 40 percent and 70 percent of these scarce resources (depending on the sector studied)—all without evidence of actually improving security.

When scarce security resources are sucked up by compliance costs, it means less time and money for actual security. Mandating compliance with outdated regulations is not only ineffective but actually counterproductive to enhancing cybersecurity. Also, organizations can overestimate the value of compliance and end up with an unjustified sense of security, which could lead them to take risks they assume are managed when in fact they are un-knowingly vulnerable.

Undermining of Partnerships

The compliance/penalty culture, which is an inherent part of the regulatory structure, is especially problematic in the cyber domain. The mindset of the regulator tends to be like a parent who feels they must discipline their unruly, industry child. In cases of actual criminal or fraudulent behavior, this is appropriate. However, in cybersecurity, the problem is more often the unequal balance between the corporate (and governmental) defenders and the attackers who are focused on inherently vulnerable systems, have first mover advantage, and are often better resourced. This is especially the case for major cyber events, such as SolarWinds, which naturally are the ones of highest concern to the government.

Too many regulators feel the need to blame the victim of the attack, incorrectly presuming that severe penalties will drive better security. More-over, the adversarial nature of the compliance/penalty culture is counter-productive to the sorts of collaborative partnership that industry and government need to evolve in order to create a sustainable collective defense model. Simply the perception of the big stick of penalties and enforcement will intensify the pre-existing attitude of fear and mistrust which undermines the widely accepted wisdom that neither government nor industry can main-tain a secure cyber system unless they act together in true partnership. The former director of the Cybersecurity and Infrastructure Security Agency, Christopher Krebs, put this concept succinctly: "Protecting privacy is at the cornerstone of everything we do as an agency that depends entirely on maintaining the trust necessary to work with industry through our voluntary programs."[18] Krebs's view was echoed in the 2020 study by Atkins and Law-son: "For their part government officials lament that mandates encourage a 'compliance mentality' among firms leading to minimalist approaches rather than a concerted effort to secure their systems, cooperate with other firms in their industry or collaborate intensively with federal authorities."

In instances such as the Enron, WorldCom, and Volkswagen scan-dals, regulators stand in for consumers and protect them from malfeasant corporations—as they should. However, in today's cybersecurity environ-ment, the opponents are not mainly corporate cheats but rather vast crim-inal syndicates and increasingly nation-states and their surrogates that are stealing and corrupting personal data, corporate intellectual property, and national secrets. The reality, often articulated but rarely implemented, is that government, consumers, and industry are actually on the same side. They need to work together.

As we detail in chapter 5, a new paradigm that moves away from the traditional adversarial regulatory model and instead steers organizations to effectively use cybersecurity techniques based on empirical assessments of their legitimate business goals will lead to a more fulsome partnership between the public and private sectors—a social contract is a more effective model for the digital age.

Government Failure in Regulating Industry

The foundational assumption of the expert agency model is that government knows what to do; all that is needed is to compel a recalcitrant private sector to follow government mandates. There is no evidence that government has attained that degree of expertise in cybersecurity. In fact, the data suggest the opposite. As noted previously, the SolarWinds attack of 2020 compromised multiple significant government agencies, including DHS, and the government was completely unaware of the attack until informed by private sector victims.

An April 2020 report from the Government Accountability Office (GAO) on the Defense Department's cybersecurity found that the Pentagon had not even fully implemented its own initiatives and practices related to improving cyber hygiene, leaving the department in the dark as to how and when to respond to breaches. According to the report, "The department does not know the extent that cyber hygiene practices have been implemented to protect DOD networks from key cyberattack techniques."[19]

A 2019 US Senate Investigations Subcommittee review of agencies' cybersecurity compliance with NIST standards found 88 percent of them failed to properly protect personal identification information, 63 percent did not have an accurate list of their IT assets, and 75 percent did not install security patches.[20] In December 2020, GAO reported that none of the 23 agencies in its review had fully implemented key foundational practices for managing information and communications technology supply chains. More broadly, a 2019 GAO report found:

> The White House Office of Management and Budget and DHS examined the capabilities of 96 civilian agencies across 76 cybersecurity metrics and found that 71 agencies had cybersecurity programs that were either at risk or at high risk. The assessment also stated that

agencies were not equipped to determine how malicious actors seek
to gain access to their information systems and data.[21]

As of March 2021, GAO reports that little if any progress has been made
by agencies in addressing deficiencies they had been made aware of over a
decade ago, noting, "Specifically, of the roughly 3,300 recommendations
made [by GAO] since 2010, more than 750 had not been implemented as of
December 2020," including 67 priority recommendations.[22] Moreover, even
where recommendations were implemented, agencies face the same challenges in safeguarding their information systems because many of the recommendations had been only partially implemented. When asked if agencies
are safer now than they used to be, Greg Wilshusen, director of information
security at the GAO, replied, "We believe, as we've reported last year, that
federal information security remains at high risk."[23]

This kind of lack of compliance by the government to their own standards further calls into question if the government has the ability to judge
the private sector on cybersecurity. Even before SolarWinds, the government
suffered multiple successful cyberattacks, involving the DoD, the SEC, and
the Office of Personnel Management. Given government agencies' inconsistent record of complying with their own regulations, combined with their
susceptibility to attack, we can add government to the list of sectors that are
highly regulated but fail to achieve acceptable levels of security.

Does Cyber Regulation Ever Make Sense?

There is a role for regulation in certain areas. Protecting individuals' data
rights is one example. Certainly, the requirement to inform citizens when
their personal data has been compromised is appropriate, as is the requirement to assist consumers with credit monitoring and other protections paid
for by the organization that lost the data. In fact, the most sensible policy in
this regard would be for a national statute preempting state laws and creating
a national standard for disclosure and remediation, as discussed in chapter 5.

Regulation can also be used to encourage improved cybersecurity in sectors where the economics of the industry are based on the regulatory model.
An example would be a traditional utility such as a municipal water system
or, in some states, electricity service that is provided through a traditional
rate of return (ROR) model.

In a ROR model, the entity, such as a privately owned public utility,
receives payments from consumers based on a determination made typically
by a public utility commission that includes adequate operational funds and

a reasonable ROR. In such cases, the costs of adequate cybersecurity can be assessed and plowed back into the rate base. This allows the companies to provide an adequate level of security while protecting consumers and ensuring adequate capital for investment for the critical infrastructure itself. If the core economics of the business inherently involves regulation, the intact regulatory structures can be adapted to provide the adequate financing of needed cybersecurity investments. However, this model breaks down if the security mandates are unfunded. What is required to make regulation in this type of environment sustainable is to recognize and fold the costs into the rate base.

As we discuss in chapter 5, expecting corporations to provide adequate security and meet their commercial obligations is obviously reasonable. Unfortunately, the traditional regulatory model, which applies generic requirements, fails to account for the uniqueness of technologies, business plans, and cyber threats. However, modern risk assessment models can be used to meet these needs and can be used to assure that companies meet their appropriate security responsibilities as defined in the National Infrastructure Protection Plan. Examples of these more appropriate models can be used to apply to regulated entities.

Cyber Law Enforcement Efforts

Clarke and Knake include law enforcement as part of the "limited role" government has in assisting the private sector in its cybersecurity efforts. However, a simple recitation of the basic facts makes it clear that government is not fulfilling its law enforcement duties sufficiently.

As we noted in chapter 1, cybercrime is at an all-time high, and there are no signs that it is slowing down. Economic losses from cybercrime are estimated to be as much as $2 trillion annually—and increasing to as much as $10.5 trillion by 2025. Even if that estimate is off by 50 percent, and we are losing only $1 trillion a year (and $5 trillion in four years), the cost is unacceptable. Meanwhile, the United States successfully prosecutes roughly one percent of cybercriminals.[24] This almost negligible rate of successful prosecution has not changed significantly in decades. This means that law enforcement provides practically zero deterrent power. It is obvious that we need to be far more aggressive and creative in assisting our law enforcement agents to address cybercrime.

To be clear, the fault lies not with our overwhelmed law enforcement personnel but with the antiquated systems and lack of resources they are given to do an extremely difficult and important job (fig. 4.1). Cyber law enforcement agents are competing with a sophisticated and resilient enemy, one that often has nearly unlimited resources—including at times collaboration with state actors.

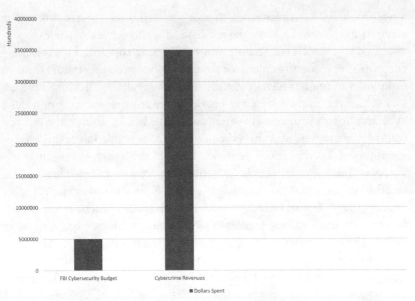

Figure 4.1. Law Enforcement Budgets versus Cybercrime Revenue

Due to the stealthy nature of modern attack methods, just detecting the attack and uncovering the crime can be difficult. Once the attack is discovered, agents may have to deal with the numerous mechanisms criminals use to hide their identity, for example, virtual private networks (VPNs) and proxies. A court order may be required to conduct a search, further delaying the investigation. If the perpetrator is overseas, as is often the case, it can become even more difficult to obtain the warrant.[25] There may be jurisdictional issues, especially if the case is international, and extradition may be required. This creates its own problems as discussed below. Law enforcement is also tasked with obtaining and safely storing the digital evidence needed to bring a case against these criminals. Obtaining and handling electronic evidence is an expensive and rigorous process.[26] Expenses include personnel costs, licenses, and equipment. If there is a mistake in the handling of evidence, a defense attorney could have that evidence thrown out. In many law enforcement departments, the handling of electronic evidence is not yet part of the core curriculum.[27] Finally, prosecution can be hampered simply because statutes are confusing or inadequate since legislators have not kept up with the digital environment.[28] While these complexities help explain why criminal prosecution is difficult, they do not explain why there has not been a comprehensive plan by government to address the situation and implement an action plan.

Funding for cyber law enforcement clearly has not been sufficient to meet the constantly growing gap.[29] The FBI, which is the federal "lead" for cybercrime, requested a $40 million increase in its cybersecurity budget, in part to tackle the growing threat of ransomware. This increase brought the FBI's cybersecurity budget to only approximately $475 million to chase down syndicates reaping trillions of dollars in profit.[30] The inadequacy of this government commitment is placed in stark relief when we realize that some individual corporations have a larger cybersecurity budget than the FBI. JP Morgan Chase, for instance, has an annual budget of $600 million.[31] And, as cars undergo a digital transformation,[32] cybersecurity spending in the automotive sector, not often thought of as on the cutting edge of digital defense, is expected to reach $7.67 billion by 2027,[33] which is roughly five times the size of the DHS's 2021 budget for cybersecurity.[34] Clearly, industry is considerably outspending the US government to protect itself and its stakeholders in the digital age.[35]

Contributing to the funding problem is the antiquated organization around cyber enforcement. In an era when cybercriminals use advanced technology to achieve heightened efficiency and effectiveness, we are still operating with a disparate and often uncoordinated law enforcement structure rooted in a twentieth-century model. While industry is increasingly reorganizing and streamlining their antifraud and cyber defenses,[36] federal departments and other government agencies remain confined to structures inconsistent with the realities of the digital age.[37] These departments and agencies include the DOJ, SEC, DHS, FBI, ICE, Treasury, USPS, and USAID. Except for the DHS, the FBI has the largest budget for cybersecurity-related matters. An overwhelming volume of reported cybercrimes are being placed on law enforcement agencies at the local, state, and federal levels. Los Angeles County Sheriff's Department chief, Bill McSweeney, said:

> There are so many cases that federal agencies skim off the high-loss cases, leaving local agencies with smaller things like forged tickets to sports or music events, losses of less than $1,000, or other relatively small scams. The volume of these cases would be way too much for federal agencies to handle. We need to either decide that we're going to empower and properly equip local police to take on these crimes, or decide that we're going to ignore them, which, for the most part, is what we're doing now.[38]

With so many domestic government entities competing for enforcement, there tends to be duplicative projects, misapportioned funds, and confusion of authority. All these issues lead to inefficiencies and a decreased chance of successfully capturing and prosecuting cybercriminals.[39]

Part of the irony is that criminal syndicates often collaborate in pursuing their criminal objectives but law enforcement, both domestic and international, often are mired in turf disputes and there has been little done to enable private sector entities, or the better resourced military, to collaborate in pursuing better resourced and internationally based cyberattackers.

International jurisdictional disputes often keep law enforcement from operating effectively. What may be legal in one country may not be legal in the United States and may be treated differently in a third country. In these instances where cybercriminals are at large internationally, countries require extradition agreements. The United States has agreements with many countries but not, at present, with China or Russia.

Brian Benczkowski, former assistant attorney general for the DOJ's Criminal Division, which focuses on developing, supervising, and enforcing federal law, stated at the 2020 Cybercrime Symposium, "One of the most frustrating challenges in bringing offenders to justice has been the willingness of some countries to protect and foster cybercrime committed by their own citizens and within their own borders."[40] To arrest cybercriminals that are foreign citizens and reside in other countries, we need diplomatic relations with the people of these countries.[41] We have to rely on countries, such as Russia, to extradite these people to be successfully prosecuted under our laws. The United States has attempted cyber diplomatic negotiations through formal state visits and treaties, but these efforts have not been fruitful. For example, in January 2022, Russia arrested an individual tied to the Colonial Pipeline ransomware attack in 2021, following negotiations between the Biden administration and Russian officials. The individual will remain in Russia rather than being extradited to the United States.[42] In an era when cybercrime is essentially borderless, administrative strictures and turf battles are further hampering an already undefended effort.

Cybersecurity and Diplomacy

Clarke and Knake suggest that government diplomatic efforts are available to assist the private sector in defending itself against cyberattackers. Unfortunately, as with the cyber law enforcement mechanisms, diplomatic efforts to enhance cybersecurity are also failing. International efforts to combat cybercrime are hindered by antiquated treaties and agreements as well as a lack of adequate structures and resources. In order to develop a truly functional diplomatic effort that will enable law enforcement, a much higher priority needs to be placed on providing a common defense, and that needs to start at the top of government. Suggestions for how this ought to begin are presented in chapter 5.

The existing treaties and agreements are not sufficient to handle the changing cyber landscape. The Budapest Convention is the only major treaty at an international scale that deals specifically with cybercrime. The goal was to gain international cooperation to have a common criminal policy to defend against and prosecute cybercrime. It primarily focuses on copyright infringement, computer fraud, child pornography, and network security.[43] It was first signed in 2001 and was ratified by the United States in 2006. Since that time, the cyber landscape has changed dramatically, and the treaty is outdated.

Toward the end of the Obama administration, there were several advancements in diplomatic cyber relations and agreements with China. In September 2015, President Obama hosted China's president, Xi Jinping, for a formal state visit. Among other things, they came to an agreement to not support theft of intellectual property and commercial hacking.[44] They jointly announced that neither government would "conduct or knowingly support cyber-enabled theft of intellectual property, including trade secrets or other confidential business information for commercial advantage."[45] Later that year, in November, at the G-20 Summit, several other bilateral agreements with China reaffirmed that commercial cyber espionage would cease.[46] Following these agreements, the amount of cyber espionage from China significantly decreased.[47] However, this success was short-lived.

In 2017, the United States warned China that it was beginning to stray from the agreement. Then, in early 2018, a report by the US Trade Representative concluded that China had continued "its policy and practice, spanning more than a decade, of using cyber intrusions to target US firms to access their sensitive commercial information and trade secrets."[48] By early 2021, reporting confirmed that an intrusion campaign, likely of Chinese origin, had stolen and pilfered the data of over thirty thousand organizations, including businesses, using Microsoft Exchange email services.[49] Cyber policy experts say that these and other attacks from China fall into a gray area of the agreement, and other critiques of the agreement also say that it is legally nonbinding, with little to no penalty against the breaching party.[50] As noted earlier, although China's attack on the Microsoft servers was condemned internationally, no sanctions were applied.

The current US strategy for managing breaches of diplomatic cyber agreements is to publicly indict the entity at fault. The strategy has seen little success and may even be counterproductive. Jack Goldsmith and Stuart Russell write:

> The publication of the many losses, followed by the invariably weak or nonexistent public response, demonstrates credibly that U.S. defenses are poor, and that the U.S. government is either unable or unwilling to retaliate even in the face of massive cyber losses. This combination of events thus emboldens adversaries and weakens deterrence, as the continuing increase in cybercrime demonstrates. Even if the United States is robustly engaging in retaliatory covert or clandestine responses, those responses cannot contribute to deterrence against the many third parties who are watching, and indeed in context detracts from it.[51]

This then gives our adversaries more of an incentive to continue to attack, because they know that there is nothing that the United States will do about it.[52]

Ironically, the United States has had successful diplomatic relations with China for decades, even in times of international stress, which suggests that even when tensions are high progress can be made. In 1972, President Richard Nixon spent over a week in China and signed an agreement with China regarding Taiwan; in 1979 President Jimmy Carter granted China full diplomatic recognition; in 1982 President Ronald Reagan reaffirmed a commitment to China and signed another agreement normalizing relations.[53] Even when tensions were high, such as the massacre of democracy protesters in Beijing's Tiananmen Square and the collision of a US spy plane and a Chinese fighter jet, we have been able to secure the release of imprisoned citizens and servicemen.[54] More broadly, despite the fairly normative stresses that tend to exist between superpower nations, the reality is that China is one of America's most prominent business partners and owns over $1 trillion of our national debt.[55]

As documented in chapter 2, China has quickly evolved as a digital power, and their initial disregard for intellectual property rights—in an era when they had little valuable digital property—may be changing as they become holders of valuable 5G and other high-end technology, with substantial commercial interest in protecting it from being copied.[56] The timing may now be right for the sort of productive engagement in mutual self-interest on a range of cybersecurity issues that could lead to a more effective international law enforcement climate.

In order for the United States to develop the ability to effectively utilize the critical diplomatic levers needed to address our cybersecurity issues, additional resources will be needed at the Department of State. National Cyber Director Inglis stated, "[The State Department] need[s] more resources, more people, more expertise . . . to raise the profile and also to be able to be proactive in being involved with international . . . groups that are involved in setting international cyber norms."[57]

In sum, we currently lack an effective strategy, a structure, and the resources to at least take a bite out of cybercrime.

Military Defense against Cyberattacks

As cyberattacks are accelerating and the lines delineating criminal activity from nation-state activity are becoming increasingly blurry, greater engagement from the military is called for. While there has been some increased collaboration between the military and the financial services and energy sectors, as described in later chapters, it is still quite limited and the rules of engagement for the military are unclear.

There would seem to be a number of instances when the advanced tools and capabilities of the military ought to be more directly engaged in what might otherwise be considered civilian cyber defense. Examples are when a company is attacked for exercising its First Amendment rights, as in the case of the attack on Sony by North Korea; or when critical infrastructure is compromised, such as the Iranian attacks on the financial services sector in response to the US-Israeli attack on Iranian nuclear reactors; or when the US government is successfully attacked via cyber methods, such as the Russian attacks on the 2016 US elections and the aforementioned 2020 SolarWinds attack.[58]

There is a wide range of military responses that can be used that fall well short of firing weapons. From this range of military options, there needs to be an improved posture that will create a greater deterrence without moving to armed conflict. The military also has sophisticated tools that could be put to greater use if the procedures were clarified. William Lynn, former deputy secretary of defense, has noted the precedent for this type of activity and how it can be successfully managed.

> During a natural disaster, like a hurricane, military troops and helicopters are often used by . . . [the Federal Emergency Management Agency] to help deliver relief. In a similar vein, the military's cyber capabilities will be available to civilian leaders to help protect the networks that support government operations and critical infrastructure. As with all cases of military support to civilian authorities, these resources will be under civilian control and used according to civil laws.[59]

These precedents need to be expanded to address the threats of the digital age.[60] NSA director and commander of US Cyber Command (CYBERCOM), Gen. Paul Nakasone, correctly said, "We are operating in a space where our adversaries are not going to stop. They are going to continue to look for ways to steal our intellectual property, to steal identification, and to try to influence our populace. We—at the same time—have to be forward, we have to be operating, and we have to be engaged with our adversaries."[61]

Given the evolution of international conflict in the digital age and the obvious inadequacy of civilian law enforcement to addres addressing international and state-sponsored attacks, there needs to be a reconsideration of what it means to defend the nation and the role of the military in this new age. In a recent white paper, Jason Healey and Erik Korn note that "the DoD has significant capabilities for responding to cyber incidents" and that "one of the DoD's key missions is for it to 'be prepared to defend the United States and its interests against cyber-attacks of significant consequence.'"[62] At the same time, the DoD has stated that it would assist federal departments such as the DHS and the FBI in the wake of a significant incident.[63]

Unfortunately, it is not clear what exactly amounts to a "significant" attack and what the roles and responsibilities for the military in civilian cyber defense are when one occurs. This ambiguity has the result of leaving both the government and critical infrastructure at the mercy of sophisticated cyberattackers. According to a panel at a 2018 strategy symposium run by CYBERCOM, "There is little consensus on what it means to defend the Nation and its interests in cyberspace, or on what role the Department of Defense should be for this mission."[64]

States in these circumstances have relied on the National Guard under Title 32 of the US Code to prepare for and respond to cybersecurity attacks. However, the DoD's guidelines under this title are ambiguous as to how exactly the National Guard should proceed in its response and what kind of reimbursements it may receive from the federal government. Further, the guidelines are unclear on how the National Guard should cooperate with other federal processes and personnel in the wake of what might be a more significant cyberattack.[65]

Information Sharing

Information sharing was one of the earliest tactics the government promoted to empower the public-private partnership, created through a series of presidential directives and later developed in the National Infrastructure

Protection Plan. The premise is that the government would collect information from companies and other agencies, combine that with threat data from government sources, and then distribute it to those interested.[66]

Among the first structures created to implement the information sharing system were the Information Sharing Analysis Centers (ISACs). Each critical industry sector was asked to create one, but there were varying degrees of success. In 2015, President Obama issued an executive order, "Promoting Private Sector Cybersecurity Information Sharing," directing DHS to encourage private companies, industries, and local governments and agencies to create their own Information Sharing and Analysis Organizations (ISAOs).[67] Providing assistance to these organizations was one of the charges DHS gave to the Cybersecurity and Infrastructure Security Agency (CISA) established in the Cybersecurity and Infrastructure Agency Act of 2018.[68]

Unfortunately, these ISACs and ISAOs have not been as effective as hoped. A 2020 study, "Success Stories in Cybersecurity Information Sharing," found that nearly a quarter century after the ISACs were founded, "most companies do not yet engage in formal information sharing."[69] The report cited three reasons for the general lack of sharing: the amount of resources such programs require, fear of liability, and lack of metrics indicating the programs are cost-effective. Still the study does describe several instances where entities have productively shared information on cybersecurity and concluded that "there is persuasive evidence ... to demonstrate that information sharing has been successful across the U.S. economy and among various sectors. . . . [W]hile the evidence is anecdotal in a sense it is collectively powerful and persuasive."

Some have suggested that the inadequate promotion of these facilities by the federal government is one reason this mechanism has not been as successful as it should be. Michael Echols, a former DHS staffer and now the CEO of the International Association of Certified ISAOs (IACI) noted that "most organizations have never heard of ISAOs and ISACs and the government has done little to raise awareness at a national, state, or local level."[70]

Although successive administrations have touted information sharing as a major tool in the fight to assist industry in protecting itself, like many other federal cybersecurity programs, the reality is that government has not fully committed to it. DHS itself has reported that the main barrier to improving the mitigation of cyberthreats is the lack of participation from government entities.[71] Of the 252 federal entities signed up for the DHS Automated Indicator Sharing platform, only four federal agencies and six nonfederal entities were actually using it.[72]

Even when the government does actively participate, government agencies and the private sector have generally found that the information shared has been of little use. The most common complaint DHS received is that the information being distributed was not timely, was not relevant, and lacked detail and therefore was not actionable. As the information was not given in context, the recipients did not understand why there was a problem.[73] In many cases, the threat indicators have already been distributed by other sources weeks or months previously. In one instance, a federal agency received over eleven thousand cyber threat indicators from DHS in one year, and only two or three of them were actionable.[74]

Finally, for these organizations to work properly there needs to be a high level of trust among the participating entities. In short, the sharing entities need to know that the sensitive threat information they share will be handled adequately. However, the necessary level of trust, even after all these years, still has not been achieved. Jonathan Couch, senior vice president of strategy at ThreatQuotient, notes that when you bring in these tens and hundreds of companies and organizations that may not know each other, it is hard for the ISAC or ISAO to broker trust among them.[75]

There is little disagreement that regardless of its imperfections information sharing can be and sometimes is a useful tool in a comprehensive cybersecurity strategy. There is fairly common agreement that the financial services information sharing programs, particularly the outreach programs large banks fund to support smaller firms and some of their specialized government programs, could be a model for industries less mature in a cybersecurity sense if they are properly structured and funded.

An example of successful information sharing was detailed at a conference at the University of Albany in 2019. In 2018, a member company of the IT-ISAC asked the ISAC for information on the "Golden Niagara" threat. The ISAC sent inquiries to its member companies and was able to collect several reports from intelligence providers, which they shared on the ISAC threat intelligence platform for all members. As a result, the ISAC was able to confirm the actors involved in the threat and obtained updated indicators associated with an active campaign, which they were able to disseminate to the full membership. ISAC members confirmed that the sharing was "very valuable and had prevented harm."

Fundamental Change

As we noted at the outset, Clarke and Knake verified that US cyber policy has changed "very little" in the past thirty years. In contrast, during that time the world itself has changed quite dramatically. In this vastly changed digital world, the "limited role" and "nudges" Clarke and Knake suggest as the basis for government support of the private sector are obviously inadequate. Government's role in collective cyber defense is more challenging than simply setting regulations and assessing if industry has followed them or nudging investment with some seed money. As we lay out in chapter 5, government engagement requires true commitment, including a financial commitment corresponding to the costs of cyberattacks and collaboration with industry partners—not stakeholders.

The US cybersecurity effort over the past thirty years largely comes down to a series of modest, disjointed, incremental tactics. Unlike the Chinese, we have not operated from a thoughtful, comprehensive strategy that appreciates the extent of the impact digitalization has on everything and leverages our economic advantages, technical expertise, and political philosophy in a pragmatic effort to secure our nation. It is time for change.

CHAPTER 5

REINVENTING CYBERSECURITY

A Strategic Partnership Approach

Larry Clinton and Alexander T. Green

The Preamble to the US Constitution describes the essential structure and purpose of the US government: "We the People of the United States, in Order to form a more perfect Union, establish Justice, ensure domestic Tranquility, provide for the common defense, promote the general Welfare, and secure the Blessings of Liberty to ourselves and our Posterity, do ordain and establish this Constitution for the United States of America." Although the Constitution clearly states that among government's obligations are the defense and the promotion of the welfare of the people, it also implies that the private sector—"We the People"—has a responsibility to help achieve those goals. This has never been truer than in the digital age when the cyber systems operated by both the private and public sectors to promote the general welfare are under constant attack and demand a modern, truly collaborative defense model.

Our analysis of the US cybersecurity situation clearly shows that it is dire. However, from this point we turn to how government and industry, working together, can create a more robust, modern, and comprehensive defensive system. We begin by suggesting that US digital policy needs to be competitive with that of the Chinese government and other adversaries. This digital policy would encompass cybersecurity, but it would not be limited to it. Just as cybersecurity is not the sole province of IT, so, too, a digital strategy cannot be confined to traditional conceptions and structures for national defense.

Although the US strategy needs to be as sophisticated as, for example, the Chinese, US strategy cannot be a mirror of the Chinese strategy. Rather than mimic the model of centralized government control and mandates, the United States needs to instead leverage the unique and powerful advantages of Western democratic norms and market economies to "secure the Blessings of Liberty" for ourselves and future generations.

To accomplish this, the policy reform must be accompanied by structural reform such as the creation of a new White House Office of Digital Strategy and Security (ODSS).

The new National Cyber Director (NCD) established in the White House by the FY2021 National Defense Authorization Act is charged with leading the coordination and implementation of national cyber policy and strategy, including assessing the effectiveness and cost-effectiveness of cyber policy by federal departments and agencies. The NCD is explicitly authorized to coordinate the streamlining of cybersecurity regulations, which creates an opportunity to begin the process of eliminating duplicative, wasteful, and ineffective cybersecurity regulations. As of this writing, the office's first director, Chris Inglis, has been confirmed but the office itself has not been fully staffed or funded. As a result, it is uncertain how many of the functions we have envisioned for the proposed Office of Digital Strategy and Security (ODSS) will be assumed by the Office of the National Cyber Director.

It is doubtful that the director's office will have nearly the comprehensive mandate, impact, or budget envisioned for the ODSS. The director's office will not have the extensive public-private partnership model we are calling for. Moreover, the federal government is replete with various cybersecurity responsibilities mandated by Congress and unfulfilled, in some cases for over a decade. The authors of this volume are not concerned about what the institution that carries out the functions described in this and succeeding chapters is called—National Cyber Director Office or Office of Digital Strategy and Security—it is the functions themselves that are of import. As a matter of convenience given the uncertain development of the NCD, we list a variety of functions assigned to the proposed ODSS.

Reform of the Current Partnership Model

It has often been said that every great plan eventually devolves into actual work. However, many important recommendations of previous "cyber commissions" have fallen by the wayside because there have been no effective institutional mechanisms to follow through on them. For example, multiple industry and bipartisan congressional and presidential commissions embraced the economics-based approach to cybersecurity defined by the social contract.[1] Despite the various reports and recommendations, there has been scant actual policy implemented addressing the core economic issues that, as we have shown, generate many of our cybersecurity problems.

The internet is structured on an interconnected multisector model, yet our security strategies have historically been based on a traditional independent sector model. The notion of independent industry sectors is increasingly outmoded, yet our security partnership model is still based on these outmoded constructs. While many sectors retain unique characteristics, many others have evolved in ways that transcend traditional boundaries. For example, the financial services firm JP Morgan employs more technologists than does the "IT" firm Google.[2] From a cybersecurity perspective, there is actually a great deal of similarity irrespective of industry sector regarding what technologies are used, how attacks are launched, and the structural problems of economic scope and scale that hinder systematic security.

Based on a set of presidential directives going back twenty-five years and subsequently folded into the National Infrastructure Protection Plan (NIPP), a superstructure has ostensibly been designed to implement a government-industry partnership model for critical infrastructure security. Each critical infrastructure sector has an industry sector coordinating council with a corresponding government coordinating council. There is also a cross-sector entity originally called the Partnership for Critical infrastructure Protection and later renamed the Cross-Sector Council to provide intersectoral exchange. However, in practice the government and industry councils in most sectors rarely meet and, with some exceptions, do not communicate or coordinate on major projects. The Cross-Sector Council has no clear mission or measurable goals and objectives, has no budget, and has only voluntary participation.

Similarly proposed specific cyber strategies, lacking institutional follow-up, have failed at the implementation phase. For example, the 2018 National Cyber Strategy outlined the Trump administration's plan for cybersecurity through various priority actions, including centralizing management and oversight of federal civilian cybersecurity. Unfortunately, a Government Accountability Office (GAO) analysis found that "the strategy lacks key elements that we have previously reported can enhance the usefulness of a national strategy, including clearly defined roles and responsibilities, and information on the resources needed to carry out the goals and objectives," and further that "it is unclear what official maintains overall responsibility for coordinating these efforts."[3] The same lack of defined roles and responsibilities regarding cybersecurity exists even in the most structured domains of government, such as the DoD, according to Healy and Korn's detailed analysis of DoD procedures for civil support in cyber incidents detailed in chapter 4.[4]

It is abundantly clear that the traditional independent and federated structures have not only been unable to implement a coherent and effective digital strategy; they have operated too often at cross purposes and created inefficiencies that have actually undermined US security efforts. While these existing structures could be integrated into the broader and more empowered structure being proposed here, they have no practical capacity currently to fulfill the roles contemplated for the ODSS.

Creating a National Strategy: The ODSS

Presidential-level involvement in creating a digital strategy is crucial. Much as the CEO of a major enterprise is directly involved with the board and its main partners in creating a digital transformation strategy, so, too, the president, working with Congress and the private sector, needs to lead the government in a digital transformation similar to that being developed in much of the private sector—as well as by our major adversaries.

Creating and implementing this strategy cannot be accomplished by an ad hoc commission or existing incremental and often disembodied government structures that were designed for the industrial age. It requires a permanent collaborative structure in the executive branch that can analyze multidimensional digital issues in a holistic fashion. Leaving aside the uncertainties of the new National Director's Office, the closest current model might be the Office of Management and Budget.

The ODSS would be charged with proactively crafting, assisting in implementing, and evaluating a sophisticated and integrated national digital transformation strategy. This strategy would seek to leverage US democratic and economic traditions and enhance our competitive posture relative to our adversaries. It would describe how digital technology has changed the world and how the United States will utilize modern market-based methods to respond to these changes and enhance its own national and economic security placing the United States in position to maximize Western democratic goals in the twenty-first century. The strategy would be to take a holistic view of how the government in partnership with the private sector needs to address major issues created by modern digitalization and leverage them to better achieve national goals.

Responsibilities and Goals of the ODSS versus the NCD

The ODSS would differ considerably from the newly created Office of the National Cyber Director (NCD), codified in the 2021 National Defense

Authorization Act (NDAA).[5] The NCD, as the principal adviser to the president, is tasked with leading the coordination and institution of national cyber policy and strategy. The NCD is also in charge of cyber incident responses and ensuring continuity of the economy in response to a cyberattack of national significance. In contrast, the ODSS would be charged with implementing a broader national digital strategy, the cybersecurity components of which should be coordinated with the NCD.

The NCD is charged with leading the *federal* cyber policy and strategy and coordinating government *response* to cyber acts of national significance. However, the NCD authorities do not provide the fullness of a truly national digital strategy and are not nearly broad enough to provide ample defense against the sorts of sophisticated cyberattacks that are becoming increasingly common against both industry and government. For example, the Russian cyberattack on SolarWinds in 2020 was a systemic attack that impacted multiple government and private cyber systems. SolarWinds is a private organization that serves both the public and private sectors. It is an example of a growing number of core elements of the internet, discussed more fully in chapter 3, whose compromise creates risk not just for the entity being attacked, but for the broader interconnected system. Attempting to design a strategy that artificially segments significant attacks on government from identical simulations of attacks on private entities—as in the Solar-Winds case—creates awkward hair-splitting and unnecessary confusion and inefficiency.

ODSS, by contrast, would be charged with developing a strategy designed to deal with systemic risk, not merely from the perspective of keeping the government operative, but, more broadly, from the perspective of the national interest—including, and involving the private sector. Working with the Cybersecurity and Infrastructure Security Agency—the operational cyber arm of DHS—this strategy could then be implemented

To fulfill a similar function, the NCD office would need to be expanded and repurposed. This broader perspective would include cybersecurity as one aspect of that overall strategy but not be artificially limited to technical issues or government systems as though they were independent from private systems (they are not).

In contrast to the NDC, the ODSS would be charged with using the partnership processes identified in joint government-industry research to create a truly collaborative and comprehensive digital cybersecurity strategy.[6] Moreover, this White House office would be charged with using modern management techniques and agile management processes within an inclusive public-private structure.[7] Critical to its success will be the degree to which the

ODSS has adequate staffing and budget and authority to carry out its mission, including regular assessment and agile modification of cybersecurity programs. The ODSS mission would be that which is specifically articulated in the joint DHS-IT Sector Coordinating Council White Paper on Collective Cyber Defense: "To integrate advanced technology with business economics and public policy to create a shared and sustainably secure cyber ecosystem that shifts the advantage to cyber defenders."[8]

Locating the ODSS in the White House enables it to coordinate easily with the NCD and the National Economic Council and access the interests of Commerce, Defense, Homeland Security, and other department perspectives while overcoming turf issues that have up until now plagued the implementation of effective cyber policy.

Government Digital Transformation

One reason US cyber policy has been ineffective is that it has taken a primarily narrow technical/operational approach to the issue. The US conception stands in stark contrast to the Chinese's Digital Silk Road strategy, which, as described in chapter 2 integrates economic, technical, and geopolitical concepts in a coherent plan.

Until recently the private sector has suffered from a similarly narrow conceptualization of cybersecurity, but that view has been changing. For several years leading private organizations have been conceptualizing cyber issues in broader strategic ways and implementing innovative structural reforms that help institutionalize a broader, more integrated approach to digital transformation. The movement toward digital transformation that integrates cybersecurity in strategic terms has been led by corporate boards, starting with the National Association of Corporate Directors (NACD) in the United States, but has now been embraced by similar directors' organizations around the world.[9]

The directors' organizations have articulated the model for addressing cyber risk in a series of publications, all advancing the strategic approach. The publications, in several cases developed with governmental partners, are now available on four continents and in five languages. Pricewaterhouse-Coopers (PwC) has independently assessed the use of this approach and found that organizations that use the methods outlined in these publications end up with larger cybersecurity budgets, better cyber risk management, closer alignment between cybersecurity and overall mission goals, and a better developed culture of security throughout the organization.[10]

The NACD's most recent publication on the subject, "Cyber-Risk Oversight 2020," suggests that this strategic understanding of cyber risk is the number one principle organizations ought to be following as part of their digital transformation.

> Over the last several years technology and data have moved out of their supporting roles and taken center stage as critical drivers of strategy. . . . [T]he business community's level of awareness of the importance of information security in general and the cross functional nature of cybersecurity in particular has taken a similar path. . . . The key questions for the board are no longer limited to how the technological innovation can enable business processes but how to balance their own major digital transformation with effective management of inherent cyber risk that can compromise the enterprise's long-term strategic interests.[11]

Although several government agencies, including DHS, DOJ, the German Office of Information Security (BSI), and the Organization of American States, have endorsed the approaches advocated by the board and industry associations,[12] there is little evidence that the governments themselves have altered their focus from their traditional operational emphasis.

Chapter 2 explains the lengthy and comprehensive process that the Chinese government went through as they evolved the Bridges and Roads Initiative (BRI) and the Digital Silk Road (DSR). These programs demonstrate that the Chinese, and other adversaries, see cyber issues not simply in terms of traditional military functions and operational tactics, but in subtler and more sophisticated ways. In the Chinese model, cyber is a mechanism that can be compromised for intelligence but also a sweetener for major infrastructure projects, a tool of foreign policy, and a pathway to long-term impact through soft power in standards development processes and more. Although the United States has at times demonstrated awareness of the ability to use digitalization in these contexts, the more extensive degree and sophistication being demonstrated by our adversaries compared to traditional US cyber policy is apparent.

Issues for the Office of Digital Security and Strategy

The ODSS would be designed to consider issues that while multidimensional have a critical digital nexus. The agency would be charged with developing strategies and policies and advising on how to deal with a wide range of cyber issues that are not currently being explored in comprehensive fashion. It would also be charged with systematically assessing cyber programs for effectiveness and cost-effectiveness and recommending changes. This process is especially important in dealing with digital issues as the digital environment is known for constant change. The process would emulate the agile management systems commonly used in the private sector

At a strategic level, the ODSS would consider how to fund the needed national security obligations that private sector companies are inheriting in the digital age but are clearly incompatible with the economic business models designed for decades past. Such a strategy would include practical answers on issues such as how to fund the growing critical infrastructure security requirements. For example, as discussed in greater detail in chapter 10, utilities that operate on economic models designed to provide only commercial-level security may need to fund vastly increased security to prevent cyberattacks that could threaten large numbers of people. The current, government-approved economic models are not designed to accommodate spending on this level, yet the threat is growing. This is a multidimensional problem that includes governmental jurisdictional issues that require more than a patchwork solution.

This is similar in some respects to a burgeoning array of digital issues that are currently being bootstrapped to outdated governmental structures. Among these issues are how to protect hospitals and local governments from ransomware attacks, how to assure the safety of intellectual property that is the basis of the countrly's economic vitality, and how to effectively address the cybercrime epidemic.

The ODSS would provide the United States with a specific location for the creation of a coordinated, integrated, and funded strategy to address these issues in a more fulsome public-private partnership model and from a multidimensional perspective consistent with the digital age. The agency could advise on executive action and recommend legislation to the appropriate congressional committees as required. Another major project for the ODSS would be to clarify the roles and responsibilities of government and private sector entities in implementing a true collective defense model by pragmatically addressing the changing digital economics that will be required to make the security model both successful and sustainable.

The digital era has obviously changed the threat picture for the twenty-first century and further adaptations are required for government to effectively fulfill its constitutional obligations. When creating the joint industry-government Policy Leadership Working Group, DHS Assistant Secretary for Cybersecurity and Communications Jeanette Manfra noted, "Government and industry must work together now more than ever if we are serious about improving our collective defense. We cannot secure the homeland alone and a company can't single-handedly defend itself from a nation state attacker."[13] Recognizing that a collective defense model is required, the strategy developed by the ODSS must carefully navigate the appropriate roles and responsibilities for the public and private sector. The National Infrastructure Protection Plan (NIPP), first crafted in 2012, under the Bush administration and then confirmed in an Obama administration update in 2016,[14] provides a thoughtful analysis that clearly delineates the appropriate role for private companies providing commercial-level security and where the national security concerns, and hence governmental responsibilities, take over.

The NIPP notes that industry and government have legitimate differences in how they assess and manage cyber risk. These differences create a gap between the security the private sector can reasonably be expected to bear and what the government needs to fulfill. The private sector is responsible for commercial-level security wherein each entity balances the financing needed to secure its systems with investment to maintain growth and profit and thereby attract private capital, create jobs, grow the economy, and fund the government by means of resultant taxes while providing citizens with goods and services.

As a result, private sector security risk assessment, and subsequent investment, is "appropriately" based primarily on an economic calculus. For example, everyone knows that a certain percentage of private inventory "walks out the back door." The reason private entities tolerate this pilferage is that they have calculated that additional security mitigation such as hiring more guards or placing more cameras costs more than the loss of the inventory. In short, it is more economical, and from a business perspective more reasonable, to tolerate a lower level of security.

The public sector has many additional security considerations that the private sector does not have: national security, economic safety nets for the disadvantaged, securing public services such as elections, and so on. Chris Krebs, former director of DHS's Cybersecurity and Infrastructure Security Agency, noted that "private companies fund security at a commercial level appropriate to their needs while the government funds at a higher, national security level. To create a sustainable 'collective defense' we must find a way to fill this economic delta."[15]

While it may be true, as some security experts have noted earlier, that a handful of companies with massive economies of scope and scale, like Microsoft and Google, might be able to finance security at levels approximating the national security level, this is not a practical option for the vast majority of the private sector. Such expenditures by the private sector would inherently divert resources from other pro-societal requirements they must meet such as innovation, capital formation, job creation, and overall economic growth.

It is the responsibility of the government, constitutionally charged with providing for the common defense, to fill this gap. If government attempts to shift this responsibility and exert greater control over private industry (e.g., via uneconomical security mandates), the unintended consequences would be disruptive to the other critical roles industry is charged with fulfilling (see chap. 4). The joint industry-DHS Collective Defense White Paper concluded, "In a world in which reliance on critical infrastructure is shared by industry and government and where industry may be on the front lines of national defense, such as in a cyber-attack, a sustainable partnership must be developed to address both perspectives by finding creative mechanisms while taking into consideration the issue of limited resources for industry and government."[16]

For well over a decade a series of industry and government reports, including the ISA's Social Contract (2008/9), The Pan-Industry Cybersecurity White Paper (2009), the House GOP Cybersecurity Task Force Report (2010), President Obama's Executive Order 13636 (2013), and the Cyberspace Solarium Commission established by the 2019 Defense Authorization Act have all called for a set of economic incentives to promote cybersecurity. Even more recently a multidimensional study by Atkins and Lawson concluded: "The core of policy challenge is that private owner-operators do not have the incentive to take into account the larger societal consequences of a disruption in their operations."[17] As a result, they are likely to underinvest in cybersecurity for their systems.

Yet, as noted, there has been scant work to develop such a model. Taking these broad recommendations and turning them into concrete policy proposals is a project squarely within the ambit of the ODSS. As the joint industry-DHS Collective Defense White Paper noted:

> The broader economy and US history have plenty of examples of nonregulatory market incentives, many of which are at a low cost to government and have promoted important outcomes that would have been challenging on a purely commercial basis. Incentive models in varying forms exist in many industries and sectors including agriculture, aviation, pharmaceuticals, transportation, and even physical security.[18]

The ODSS should be charged with examining existing market incentive programs in various industries and determine how they can be adapted to enhance cybersecurity.

A greater degree of government support and collaboration with industry through pro-market incentives is consistent with the traditions of the American economic system and has often proved quite successful, as we discuss below. Developing these economic incentives, without bankrupting the government, should be a responsibility of CISA and the ODSS.

Response to Nation-State Attacks against Private Infrastructure

The history of cyber public policy in the United States has been dominated by traditional military/DoD perspectives and the protection of critical infrastructure. While these domains are obviously vital and ought to be prioritized, criminal attacks, including those by nation-states, on the private sector have not received the attention they deserve.

Virtually no commercial-level cyber defense is a match for cyberattacks launched by nation-state actors. The global costs of state cyberattacks run into the trillions of dollars, and we have already documented the near-zero rate of successful criminal prosecutions in cybercrime cases. Perhaps most curious is that there seems to be no concentrated effort to develop "solutions" to this problem—even if "solution" is defined as allowing only 95 percent of cybercriminals to escape prosecution. This alone would be a massive improvement. The national digital security strategy needs to map out a program to effectively address cybercrime.

As part of the overall digital transformation strategy, the president should appoint a separate commission within the ODSS charged with developing a practical plan for improving prosecution of cybercriminals in a sustainable format. This separate commission should be composed of sixteen individuals: four former law enforcement officials, four former military officials, four representatives of industry (no more than one from each sector), and four representatives of victims of cybercrime. None of the civilian representatives should have government experience. The commission should include in its deliberations how military and law enforcement may collaborate more effectively to pursue cybercriminals, how domestic and international law ought to be changed to effectuate the strategy, and how to develop an international political consensus to make the plan workable.

The Role of the Military in Cyberattacks of National Significance

As commander in chief, the US president is the ultimate strategic player in defending the country. *Merriam-Webster* defines *warfare* as military operations between enemies, and as an activity undertaken by a political unit (such as a nation) to weaken or destroy another. By these definitions, the United States has suffered multiple cyberattacks that could easily fall into the category of warfare. Although as of this writing the full implications of the SolarWinds attacks are not fully known, it has been suggested that they are tantamount to acts of war. Certainly, the Chinese attacks stealing the plans for the F-35 fighter, as directed by the Communist Party, were designed to weaken the United States. The 2016 attacks on the US electoral system conducted by "Fancy Bear" under the direction of the GRU—the Russian military's intelligence unit—similarly were designed to weaken the United States. In 2020, the Russian and Chinese governments attempted to steal US intellectual property involving a vaccine for COVID-19. There are numerous other less high-profile examples. Obviously, the deterrent factor of having the world's largest, best-funded and best-equipped military has not proven effective regarding cyberattacks.

In addition to cyberattacks, the nature of nation-state warfare has changed, and we have not yet determined how the military should change in this new era. As noted in chapter 4, there is "conceptual confusion" surrounding the military's role in cyber defense and little consensus on what the Department of Defense role should be for this mission. Similarly, a recent GAO report identified key challenges and shortcomings in DoD's current approach in cyberspace, highlighting a lack of definition in organizational roles and responsibilities for providing civil support during a cyber incident of national significance.[19] Analysts have speculated about whether the Pentagon can recognize that these gaps exist and adapt and seize new opportunities to provide more effective support functions during significant cyber events or whether it will fall back into the trap of institutional norm.

The details of how these complicated issues ought to be resolved are beyond the capacity of this volume. However, a practical and efficient way for law enforcement and military organizations to protect the United States from cyberattacks by nation-states or state-affiliated actors is long overdue.

Among the issues a review of the military's role in cybersecurity should address is the definition of the role of the military and the meaning of terms like "significant attack" and "critical infrastructure," so that clear jurisdictional and actionable guidelines are created that enable greater synergies on how to assist and operate with the private sector to prepare for, protect against, and respond to cyberattacks.

The ODSS would consider how we are to compete with the Chinese government, which, as described in chapter 2, is engaging in a multidimensional campaign against US national interests. The Chinese are cross-subsidizing their technology companies and creating an inequitable playing field, with serious national security as well as competitive implications. While the Chinese program obviously has relevance to the Departments of State and Defense, it also has an impact on commerce, finance, trade, and technology. This is an example of how a major competitor is succeeding in a geopolitical space in large part thanks to a better-designed organizational structure. The ODSS would not usurp the roles of the established government structures but rather bring them together, with the equally interested private sector partners as envisioned in the National Infrastructure Protection Plan to develop a coherent and pragmatic strategy.

Government Digital Transformation through Modern Management Techniques

For several years, leading enterprises have been implementing agile organizational structures to enhance efficacy and effectively respond to the digital age. Government can start a similar transformation by tasking the ODSS to utilize modern, agile organization practices in its evaluation of the federal government's digital transformation. The agile organizational model strives to be both dynamic and stable at the same time. It needs to include a stable backbone— which exists in the traditional governmental framework—but one that evolves to support dynamic capabilities that can quickly adapt to new challenges.

Obviously, China operates according to a very different set of values and policies from that of the United States. It also operates under a very different organizational structure from that of modern Western private sector institutions. From an organizational development perspective, the Chinese structure could be characterized as following the "machine" paradigm with a strict hierarchical and specialized structure.[20] While this structure has worked well for the Chinese, with their planned economy and restrictive culture, it is not a model that can be usefully applied to Western institutions in the digital age. A series of studies by McKinsey found that when Western companies tried to use machine-style organizations, it has not worked out well.[21] The US government has similarly attempted to operate in its traditional, hierarchical, machine-like structure, and as we have demonstrated at least with respect to cybersecurity, it has not worked out well either. Instead, the ODSS should follow the model that leading corporations are adapting for their own digital transformation that stresses agility over strict hierarchical structure and is more akin to a living organism than a machine.[22]

The NACD "Cyber-Risk Handbook" outlines how to institutionalize the broader strategic approach to cybersecurity by laying out specific steps entities ought to use to implement the strategic approach on an organizational level. The recommended process calls on leaders to "appoint a cross-organizational cyber risk management team. All substantial stakeholders' departments must be represented including the business units' leaders, legal, internal audit and compliance, finance, human resources, PR, IT, and risk management."

In the governmental context, this might include representatives of cabinet-level agencies. However, because in the United States as much as 90 percent of critical infrastructure is owned and operated by the private sector, the US model needs to also include private sector participation, equivalent to that of the government. Indeed, joint industry-government research has demonstrated that when cybersecurity programs are managed in a fulsome partnership model—including cochairing of project teams by government and industry—the effectiveness and satisfaction with the projects is enhanced.[23] Chapter 3, on systemic cyber risk, notes multiple areas wherein a more intensely collaborative structure will be needed to manage this increasingly interdependent problem. Similarly, as detailed in chapter 8, on the defense industrial base (DIB), when the Pentagon instituted a process wherein there was equivalent representation on development teams in creating their new supply chain cyber risk management system (CMMC) it led to broader success than previous, more traditionally structured programs had.

Who Should Lead in Digital Strategy?

Leadership is a critical aspect of developing a more strategic approach to cybersecurity. Here again US adversaries seem to ensure that the broader strategic perspective is used by involving senior, organization-wide leadership in developing policy. For example, as previously noted, President Xi personally oversees the Military-Civilian Blending in China. In the US government, it is still routine to look to technologists for leadership on cyber issues. Conversely, in upper levels of business there is a conscientious move away from having technologists lead on cyber issues.

Again, quoting the NACD Cyber-Risk Handbook, "The basic management (structural) model stresses not only that multi-stakeholders ought to be involved in developing cybersecurity policy but also advocates for an identified leader—not from IT—who has cross organizational authority."[24] While IT people obviously need to be centrally involved, the NACD advises corporate boards not to put them in charge of decision making because they tend to see issues primarily in operational and technical terms and can miss the larger strategic insights necessary for effective digital policy.

As we have seen, China has taken a sophisticated and integrated approach to the digital age exploiting its vulnerabilities and providing massive subsidies, tax breaks, and favorable credit lines to their domestic IT companies. A recent article in the *Harvard Business Review*, "Three Lessons from Chinese Firms on Effective Digital Collaboration,"[25] highlighted a range of collaborative models pioneered in China. It notes that these collaborations have been "effective in China's leveraging coalitions to scale business activities in pursuit of broad 'whole of society' goals," a category cybersecurity would seem to fit well in. It also notes that the models harken back to large collaborations that were once more common in the West, for example, that involved the race to the moon. The *Harvard Business Review* stated: "We recognize that a natural reaction of many non-Chinese readers will be that the Chinese context is unique, and therefore collaboration strategies that may work in China may not work in the West. Yet, while there certainly are differences in business practice cultural context and applicable regulations the broad principles described in these models are universal." A National Digital Security Strategy that facilitated such collaborations could be extremely helpful in addressing the issues of scarce cybersecurity resources.

Among the transferable items are also best practices for partnership programs. The *Journal of Strategic Security* has published several studies documenting industry and government studies outlining the impact of improved best practice for government industry collaboration which ought to be integrated into partnership programs.[26] The ODSS would systematically evaluate progress in implementing the US digital strategy and update the strategy and implementation plan annually.

Program Evaluation and Modification

In its study of organizations using agile principles, McKinsey found that the successful entities "regularly evaluate the progress of initiatives and decide whether to ramp them up or shut them down."[27] This aspect of agile organizations can enhance the efficiency and cost-effectiveness of cyber programs and is a fundamental element of good cyber risk management. Unfortunately, it has generally been absent from government-industry partnership programs. For example, the NIST CSF—one of the most heavily promoted government cybersecurity programs—has never been assessed to determine which aspects of the CSF are cost-effective for different-sized enterprises, despite the fact that this was called for in Executive Order 13636.

Figure 5.1. Evolution of the Cybersecurity Social Contract

The ISA first recommended using NIST to create a set of cybersecurity standards and practices for voluntary adoption by industry in its initial Social Contract white paper in 2008.[28] NIST created the Cybersecurity Framework in response to Presidential Executive Order 13636 in 2013, and it has been added to substantially since its inception. Notwithstanding nearly a decade of extensive promotion by the government, there is little empirical evidence that the content of the CSF is being widely adopted or enhancing security (Fig. 5.1).

The recent joint industry-DHS Collective Defense White Paper noted that "many small and medium-sized businesses (SMBs) are still unaware of the Framework. Many SMBs that do attempt to use the NIST Framework find that it could be more user-friendly and may not have the expertise to implement it.[29] And a 2021 study by the US Telecom Association found that only 13 percent of small businesses in critical infrastructure industries rely on government advice in developing their cybersecurity programs.[30] Further, as documented in chapter 4, in 2020 ESI found that the relationship between companies that do use the NIST CSF and effectiveness in actual security is weak and that CISOs generally acknowledge that adhering to the NIST is not enough to provide security against advanced threats.[31] While these findings may be underwhelming, they should not be considered as too harsh a judgment on the NIST CSF. It is quite possible, even likely, that NIST CSF can enhance security given specific uses of the expansive list of options and the specific needs of various companies and industries.

What is required to maximize the security utility of a tool like the NIST CSF is research that documents what variations of the framework (and there are many possibilities) show cost-effectiveness for specific user populations. The ODSS should undertake this research and engage in outreach backed by empirical data for specific populations.[32]

Private organizations, particularly smaller ones, which are most in need of cybersecurity advice, are primarily influenced in spending decisions by data. Research that documents the use of specific elements of the CSF to security outcomes would be a strong lever for increasing the voluntary use of the NIST CSF. This practice of evaluating government-industry programs for cost-effectiveness, and of modification based on the results, should be applied to all such programs.[33]

The agile organizational model suggested for the ODSS would enable the creation of quick and flexible teams to engage in the needed evaluation of innovative programs and suggest how they can be adapted to the unique needs of various sectors. The ODSS can be a vehicle for sharing not just technical threat data but also innovative cyber people, processes, and technologies, along with the evaluative data to indicate how they might be usefully adapted to diverse sectors. No such evaluation process entity currently exists in the federal government.

CHAPTER 6

THE CYBERSECURITY POLICY WE NEED

Incentivize, Modernize, Economize

Larry Clinton

In the previous chapter, we proposed that government create a comprehensive and inclusive digital strategy in full partnership with the private sector. We also proposed creating a structure consistent with contemporary organizations' efforts to enact a digital transformation strategy to help manage, evaluate, and implement that strategy. We now turn to a series of reforms we believe ought to guide that strategy. The policy proposals articulated here are somewhat broad; details are provided in the subsequent sector-specific chapters. The policy prescriptions we propose follow three general principles.

- We need to devote far greater resources to addressing the digital threat.
- Needed efficiencies can be generated by systematically evaluating and reorganizing a number of current cyber programs.
- We need to modernize our approach to cyber defense.

In essence, these principles can be stated succinctly: incentivize, modernize, and economize. Even then, however, the government will have to spend more money.

Incentivize

President Joe Biden has often said, "Don't tell me what you value; show me your budget, and I will tell you what you value." Based on this criterion and comparing what the US government has spent on cybersecurity to the expenditures of its major adversaries, a reasonable conclusion is that the United States has not placed a high value on cybersecurity.

If the United States is going to value its security in the digital age, it is going to have to pay for it. Nothing incentivizes as directly as money. By Biden's scale and notwithstanding some initial steps by the Biden administration, the US government is not valuing its cybersecurity because it is not devoting adequate resources to secure cyberspace. Also, by virtually any measure, it is the private sector that has been leading in the commitment to fund cyber defense. A core element of the national digital strategy has to be how we are going to amass the required resources to make it work. This critical element has been the missing link in virtually all the previous commissions and strategies on this topic.

The federal government will need to substantially increase its own spending on cybersecurity in order to begin to strengthen the system. But it can turbocharge its investment if it is coupled with appropriate market incentives for the private sector to invest beyond their commercial needs.

It is simply unrealistic to expect law enforcement, led by an FBI with a cyber budget of roughly half a billion dollars,[1] to be able to bring to justice a criminal empire generating over $2 trillion in economic damage annually. The fact that we prosecute about 0.3 percent of cybercriminals makes this need unassailable.[2] Similarly, it is impossible for the United States to keep up with our adversaries, who, as James Lewis from CSIS estimates, are outspending us by a thousand to one on next-generation technologies.[3] And it will be impossible for American companies to compete internationally when they are faced with competitors who receive massive state-supported cross-subsidization that creates dramatically uneven playing fields and weakens the geopolitical standing and security infrastructure of the United States and other Western countries.

As stated in chapter 5, the financial commitment to enhancing our nation's digital infrastructure needs to originate in an industry-government partnership. However, simply mandating increased private sector investment to make up for massive underinvestment by the government is not a sustainable strategy. In a market economy, private sector spending needs to be justified economically by a company's business plan. The private sector's main focus is to keep the American economy healthy and Americans employed. Security investment is part of that, but it needs to be integrated appropriately into enterprise business plans.

If corporations in a market economy are forced to continually make investments that are not economically justified by their business plans, the needed capital required to provide jobs, innovate products, and pay taxes will flee to more profitable enterprises. Although corporations can, and do, assist in securing the nation, providing for the common defense is and needs to be primarily a governmental responsibility.

In fact, the private sector both spends more and is increasing its spending on cyber defense at far higher pace compared to the federal investment. Although it is the government's constitutional responsibility to protect the general public from criminals and nation-state attackers, it is the private sector that primarily provides its own cyber defense. A recent comparative analysis of spending on cybersecurity by Forbes concluded that "as a result of government inaction, private sector companies have been forced to take cybersecurity more seriously and, according to some projections, will spend over $1 trillion on digital security globally through 2021."[4]

These estimates, when weighed against actual government spending and budget projections, appear to be quite accurate. Total federal appropriations on cybersecurity in fiscal year 2021, the last year for which we have final data, was $19.45 billion, including the $650 million in additional funding for CISA in the American Rescue Plan.[5] About half of this money, however, goes to the Department of Defense, which, as discussed in chapter 4, has provided marginal assistance on cyberattacks to the general public.[6]

It is encouraging that President Biden's FY 2022 budget request includes a $110 million increase in funding for CISA, bringing its total funding to $2.1 billion.[7] The president's budget also proposes $20 million for a Cyber Response and Recovery Fund and $5 billion for a Critical Supply Chain Resilience Fund.[8] Even so, these numbers will undoubtedly change before a final budget agreement is reached. Moreover, cybersecurity needs to be understood as a competitive activity. Instead of looking at government budget growth rates year over year, the United States needs to see its spending in relation to what its adversaries are spending to attack it. The spending disparities between the United States and the attack community—which we have already documented—include China's announced plan to spend $1.4 trillion on its digital strategy over the next five years.[9] Add to that Russia, Iran, and North Korea, among others, and the multibillion-dollar criminal enterprises, and we can see why the threats are increasing dramatically and the system itself is getting weaker.

Meanwhile, the 2021 federal budget enacted a slight decrease in federal spending on cybersecurity, from about $18,791,600 to $18,778,80. Even if President Biden's FY 2022 budget calling for a 14 percent increase in federal civilian cybersecurity funding is enacted, US spending still pales in comparison to cybersecurity spending by US adversaries.[10] In contrast, the Chinese state-run media Xinhua projects a 25.1 percent compound annual growth in Chinese government cybersecurity spending from 2019 to 2023.[11] One might be skeptical about relying on state-run media, but a review of the Chinese programs outlined in chapter 3 (Belt and Road and Digital Silk Road) seems to verify the degree of disparity if not the exact numbers.

Under the Trump administration, DHS proposed a budget cut of 15 percent to its lead cyber research group, the Science and Technology Directorate. Within the Directorate, funding specifically for cybersecurity research was cut 66 percent.[12] This is not the only research institution that has recently seen a cut in funding. The National Institute of Standards and Technology, which is the government's main cyber standards institution, saw a cut of 10 percent in FY 2021.[13] Biden's 2022 budget included nearly $823 million for the Science and Technology Directorate, and NIST received a 30 percent increase in its budget, topping at $1 billion.[14]

In contrast to the federal government's spending on cybersecurity, US private sector spending on cybersecurity is expected to reach $207.7 billion by 2024, according to a study from Gartner.[15] Even operating from a much larger funding base than the federal government, the percentage increase in private sector spending will be about 9 percent during this time period.[16]

While CISA, the federal agency charged with cybersecurity for all non-military portions of the government and the private sector, has a proposed FY 2022 budget of $2.1 billion, the automotive industry alone is expected to spend $7.67 billion by 2027 on digital defense,[17] almost four times the entire CISA budget.

Moreover, as discussed in some detail in chapter 5, the National Infrastructure Protection Plan acknowledges that private sector security spending is appropriately focused on security at a commercial level. That will not accommodate our national security needs and illustrates what Chris Krebs describes as a gap in our nation's cyber defense between what the private sector can be expected to provide for commercial purposes and what the government is now providing for cybersecurity.[18]

The cyber investment gap manifests itself in a different sense when US spending is compared to that of its major adversaries. China, for example, has allocated billions of dollars to investments in research and acquisition of advanced technologies that are key to future economic growth, including semiconductors 5G, AI, and supercomputers at rates many times that of the US investment. Similarly, US educational spending specifically on the critical Science, Technology, Engineering, and Mathematics (STEM) curriculum is lagging. The United States ranks 30th in math spending and 11th in science spending. The enacted FY 2021 budget for STEM education was only $3.2 billion and has not seen marked increases since 2019 (figures for 2022 are not available at the time of this book's writing).[19] On the other hand, China's budgetary spending on education is around $520 billion.[20]

Further, broader R&D spending is not keeping pace with our adversaries. In 1960, the United States accounted for 69 percent of overall global R&D funding; today it accounts for roughly 30 percent.[21] While the United States maintains its overall lead in R&D spending, that lead is quickly vanishing because other countries are now realizing the importance of investing in technology.[22]

China is currently the second largest investor in overall R&D funding—over half a trillion dollars—and now accounts for about 26 percent of all global spending.[23] Since 2000, China's R&D funding has grown roughly 1,600 percent, with South Korea right behind, having grown just over 400 percent, and the United States further down on the list, having grown roughly 100 percent.[24]

Determining the National Cyber Risk Appetite

By almost any measure, federal government spending on cybersecurity is inadequate and noncompetitive with our major rivals. One of the most important aspects of the proposed national digital strategy is to develop a realistic cyber risk appetite. This is one of the foundational principles of the economics-based risk assessment methods we describe below and is increasingly being adopted by the private sector. Entities that are serious about cyber risk management go through a prescribed series of steps to determine their cyber risk appetite, which helps determine how much money it will take to avoid, mitigate, or transfer their cyber risk to an acceptable level.

Working with the appropriate federal agencies to ensure that they are doing sophisticated, not purely technical, cyber risk assessments should be a prioritized goal for the new Office of Digital Strategy and Security we propose. This would lead to realistic estimates of what will be needed for the United States to achieve an acceptable level of cyber risk.

Paying for Cybersecurity

In the sections that follow, we present a number of examples of how cost-effective spending, including by the private sector, can be pursued. Additional examples are provided in part 2 of this volume.

The nation's leading law enforcement agency for cybersecurity, the FBI, has an annual cybersecurity budget of about half a billion dollars. The director of the National Intelligence Agency has called cybersecurity our greatest national threat, yet based on the most recent numbers, we spent less than $19 billion on cybersecurity, whereas we spent $175 billion on international terrorism.[25] No one wants to argue for spending less to fight terrorism, but at least an equivalent expenditure on cybersecurity is appropriate based on the assessments of the US government's own threat experts.

The obvious answer to this conundrum is, of course, that the government feels the federal budget simply cannot accommodate that level of spending. However, in light of the documented nature of the cyber threat and recent government spending initiatives, this spending restraint needs to be called into question. Moreover, a significant effect can likely be achieved with spending increases that are modest in comparison to other elements of the budget. For example, phasing in a doubling of the FBI's cybercrime budget would cost less than a billion dollars. Providing federal grants to build our cyber workforce would be similarly cost-effective. Funding research to determine the cost-effectiveness of our cybersecurity programs and analyzing how to adapt existing market incentive programs to the cyber domain also require similarly modest outlays—especially in comparison to the costs of the attacks we are suffering.

Other investments such as tax breaks for small- and medium-sized companies that suffer from sophisticated cyberattacks but cannot afford sophisticated defenses should also be considered. A recent study by IBM found that 52 percent of critical infrastructure SMBs experienced a cyber breach in the last year.[26]

The study also found that a majority of those surveyed believe their company is not prepared to prevent or recover from a cyberattack. For these SMBs, the pathway to needed security enhancements clearly does not lie in traditional government awareness programs. What is required are empirically proven methods of improving security and the funding to make these investments practical. The study concluded that "SMBs may not be able to sustain uneconomic investments in cybersecurity beyond minimum requirements. Consequently, consideration must be given to what incentives may be required."[27] When compared to the extent of SMB interface with critical infrastructure and current government spending patterns, the sorts of modest tax incentives required to provide adequate security seem to be more than affordable.

Another area where comparatively modest government spending could bring long-term benefit is investment in advanced technologies at a rate equivalent to our major adversaries and developing a digital foreign policy competitive with our geopolitical adversaries.

It is beyond the province of this volume to dictate the specific spending levels that will be required. These need to be analyzed and suggested based on the cyber risk assessment methods and the digital transformation plan we are calling on the White House to develop through the ODSS. However, this analysis of current spending, in light of the extent of the growing threat and the substantially higher investments of our major adversaries, clearly demonstrates that the US government must increase its cybersecurity spending in multiple areas if we are to maintain the world leadership position we have held since World War II.

The question is not really if we have the money to spend on creating a cyber secure system but rather, to paraphrase Biden, do we truly value our own security?

Market Incentive Models

Government can potentially stimulate an increase in overall cybersecurity investment by addressing the economic gaps between commercial- and national-level cybersecurity needs discussed in the NIPP. This can be done by creatively developing economic incentives that will make private sector cyber investments, which may be unjustified on a commercial basis, more economically viable. While tax policy is the most direct market incentive and may be appropriate in some cases—such as with small companies—non-tax incentives can also be creatively deployed to generate increased private sector cybersecurity spending in the national interest.

As detailed earlier, there have been numerous government and industry commissions and reports advocating the development of a pro-market incentive model. Unfortunately, apart from one bill passed in 2016 that provided a limited liability exception to industry participants in one of the government's information sharing programs, there has been no serious consideration given in Congress or the executive branch to developing the menu of incentives that could substantially improve the nation's security without having a serious impact on the federal budget. As this book goes to press the Biden administration and Congress, perhaps recognizing the movement toward a more economics-based model of cybersecurity, have floated several ideas for injecting market incentives into the cybersecurity ecosystem. These range from grants to small telecommunications companies to "rip and replace" Chinese technology in their networks to liability protections for promptly reporting cyber incidents to financial incentives for voluntarily enhancing security in the energy transport system and even substantial payments for tips on international malicious cyber activity.[28] Unfortunately, as of this writing none of these incentives has been enacted, but the proposals suggest a productive trend toward addressing and rebalancing the economics of cybersecurity.

There are multiple models of incentive programs that have been used on various industry sectors to generate pro-social benefits. These models ought to be studied within the ODSS and adapted based on that analysis to promote increased cybersecurity expenditure by industry by making such expenditures economically attractive. The joint industry-DHS Collective Defense White Paper cited in chapter 5 identifies a range of sectors that are worthy of serious investigation

A few additional examples are given below.

- In the pharmaceutical industry, companies can earn the right to access a fast track for valuable patent approval for new drugs. This can be a substantial market incentive for pharmaceutical companies since getting products to market quickly is a major goal. As we documented in chapter 1, getting products to market quickly is also a major goal in the IT industry. The ODSS should study how this model could be adapted to cybersecurity by creating incentives to build security into IT products before bringing them to market.

- After 9/11, Congress passed the SAFETY Act, which provided marketing and insurance incentives for the development of antiterrorism technologies. The SAFETY Act, however, is built on a terrorism model inconsistent with the chronic economics-based cyberattacks we experience. The ODSS, in consultation with DHS, should study how the act could be altered to make it more useful for the realities of the current cybersecurity environment.

- In the energy industry, a creative program was developed for emissions trading that accessed the greater economies of scope and scale for larger utilities, enabling them to profit from exceeding their needs for regulatory compliance and assisting other entities in meeting their obligations. This resulted in expanded environment improvement overall. Major financial institutions are currently adapting this model to develop offsets to help reduce their carbon footprints.

- Similar small company/large company disparities exist with respect to cybersecurity in many sectors. Finding ways to leverage the economies of scale larger firms enjoy, making it profitable to sell or share cybersecurity methods or tools, is another worthy area of study. Chapter 8 on the defense industrial base (DIB) offers one such proposal which may be adaptable to other sectors also.

This is just a sampling of the creative programs available for use by the federal government to incentivize greater cyber spending by the private sector without engaging in the sort of state mandates and nation-state requirements characteristic of governments like China. Successive chapters on the defense, energy, healthcare, and others provide a range of sector specific programs that can also free capital for more private cyber spending.

There are three essential elements needed to make an incentive program a success.

- There needs to be a "cyber strike zone," that is, a qualifier for earning the incentive. Aside from special instances (e.g., small companies) we anticipate incentives for "good actors." The bar could realistically be set based on results of a DHS-certified sophisticated cyber risk assessment, as discussed below.
- The incentive needs to be appropriate for the industry. For example, procurement incentives might be best for DIB companies; regulatory forbearance for traditionally regulated entities; and patent or permitting "fast tracks" for other unregulated entities.
- The incentive needs to be economically powerful enough to change behavior.

What is required is a plan—a digital strategy—and a conscientious program for implementation and evaluation as exists in the private sector.

Modernize

Use of modern comprehensive cyber risk assessment programs that define an entity's appropriate risk appetite on empirical and economic bases should replace the traditional checklists of requirements as the preferred regulatory yardstick. As demonstrated in chapter 4, the traditional regulatory paradigm, which is typically based on compliance, with an extensive checklist of mandated requirements, is ill-suited to managing the dynamism of the cyber threat. Not only has it been shown to be costly and ineffective in sectors that have attempted to use it,[29] but it fosters mistrust and alienation among parties that need to be collaborating. A more extensive discussion of the inadequacy of this compliance model, even when applied in a highly regimented sector, is provided in chapter 8 on defense.

In earlier eras, cyber checklists were state of the art. However, in recent years, risk assessment models that enable organizations to conduct empirical and economics-based cyber risk assessments are now available and are being widely adopted, including by critical infrastructure and the insurance industry. Models such as Factor Analysis of Information Risk (FAIR) and X-Analytics are a far more appropriate method for cyber risk assessment, and these and similar tools should replace the antiquated checklists.

It should be understood that the use of these tools does not obviate the use of more standard frameworks such as NIST, ISO, and SANS. The broader methodologies suggested here typically map onto all the major frameworks. Use of these tools simply enables organizations to make more strategic use of the standard frameworks based on empirical and economic factors. This further enables industry and government to strategically determine how to best deploy scarce cybersecurity resources. Standard checklists do not enable needed economic prioritization.

All indications are that the market will be increasingly generating such tools, making them even more widely available, targeted, and affordable (some of the tools are already open source). DHS has a modality under the SAFETY Act that can be modified and used to designate and certify the models as qualifying for determining access to incentives.

As described in the NIPP, private entities should be expected to achieve commercial-level security. The appropriate level of commercial-level security—the risk appetite—is defined by the unique business model or organizational mission. Another flaw in the current regulatory system is its tendency to treat all companies in a broad industry sector the same, with some allowances for size. Companies in the same economic sector can have appropriately different risk appetites based on a wide range of differences in business plan, culture, and location, as well as many factors.

Even in most regulated sectors, such as finance and healthcare, the more contemporary model for regulation advocated here needs to be adopted. In fact, many companies are already using these models, in addition to the government mandates, because they realize the government structures do not provide the needed information to do effective cyber risk management and budgeting. For many of these companies the government checklists are little more than a compliance item, not a fundamental risk assessment tool.

Regulated entities could reasonably be required to demonstrate that they have met that level of commercial security as determined by the sophisticated risk assessment tools certified by DHS under the SAFETY Act, which would presumably include provision for consumer security. This would relieve them of the burden of government checklists.

By calibrating cybersecurity decisions on the use of these rigorous, empirical, entity-specific risk assessments, government will assure greater efficiency in cyber risk expenditures and thus enhance overall ecosystem security. Moreover, these more precise assessments will properly enable the setting of risk appetites in accord with the organization's legitimate business plan. This will facilitate the use of the incentive models the ODSS could create. These models provide a clear measurement of the amount and type of market incentive that can be used to urge an organization to make security investments that go beyond their core commercial interests and meet broader national security needs if this is required.

Creating a structure that systematically addresses how to bridge the gap between legitimate industry spending on cybersecurity and the government's needs is an important first step. Additional gains can be made by modernizing the process for addressing cyber risk in a truly collaborative industry-government partnership as opposed to the current compliance-based punitive model.

The Biden Administration's Approach to Cybersecurity

The SolarWinds and Microsoft Exchange attacks revealed major vulnerabilities in the US government's software supply chains, and in response to these incidents, the Biden administration released its Executive Order on Improving the Nation's Cybersecurity in May 2021. The executive order seeks to protect and modernize federal information systems by preventing, assessing, detecting, and remediating cyber incidents within them. It also acknowledges that effective cybersecurity policy is "essential to national and economic security,"[30] a central tenet of this book. In particular, the executive order takes steps to remove contractual barriers to threat information sharing between executive agencies and their IT/OT contractors (many contracts explicitly preclude companies from sharing such threat information); secure the integrity of software supply chains; and establish a Cyber Safety Review Board to investigate and mitigate the potential significant cyber incidents. The executive order also takes the largely unprecedented step of setting requirements for federal contractors to promptly report cyber incidents to CISA and the FBI.

While Biden's executive order is applicable only to contractors to executive agencies such as DoD, DOJ, and DHS, it, along with Biden's proposal to increase federal cybersecurity spending to $9.8 billion, suggests an increased recognition that cybersecurity is a national security issue. To build on the executive order's objective, in January 2022, Biden signed the National Security Memorandum, aimed at better securing systems containing classified data across federal agencies. The memo includes various security requirements that must be implemented for national security systems within 180 days.[31]

Managing Systemic Cyber Risk

Most cyber risk management efforts have focused on codifying firm-specific best practices and incentivizing individual companies to adopt them. Systemic technology failures go far beyond economic disruption; they jeopardize human life and property. A sector-specific view is incomplete as multiple industries interact to deliver the same critical service.

Fortunately, the number of historical cyber events causing systemic property damage or loss of life is limited. Unfortunately, this is likely to change as we transition to 5G cellular wireless and rely more on connected devices in critical applications such as transportation.

The risk of systemic attack is also increasing as sophisticated attack tools become increasingly available to nontraditional "asymmetric" players. For years the technical ability to cause systemic attacks was limited to major nation-state actors. However, the economic interdependencies of nation-states like the United States and China made such potentially devastating attacks counterproductive as devastating economic impacts could rebound against the attacker. Terrorists, however, may have no such qualms, and as sophisticated attack tools become increasingly user-friendly the opportunity for systemic attack grows.

As more of our critical infrastructure and service providers become connected and leverage common hardware, software, and vendors, the nation's risk level increases. It is likely that we will see more and larger systemic cyber events similar to SolarWinds in the future, and it will require governments, corporations, and citizens to work together to assess, prepare for, and manage this risk.

Cyber risk management needs to advance materially and marry company- and systems-level views of cyber risk. DHS's National Risk Management Center has done some great initial work in this area. However, to achieve a full understanding of the "fabric of the world," it will be necessary to evolve the National Critical Functions to a set of end-to-end "maps" of critical systems. Continued work is needed to accelerate understanding of and action on systemic cyber risk. The federal government is in a central position to organize this effort in collaboration with private industry and academia.

The complexity of addressing systemic risk also illustrates the need for a multidimensional process that considers the interactions of technology, economics, and security. For example, consider the Orion software that was the focal point of the SolarWinds attack. A traditional regulatory approach might be to mandate that all such software be restricted to assure security. However, this solution would amount to a substantial curb on innovation, which is the lifeblood for competitiveness in the digital world. The software was judged by the market, including multiple government agencies, to be adequately secure for widespread adoption. However, the software became a more attractive target in large part due to the market penetration it had achieved. A more sophisticated approach might be for critical elements of systems to be monitored for market penetration, and when a systemically dangerous level of penetration is reached a collaborative—government and industry—process would determine if adjustments need to be made to protect the system. In SolarWinds, it is likely that a more carefully calibrated configuration would have provided greater security, thus mitigating the risks.

There are a relatively small number of core system components that due to their market penetration might qualify for this special treatment and may enable greater management of systemic risk without unduly curbing beneficial innovation (see chap. 3). No such process currently exists but could be an element of the ODSS.

An International Legal Structure

The president should immediately resume a dialogue with our allies and adversaries to work toward signed agreements outlining a practical international legal structure to fight international cybercrime. The last such agreement, the Budapest Convention on Cybercrime, is nonbinding and is ill-equipped to handle the scale and systemic nature of the international cybercrime threat.[32]

As stated in chapter 5, the president should convene a multi-stakeholder commission specifically charged with determining what the United States sees as a functional international cyber law system. The necessary follow-up step would be the diplomatic effort required to put that system into effect. The administration should create an assistant secretary–level position for cybersecurity within the State Department with an adequate budget to follow through on the cybercrime initiative. While it is understood that such a framework will be difficult to erect, especially in the current international climate, the long-standing status quo cannot be considered tolerable. A concerted effort to create a workable international cybercrime enforcement system is needed. Ideally, these agreements would have clearly defined terms and consequences for violations. Extradition needs to be addressed, thus enabling its law enforcement agencies to prosecute and protect against individuals who commit crimes and seek protection in foreign countries.

It is noteworthy that previous generations operating in similarly tense periods of international animus have succeeded in achieving workable international agreements such as nuclear test ban treaties, nonproliferation pacts, and international inspection systems. Although the terms of cyber-crime agreements would be different, the previous agreements were similarly difficult to negotiate in their era and were accomplished, even if imperfectly.

Law Enforcement

We have outlined the multiple challenges law enforcement faces fighting cyber-crime, including inadequate resources and organizational misalignment among disparate law enforcement entities. A compelling example of how digital crimes are growing and morphing into ever more sophisticated forms is the dramatic increase in ransomware attacks.

On May 7, 2021, the Colonial Pipeline, which supplies 45 percent of the East Coast's supply of diesel, petrol, and jet fuel, announced its networks had been compromised and much of its data taken for a $5 million ransom by a criminal group called DarkSide.[33] For nearly a week, the pipeline remained offline, causing severe fuel shortages and panic buying throughout the southeastern United States. Eventually, Colonial Pipeline paid the ransom, though fuel shortages continued for weeks after the company went back online. Later that month and after an extensive investigation, the FBI was able to recover about half of the ransom payment, which the bureau touted as a success story in information sharing and public-private collaboration.[34]

The Colonial Pipeline incident, however, was just one event. Less than a month later, on May 30, JBS, the world's largest meat supplier, announced that several of its plants were shut down by cybercriminals demanding an $11 million ransom.[35] The plants, which provided nearly one-fifth of the US meat supply, were shut down for nearly three days before JBS agreed to pay the ransom. As of this book's writing, neither JBS nor the FBI has recovered the ransom payment.

While the Colonial Pipeline and JBS incidents caught widespread attention in the media for their impacts on everyday consumer goods, they represent a very small portion of the hundreds of thousands of ransomware incidents that have occurred over the past eight years. In 2020 alone, there were as many as 65,000 successful breaches totaling $350 million in ransom payments.[36] These figures are not likely to abate. And by 2031 global ransomware payment costs are predicted to exceed $265 billion.[37]

Since ransomware first emerged in 2013, attacks have become easier—and cheaper—to perform. The emergence of ransomware as a service (RaaS), in particular, represents a major shift in the ransomware "business model." Under a RaaS model, malicious actors who lack the skill or time to develop their own ransomware strain can rent or buy one from a variety of vendors on the dark web.[38] For a monthly fee as low as $40, ransomware developers will provide 24/7 service, user reviews, and user forums. Since 2020, RaaS has flourished as a competitive market with significantly lowered barriers to entry and fierce price competition.

Indeed, the accessibility of ransomware to everyday individuals—combined with the anonymity of both the dark web and ransom payment systems like cryptocurrency—poses a conundrum for law enforcement, which, as we have noted repeatedly in this book, remains uncoordinated and underresourced as cybercriminals grow ever more sophisticated. While the FBI's recovery of some of Colonial Pipeline's ransom payment is a positive development, that case remains an outlier. Thousands of ransomware attacks happen every year, and at current funding levels the FBI—or any law enforcement agency, for that matter—cannot address each case with the attention it gave to the pipeline case. What the Colonial Pipeline case did demonstrate, though, is that with the proper resources and organizational alignment law enforcement can play an active, productive role in promoting effective cybersecurity.

Adapting Effective Law Enforcement Techniques to Digital Issues

In May 2021, the FBI was quickly able to retrieve around half of the money originally lost to a massive ransomware attack on Colonial Pipeline. If this were a drug seizure, as opposed to a digital recovery, law enforcement would be able to keep a percentage of the recovered funds. Such a system adapted for ransomware recovery could expand law enforcement's ability to protect the public from these attacks. A portion of recovered ransom money could be placed in a revolving fund to subsidize future law enforcement efforts. The success in the Colonial Pipeline case demonstrates that given adequate resources, law enforcement can assist cybercrime victims, significantly diminish the profit for the criminals, and thus substantially reduce the incentive for these attacks. If law enforcement always had the resources to recover a portion of ransomware payments and pursue cybercriminals, the entire nation would benefit from fewer such attacks.

Law enforcement might also benefit from adopting organizational innovations currently being used in the private sector. Major financial institutions, some operating with cybercrime budgets of similar size to the FBI, have been facing similar stress in attempting to maximize scarce resources to fight cybercrime. As is so often the case, it is leadership that is the key to progress. Research by McKinsey found that "as criminal transgressions in the financial sector become more sophisticated and break through traditional boundaries, banks are watching their various risk functions become more costly and less effective. Leaders are therefore rethinking their approaches to take advantage of synergies.... Most forward-thinking institutions are working toward integration, creating, in stages, a more unified model across domains based on common processes, tools and analytics."[39] This research showed that these organizational innovations can improve the efficiency and effectiveness of anti-cybercrime efforts. Similar innovations in law enforcement organizations could be helpful in addressing the issues documented in chapter 4.

The McKinsey research describes several models that can be used, based on the size and sophistication of the financial institution, to move through stages of integration based on the institution's unique circumstances. It notes that many financial institutions are integrating previously disparate criminal divisions to leverage better use of modern analytics and stimulate increased teamwork to fight cybercrime. The existence of multiple models is convenient as law enforcement organizations also have a variety of structures and can adapt the private sector model that most closely replicates their unique situation.

> The integration of cybersecurity with other crimes is an imperative step now since the crimes themselves are already deeply interrelated. The enhanced data and analytics capabilities that integration enables are now essential tools for the prevention, detection, and mitigation of threats. . . . Most banks begin the journey by closely integrating their cybersecurity and fraud units. As they enhance information sharing and coordination across silos, greater risk effectiveness, and efficiency becomes possible. To achieve the target state they seek, banks are redefining organizational lines and boxes and utility.[40]

Among the noteworthy outcomes McKinsey found was that personnel freed from some organizational constraints felt better able to "think like the criminal" and anticipate criminal activities, which enhanced risk management. Its report cites one leading US bank that set up a holistic cybercrime "center of excellence" and made "significant efficiency gains," while another major institution went "all the way," combining all their operations related to financial crimes and reducing operating costs by approximately $100 million. Such a saving in efficiency if applied to the FBI's 2022 budget would be the equivalent of a roughly 20 percent increase.

Military and Civilian Law Enforcement

In chapter 8, on defense, we lay out an approach to collective cyber defense to assist smaller businesses in the supply chain that lack the time and resources to commit to addressing cybersecurity. This same challenge exists in the law enforcement arena as well, as state and local law enforcement agencies can often be the first point of contact for a business but lack the same level of resources as other federal agencies leading on cybersecurity such as the FBI. To create a "collective defense" that elevates the security of both small and large entities in the DIB, we propose several models that could be adopted, including the development of a centrally managed working environment that would help defend the entire DIB ecosystem. A similar model could be adapted to the law enforcement community. Larger federal law enforcement agencies could create a similar type of working environment that would provide state and local law enforcement agencies access to the tools, tactics, and services to investigate cybercrime on a smaller scale.

Alternatively, the RAND Corporation has proposed a similar model for how to more holistically address the cyber threats in the defense sector through a DIB Cyber Protection Program (DCP2).[41] RAND proposes the use of a cloud service to disseminate essential cybersecurity tools and information to smaller firms in the DIB supply chain. The DCP2 would provide tools such as vulnerability scanning and software patching, as well as advanced email security, data filtering, and data loss prevention software. DIB firms also leverage security information and event management (SIEM) tools to track malicious attackers and eradicate malware from their networks.

These models could be further tailored based on recommendations in the joint DHS-industry Collective Defense White Paper.[42] The White Paper suggests additional outreach to large and small businesses, as well as smaller state and local law enforcement agencies and organizations such as the International Association of Chiefs of Police, to expand capabilities and share information across jurisdictions.[43] This includes increased coordination, development, and updating of best practices; promoting use of cyber insurance; and communicating protocols for reporting cybercrimes and requesting law enforcement support.

We documented similar issues with smaller law enforcement agencies lacking the funding for cybercrime initiatives that larger ones possess in chapter 4. Proposals such as these laid out in the DIB should be used as a model and applied to law enforcement, with the FBI taking the role of establishing a scalable cybersecurity service and tool for smaller law enforcement agencies. The Pentagon could even serve as a conduit for the provision of tools and information directly to law enforcement, in some cases with costs on a sliding scale for private as opposed to public entities. The goal would be, through cooperation, to share cybersecurity infrastructure and techniques for the public benefit and lower costs by expanding scope and scale.

While there are obvious differences between law enforcement, banks, and defense contractors, there are similarities in terms of budget and organizational stresses. These alternative approaches are unlikely to be suitable to simply cut and paste in the law enforcement community; however, thoughtful review should be conducted to find the appropriate areas of convergence. The ODSS could provide the home for analysis and coordination between the public and private sectors to facilitate the adaptations that are most suitable to the adaptations the cybercriminal community are making.

Cybersecurity Education

There is a severe market failure with respect to the nation's cyber workforce. This failure makes the already difficult job of securing networks from constant and sophisticated attacks much harder. According to statistics compiled by the job aggregator CyberSeek, 522,000 cybersecurity jobs remain unfilled,[44] while the Bureau of Labor Statistics (BLS) claims that postings for cyber jobs will increase by 31 percent through 2029.[45]

Government is faring no better than the private sector—many think it is faring worse—in terms of cyber workforce development. A 2019 GAO report stated:

> DHS and the Department of Defense had not fully addressed cybersecurity workforce management requirements set forth in federal laws. Further, as of June 2018, most of the 24 major federal agencies had not fully implemented all requirements associated with the Federal Cybersecurity Workforce Assessment Act of 2015. For example, three agencies had not conducted a baseline assessment to identify the extent to which their cybersecurity employees held professional certifications. As a result, these agencies may not be able to effectively gauge the competency of individuals who are charged with ensuring the confidentiality, integrity, and availability of federal information and information systems.[46]

As of 2021, these agencies had made only marginal progress in addressing these deficiencies and "continue to face challenges in ensuring that their cybersecurity workforce has the appropriate skills."[47]

Much of this problem has to do with the lack of curriculum in schools and universities. According to *US News & World Report*, none of the top ten US computer science programs requires a single cybersecurity course for graduation. Only one of the top five schools offering the most cybersecurity electives is ranked among the top fifty computer science programs. Schools were being squeezed for funds even before the COVID-19 pandemic. In its aftermath, the incentive to launch new programs with substantial upfront cost and uncertain promise of long-term payoff further complicates a bad situation.

There are a wide range of opportunities to begin to fill these gaps, particularly with more creative thinking about the problem. For example, the accounting profession had a similar problem attracting individuals into the field, which many millennials deemed unexciting or excessively technical. The Center for Audit Quality designed a creative marketing program featuring approachable "cool" men and women in a targeted PR campaign. The young representatives personalized the benefits of the profession and expanded the candidate pool.[48] In another direction, there may be a massive pool of interested young people active in online gaming who could be attracted with the prospect of making a living practicing many of the same skills they have developed in their pastime.[49]

Traditionally underserved populations should also be targeted. To address the curriculum gap discussed earlier, existing curriculum programs developed at major universities should systematically be shared and supported at Historically Black Colleges and Universities. Such outreach should provide teaching techniques and scholarships targeted at inner cities to more aggressively fill the large cyber workforce development gap and generate needed diversity and economic development.

Government agencies can also create a public-private partnership in which recent graduates work in cybersecurity in the federal government for a certain period, then have the opportunity to work in the private sector. Starting in summer 2020, Microsoft and MasterCard initiated programs in which after two years with the federal government, students could work in cybersecurity in their corporations and also have an opportunity to receive student loan forgiveness for up to $75,000.[50] The second cohort is expected to be placed by summer 2022. To better meet the growing needs in the cyber workforce, both in the public and private sector, this type of initiative needs to be broadened and have more participation across industry sectors. A program like this would incentivize the younger generation to study cybersecurity because they know that they will have a better chance of securing a job after graduation.[51]

Economize

Many cybersecurity issues are complicated by major nation-state actors interwoven with criminal syndicates operating under outdated and haphazardly defined economic and legal structures. These issues cannot be addressed with the current technical/operational model we have followed for nearly thirty years. These are difficult issues that will require investment, as well as creative and innovative programs, to leverage the best of our public and private sector initiatives.

However, there are also significant cybersecurity issues that exist primarily because well-intentioned government institutions have not matured to the level that allows them to operate effectively in the digital world. Government can solve these problems with political will and hard work.

Streamlining Existing Regulatory Structures

One of the largest government-created cybersecurity challenges is that of conflicting and duplicative cybersecurity regulation. As stated above, the entire regulatory model needs to be modernized, with the inefficient checklists being replaced by modern cyber risk management systems that put cyber risk in empirical and economic terms. While waiting for that to happen legislatively, the current system can be streamlined largely though administrative action.

There is widespread consensus on the overall lack of cybersecurity resources and personnel available to deal with the ever-increasing number of cyberattacks. Cybersecurity regulations that conflict or duplicate each other actually hurt our security by diverting scarce cybersecurity resources to compliance exercises that, because of their redundant nature, do not enhance security.

As explained in the chapters on financial services, healthcare, retail, and energy in part 2, streamlining cyber regulatory processes will do away with unnecessary redundancies and achieve dramatic savings, with estimates of up to 40 percent, without sacrificing effectiveness. This means security teams are now spending nearly half their time on duplicative audits and compliance measures rather than implementing controls to secure their networks. The efficiencies from streamlined regulation can, and should, be channeled back into effective security.

The problem is not unique to the private sector. The same challenge is affecting state and local governments. The National Association of State Chief Information Officers prioritized in its 2021 agenda harmonizing the duplicative and conflicting federal regulations states must comply with.[52] A 2020 Government Accountability Office report reviewed cybersecurity regulations across the Centers for Medicare and Medicaid Services, the Internal Revenue Service, the Social Security Administration, and the FBI and found that between 49 and 79 percent of cybersecurity regulations were either duplicative or in conflict with each other.[53] The GAO recommended that OMB coordinate the regulatory agencies "to the greatest extent possible and direct further coordination where needed."[54] Similar recommendations have been endorsed by the bipartisan leadership of the Homeland Security Committee and the bipartisan Cyberspace Solarium Commission.[55]

Enough research has been done on this. OMB should require that all new federal cybersecurity regulation be certified as being neither redundant nor in conflict with any already existing regulations. Beyond that, the proposed ODSS should begin the long effort of untangling the existing regulatory duplication as part of the National Digital Transformation Strategy.

A National Data Protection Law

There are fifty individual data protection plans proffered by the states, meaning that multistate entities need separate regulatory structures and procedures to accomplish basically the same functions. This waste and duplication, as in the case of federal requirements, creates an antisecurity environment by diverting scarce cyber resources.

Congress should pass and the president should sign a data breach protection law that provides a national standard preempting state action and simplifies and clarifies data security for the organization and the consumer. It is true that states are traditionally a laboratory for new regulatory initiatives, but in this case—after more than a decade—the age of experimentation is over. Cyberattacks clearly transcend state boundaries and hence ought to be the province of the federal government. Multiple state laws are, at this stage, contrary to the public interest and need to be preempted.

The specifics of the requirement should meet the justified needs of both industry and consumers; however, redundancies and state variations need to be eliminated. Backed by a national data protection law, organizations will be able to more effectively implement consumer protection as determined by the US Congress.

PART TWO

SECTORS OF CYBERSECURITY

CHAPTER 7

HEALTH

Cybersecurity as a Core Element of Patient Care

Lou DeSorbo and Jamison Gardner

The healthcare industry is losing the battle in cyberspace. Over the past decades, healthcare has become increasingly intertwined with technology. The increased use of technological solutions can lead to better care and outcomes for patients. However, this integration of technology also creates significant security vulnerabilities that can generate negative outcomes. In the twenty-first century, cybersecurity has become an integral part of comprehensive patient care and one of the foremost challenges facing the entire healthcare industry. Currently, the industry as a whole seems to be losing the cybersecurity battle. Here are just a few key metrics to substantiate that point.

- Since 2015 over 300 million patient records have been stolen.[1] In a 2017 survey, 81 percent of the 220 healthcare organizations surveyed reported a security breach resulting in data being compromised.[2] In 2020 the healthcare industry experienced a 55 percent increase in cyberattacks, leaving an estimated 26 million patient records exposed.[3] In 2021, more than 40 million patient records were compromised.[4] Data from the Department of Health and Human Services shows that in almost every month of 2020, more than one million people were affected by data breaches at healthcare organizations.[5]
- A recent Black Book survey revealed that 96 percent of almost 3,000 security professionals indicated that their organizations are not able to keep up with the ever-growing cyber threats in the healthcare field.[6]
- Interpol's Cybercrime Threat Response team reported that the COVID-19 pandemic has spurred increased targeting of vulnerable hospitals by cybercriminals around the world. By the end of March 2020, only weeks into the pandemic, cyberattacks against

the healthcare industry had increased by 150 percent.[7] Ransomware
attacks against the healthcare industry continued to grow in 2020:
in October alone "there was an increase of 71 percent."[8] Overall, the
healthcare sector experienced a 55 percent increase in data breaches
since 2019 and a 10 percent increase in the average cost per breach
in 2020.[9] These growing ransomware attacks create a dual threat to
the healthcare system. First, ransom demands, which started at a few
thousand dollars, have grown to seven figures, in some cases stripping
vital resources from overwhelmed healthcare facilities.[10] Second, the
threat of the altering of patient information creates the paralyzing
prospect that care will not be able to be provided with confidence.

This trend of increasing cyberattacks against the healthcare industry is not
expected to stop anytime soon.

Healthcare in particular is being heavily targeted by cybercriminals
because "it is a rich source of valuable data, and it is a soft target."[11] As is the
case with all sectors of the economy, the economics of cybersecurity in the
healthcare field weigh heavily in favor of the cybercriminals. Patient datasets are extremely valuable to cybercriminals and nation-state actors alike.
The costs associated with launching an attack are relatively low while profits
from stolen patient datasets are very high. This data can fetch over $1,000 on
the black market because the information contained in them can be used in
several lucrative ways, including to submit false medical claims, acquire prescription drugs, and obtain credit.[12] To add some perspective, it is estimated
that a person's medical information is at least twenty times more valuable
to criminals than a person's financial information.[13] In the world of nation-
state threat actors, healthcare records are an excellent source of intelligence
for building out target folders on individuals those nations might want to
compromise in the future. Thus healthcare organizations are a prime target
for cybercriminals and nation-state actors because they present an opportunity for high returns on their attack investment. During the COVID-19 pandemic, cybercriminals are exploiting people's fear by sending phishing emails
posing as the Centers for Disease Control and other trusted sources to extort
money, information, and gain access to IT systems.[14]

While cyberattacks on the healthcare industry are a financial boon for
nation-states and criminals, they may also endanger the patients themselves.
As such, failing to secure current and future interconnected medical devices
could have significant consequences for patient health and hospitals systems
alike.

Ransomware attacks against hospitals have increased in recent months. In 2020, ninety-two US healthcare organizations suffered ransomware attacks, almost double the number of attacks reported in 2019. In 2021, nearly 42 percent of healthcare providers had faced two or more ransomware attacks within the past two years. Comparitech estimated the costs of the attacks in 2020 at almost $21 billion. The number of ransomware attacks increased by 60 percent from 2019 to 2020, showcasing how quickly this problem is growing. One explanation could be the new target for nation-state-backed hackers and cybercriminals: antibody drugs and vaccine-related research. Great Plains Health, a hospital in North Platte, Nebraska, recorded on average a threefold increase in blocked attempts to access its servers after it started coronavirus antibody drug trials in November 2020. Hackers are even targeting vaccine manufacturers themselves: AstraZeneca staff, some of whom were working on COVID-19 research, were sent emails with job descriptions laced with malicious code designed to gain access to the person's computer. It is not thought that this specific attack was successful, but other attacks to gain information likely have been. The European Medicines Agency, which assesses vaccines for approval, was attacked on December 9, 2020. The attackers were able to access some documents related to the regulatory submission for Pfizer and BioNTech's COVID-19 vaccine. Attackers are becoming more emboldened, and the possibility of gaining valuable information on vaccines will continue to be a threat, as vaccines and boosters continue to be administered across the globe.

Increased Interconnectivity of Devices

The healthcare field is becoming more interconnected every day to improve the quality and efficiency of patient care; however, these enhancements can put patients at risk. The internet of Things (IoT) is a system of internet-connected devices capable of communicating information across the internet. These technologies are making their way into healthcare at an accelerated pace. As of 2021 there were, on average, between ten and fifteen interconnected devices per hospital bed in the United States.[15] This number is expected to rise in the future as healthcare technology advances. The use of consumer devices such as wearable smart devices and mobile phones has also become increasingly prevalent in the healthcare industry over the past ten years.[16] These trends, combined with the COVID-19 pandemic, are causing an even sharper increase in the use of consumer devices in the healthcare field for telemedicine and other functions as medical care adapts to social distancing protocols.[17] Obviously, with so many IT devices intimately involved in direct patient treatment, their reliability and security is critical to the medical outcome of the patient.

In addition, there has been growing concern regarding the vulnerability and connectivity of wearable and implanted medical devices like pacemakers and insulin pumps. The FDA first addressed the possibility of medical device attacks by cybercriminals in 2013, after Jay Radcliffe demonstrated that he was able to easily hack into his own insulin pump to deliver a lethal dose.[18] Today there are thousands of implanted and wearable medical devices that may be vulnerable to attack. In June 2020, for example, the Department of Homeland Security issued an emergency alert that the vendor Medtronic had over twenty devices with vulnerabilities that could be exploited persons with a "low skill level."[19] In December 2020, DHS issued a warning about an authentication flaw found in various GE radiology devices that can allow an attacker to access and alter data or interrupt the availability of the machines.[20] Although the incentives for criminals to access standalone medical devices may be relatively low, the use of ransomware to degrade or destroy medical devices is a real threat to patient care. Further, nation-state actors may be more interested in using medical device vulnerabilities in technologies such as wirelessly accessible pacemakers to threaten harm or influence targets to take actions they may otherwise not have taken.

Many medical devices are now interconnected to a larger technological "ecosystem" in such a way that vulnerabilities in one device can put entire networks at risk.[21] The risk to the whole ecosystem exists because each connected device creates a "potential gateway to access" for cybercriminals seeking to gain access to hospital systems and other connected devices.[22] As a result, although the increase in the number of connected devices sharing information is improving patient care and efficiency, it presents an additional threat to patient data and even patient health.

The issue of interconnected devices is exacerbated by the increased lag time between a breach and the detection of that breach by the organization.[23] Thus a cybercriminal could use an unsecured medical device to gain access to a vast network of interconnected systems and use this access to significantly disrupt patient care before anyone would know that an attack had been launched. In fact, a simulated attack conducted by researchers at the University of California, San Diego, Medical Center showed how a cybercriminal could use a single point of access from a connected device to alter blood and urine test results that doctors rely on to administer correct treatments.[24] Evidence like this suggests that the future of cybersecurity in healthcare is not just about securing patient data but also about protecting patients' physical well-being.

Cybersecurity as a Critical Component of Modern Healthcare

Despite the sensitive nature of health data and the increasing number of successful cyberattacks, the healthcare industry historically has failed to adequately prioritize cybersecurity. Most hospital personnel are primarily, and understandably, concerned with preserving life and limb.

Cybersecurity should be viewed as a critical component of the care provided to patients. For example, protecting critical medical systems containing patient data or medical devices responsible for monitoring patient data and/or delivering therapies reduces the likelihood that this data may be lost, stolen, or manipulated in such a way to cause patient harm. An example of this possibility might manifest itself in an attacker manipulating patient allergy information, which could lead to serious injury or even the death of the patient. Moreover, a medical device might be manipulated in such a way as to delete or manipulate data logging of patient healthcare information or to actively change therapies (e.g., insulin pumps or pacemakers), causing patient harm or death.

Modernization of Patient Care and Added Risks

While there has been a massive push to integrate technology into healthcare in order to achieve better patient outcomes in the past two decades, the push to adopt technology to promote cybersecurity has been slower to develop. In the Do No Harm 2.0 Cybersecurity Initiative by New America, the situation is described as "an underlying culture of 'no' that has emerged around healthcare cybersecurity technology, which stands in contrast with the often-eager adoption of new technologies that promise to directly improve clinical outcomes."[25]

An EY study from 2020 found that COVID-19 "accelerated the adoption of health technology and shattered preconceptions of what it takes to create a digital-first health experience." Physicians in this study noted that telephone and video usage for appointments increased from 20 to over 80 percent. Because of the convenience digital technologies provided patients in 2020, 81 percent of physicians planned to accelerate the introduction of new digital technologies, and 63 percent stated that they will invest in digital technologies over the next three years. While the use of these technologies is likely to decline after the pandemic, video and telephone consultations are expected to remain at a higher level than before 2020.[26] In the same survey, the majority of physicians said that they recognized digital healthcare technologies will become commonplace in the next decade. Healthcare professionals know that digital change and integration is coming, and they also know they are not doing it well.[27]

Many organizations have rushed to integrate technology into almost every aspect of patient care, in many cases at the cost of neglecting the security of these devices and systems.[28] This lack of focus on security is further highlighted by the pervasiveness of "outdated clinical technology, insecure network-enabled medical devices, and an overall lack of information security management processes."[29] Unsupported legacy systems and insecure devices remain far too common among healthcare providers in part due to a "if it ain't broke, don't fix it" mind-set when it comes to cybersecurity technology.[30] Healthcare has largely fallen into a reactive state when it comes to security, opting to invest or upgrade only after a significant breach or system failure.[31] Worse, many healthcare enterprises focus on compliance with regulation instead of a risk-based approach to securing data, systems, and devices. This type of reactive, compliance-based approach to cybersecurity will never be a winning formula in a world where cybercriminals, driven by substantial financial gain, are constantly finding new ways to gain access to healthcare systems, data, and even medical devices. Instead, the United States must build capabilities that manage risk effectively by reducing the likelihood of successful attack, as well as the impact of successful attacks. This will reduce risk, resulting in continued quality patient care.

The COVID-19 pandemic expedited the integration of technology in healthcare. With hospitals and healthcare systems flooded with patients, the focus on cybersecurity, perhaps understandably, was generally not prioritized. Telehealth skyrocketed during the pandemic as healthcare systems tried to keep patients out of their offices and safely at home. The Department of Health and Human Services found that "before the public health emergency (PHE) only 14,000 patients received a telehealth service in a week but during the PHE period from mid-March through early July, over 10.1 million patients received a telehealth service."[32] That radical and unplanned jump in the use of healthcare technology raises troubling questions about the cybersecurity of millions of new access points into a healthcare system.

In addition, cybersecurity training for healthcare employees tends to be severely neglected. In a survey on the state of security and privacy in the healthcare field, almost 80 percent of employees were found to be unprepared for common security threats.[33] Even more alarming are the results of a 2018 Kaspersky study, which revealed that nearly one-third of healthcare workers had not received any sort of cybersecurity training.[34] Cybersecurity training is largely seen as another expense because it is believed that it does not directly promote better patient outcomes. However, proper training can help employees make better use of medical technology and therefore enhance patient care. Worse, using medical technology improperly can cause misdiagnosis or inappropriate interventions based on faulty information. Adequate training can also drive change in the culture of an organization and help mitigate the occurrence of successful cyberattacks. In 2017, the Department of Health and Human Services established a Health Care Industry Cybersecurity Task Force (hereafter referred to as "the Task Force"), which identified proper cybersecurity training as a key to improving the security of many healthcare organizations.[35] The low priority that this sector tends to place on training seems to be further evidence that security is often an afterthought. Although there are providers and insurers who do focus on security and make significant investments year after year, the industry as a whole does not seem to have adequately prioritized cybersecurity and is vulnerable because of it.

Increased Patient Risk from Lax Cybersecurity

The habitual lack of prioritization of cybersecurity in healthcare has naturally led to underinvestment in this area. Healthcare leaders logically tend to push the limited funds of their organizations in the direction of traditional patient care before dealing with the "problem" of cybersecurity. Until these leaders understand that securing healthcare data, systems, and connected devices is a critical component of quality care, it is easy to understand this approach. However, it is clear that a change must take place. There is an inherent tension between those providers and administrators who have learned to focus primarily on providing medical care and those cybersecurity practitioners who focus on protecting patient data, hospital systems, and connected medical devices. This tension is most likely a by-product of a lack of understanding of the need to secure data, systems, and devices. This is a critical component of providing the best health outcomes for patients. In 2021, only about 5 percent of the already limited IT budgets at hospitals was spent on cybersecurity, and that number has remained the same over the past several years.[36] As an industry, healthcare lags behind banking and financial services, retail, and the wholesale industry in security spending.

This is true despite the significant regulatory requirements and the fact that the vast majority of healthcare organizations continue to be the victims of successful cyberattacks year after year. Furthermore, in 2019, 80 percent of leaders in the healthcare field indicated that insufficient resources were allocated to cybersecurity at their respective companies, and budgets continue to fail to keep pace with the threat actors.[37]

Although more money does not necessarily equal more security, most healthcare IT departments are hamstrung by a lack of funding when it comes to hiring personnel, investing in security solutions, and keeping pace with the ever-changing threat landscape. The Cybersecurity Task Force,[38] along with others, identified a lack of financial resources to devote to cybersecurity as a key problem preventing the healthcare sector from adequately securing its data and devices.[39] Many healthcare organizations, especially smaller ones, simply do not or cannot adequately invest in cybersecurity.

To make matters worse, the lack of up-front investment in cybersecurity often leads to significant costs later. According to a 2021 study by IBM, the average cost of a data breach for a large company in the United States is around $4.24 million, a 10 percent rise from the average cost in 2019.[40] Healthcare was found to incur some of the highest per capita costs from data breaches of any industry.[41] The costs of a breach extend far beyond the immediate expenses to identify and then fix the vulnerability. They include loss of business, damage to reputation, civil lawsuits, and punitive fines from the Department of Health and Human Services Office of Civil Rights.[42] In all, the Ponemon Institute found that a breach costs almost $430 per patient record in the healthcare industry.[43] Clearly, cybersecurity underinvestment in healthcare carries substantial penalties that may not be felt for years after a successful attack.

Challenges to Improving Cybersecurity in Healthcare

The foremost challenge to developing robust cybersecurity in healthcare is the artificial separation of cybersecurity from patient care. Although healthcare leaders are gradually becoming more aware of the need for cybersecurity investment and prioritization to protect patients, there is still a disconnect between leadership and the organization's IT and security departments. One national survey of chief information officers (CIOs) in the healthcare field found that almost half are operating in a "weakened" role and are not able to participate in organizational strategy meetings.[44]

The undervaluation of IT and security personnel in healthcare is a contributing cause of the cybersecurity "skills gap," or severe shortage of qualified cybersecurity staff. This shortage is hampering the ability of most organizations to adequately protect their data, systems, and devices.[45] In a 2019 survey, C-level healthcare executives cited hiring skilled IT professionals as one of the top two drivers of their company's improvement in cybersecurity.

However, in 2018, 91 percent of healthcare executives indicated that they could not hire or retain the people they need to effectively secure their organizations' data, systems, and devices.[46] In a 2019 Ponemon survey, 75 percent of respondents indicated that hiring and retaining cybersecurity talent was a difficulty for their companies. Furthermore, fewer than a third indicated that their cybersecurity staffing was adequate for their organizations' needs.[47]

There are two key factors that make recruiting and retaining skilled cybersecurity healthcare personnel difficult. First, many healthcare providers simply cannot afford the high rate for a cybersecurity expert.[48] This inability or unwillingness to compensate top cybersecurity talent is linked directly to the lack of investment and the lack of resources discussed earlier. Second, the culture of healthcare can be a major impediment to recruiting and retaining adequate cybersecurity staff.[49] There is little incentive for highly sought after cybersecurity professionals to work for less money in organizations that have historically undervalued, and in many cases continue to undervalue, their work.

Adding to the difficulty of prioritizing cybersecurity in healthcare is a general lack of capital across the industry. Most organizations operate on tight budgets, and leadership must make difficult decisions about how their limited resources are used. The operating margins of healthcare providers are low when compared to other industries, sometimes under one percent.[50] Currently, the COVID-19 pandemic is exacerbating this issue, especially in hospitals that have seen revenues and margins fall significantly due to empty beds and a severe decline in elective surgeries.[51] With the best intentions, many healthcare leaders and practitioners funnel the vast majority of the scarce operating capital available to them into solutions that are informed by traditional short-term understandings of patient outcomes and profits. Sometimes this occurs at the expense of security, including in some cases the longer-term impact on the patient. This trend is exacerbated by an underlying culture of rejecting the adoption of cybersecurity solutions, due to the often-false perception that it is an impediment to patient care. Meanwhile this same culture is embracing the rapid adoption of clinical technology without the necessary cybersecurity required to protect patient data, the systems on which they depend, or the medical devices they interact with and that in some cases are implanted in patients' bodies.[52]

Ineffective Regulation

The rush to integrate technology into healthcare at the expense of cybersecurity is not only driven by the culture of healthcare, but also by regulation.

The Meaningful Use (MU) program is a prime example of when a regulatory push to integrate technology has taken valuable resources and focus away from security and functional interoperability. The program was an attempt to promote increased interoperability in healthcare by requiring "eligible hospitals and professionals to meet certain measures in order to demonstrate meaningful use of certified electronic health records (EHR) technology to avoid Medicare payment penalties."[53] Although this did lead to investment in IT in general, the majority of that money was spent on trying to meet the requirements of the program, with the average hospital spending over $700,000 a year to stay up to date with the requirements.[54]

Many smaller providers found that MU compliance was not feasible and opted to lose out on the promised funding rather than expend their severely limited resources on compliance. To add to the inefficiency, most MU compliant providers worked with partners who did not have the ability to receive EHRs securely.[55] This meant that the heavy investments to be MU compliant often did not translate to increased interoperability in the real world. Sadly, the government's push to increase interoperability left less capital for investment in security.

Although this program has taken a new form in 2020, the overarching theme is similar. Overall, government-mandated integration of technology at the expense of security has proven to be both costly for the healthcare sector and potentially dangerous for patients.[56]

Recommendations for Policy Makers

It is critically important that Congress and the administration focus on increasing cybersecurity investment. Options for achieving this outcome are many and varied. However, some specific recommendations include reducing and streamlining existing regulation, increasing financial incentives for meeting "cybersecurity due care," and labeling and accounting for cybersecurity spending as a portion of patient care. Each of these options has the opportunity to significantly reduce the risk to patients from a cybersecurity incident or breach. In doing so, the healthcare industry will be better able to attract the type of top-tier talent and invest in the kinds of cutting-edge technologies that are needed to secure this key component of our critical infrastructure.

Cybersecurity Investments and the Medical Loss Ratio

The Affordable Care Act mandates that health insurance companies spend between 80 and 85 percent of their revenue on patient claims and improving the quality of their services. The remaining 15 to 20 percent can be used for administrative costs and other expenses. Currently there is debate as to what should be included in the quality improvement category and what should be categorized as administrative expenses. Some argue that administrative expenses should include a wide array of expenditures in order to make sure that the 85 percent of revenue is being used solely to benefit patients. Others see such spending restrictions as unfeasible for the insurance industry and advocate a broader definition of "quality improvement" expenditures.

Although there is debate over how to structure the medical loss ratio, one thing is clear: cybersecurity is crucial to the well-being of patients and must be prioritized as a critical component of patient care. Insurance companies are responsible for huge amounts of highly personal patient data that is extremely valuable to cybercriminals. Furthermore, the type of data at stake in the health insurance industry is not easily changed, unlike a credit card number that can be canceled, resulting in lifelong consequences for those whose health data is stolen during a breach. Therefore, it is advisable that cybersecurity investments be explicitly categorized as quality improvement under the medical loss ratio. This would help ensure that healthcare insurers have adequate funds to invest in cybersecurity, which will ultimately benefit the insured without requiring direct government subsidization. Furthermore, solidifying cybersecurity as part of patient well-being in this way will help focus more attention on this issue in the health insurance field. Ransomware attacks are explicitly related to patient care because they can prevent hospitals from accessing patients' data or systems the patient relies upon for care until a ransom is paid to the hacker; over 18 million people and their records were affected by these attacks in 2020.[57]

Reduced Regulation

The American Hospital Association has identified key areas for regulatory reduction in healthcare that could help lower the cost of compliance. These areas include duplicative quality reporting requirements and stringent conditions of participation to qualify for Medicare funding. One potential solution for this could be the US government instituting merit-based incentives that correlate with overall performance of healthcare organizations in securing patient data, so-called good actor benefits. Audits, fines, and HIPAA compliance costs could then be tailored to match the overall performance of a healthcare provider and their commitment to cybersecurity. High performers could then be subject to fewer and less time-consuming audits and the heavy fines would be reduced or reinvested in the cybersecurity controls found to be deficient. This could free the organizations from many of the costs associated with government intervention as an incentive and result in a significant continual investment in cybersecurity. This type of results-oriented policy would also result in less spending for the providers and the government in the long run. This model would function more similarly to how cybersecurity insurance was supposed to work and how the fast-track system for prescription drugs functions today. It would incentivize greater investment in cybersecurity to avoid high premiums or, in the case of health-care and pharmaceuticals, the high costs of compliance. In addition, it would actively redirect any fines back to those organizations as required investments to shore up any control deficiencies.

MU Health Information Exchanges

MU requirements should be reduced or eliminated in order to allow for investment and use of health information exchanges to increase secure interoperability in the healthcare field. As stated previously, the average-size hospital spends over $700,000 a year to comply with MU. However, the MU program has not resulted in a significant increase in interoperability and has left less capital to invest in security. Many smaller providers do not have sufficient revenue to comply with MU, and others, such as third-party applications, are not required to do so. As a result, many of the providers who are compliant cannot securely share patient information with smaller providers or third-party applications. Thus the cost of compliance is high and has poor return on investment to date.

One part of the way forward to achieve secure interoperability in the healthcare field is to leverage HIEs. An HIE facilitates the secure and efficient collection and transmission of crucial healthcare data such as. HIEs have already shown promise. In Indiana, they provide a low-cost solution to allow both large and small healthcare companies to securely increase their interoperability. In Texas, larger healthcare providers, referred to as anchor hospitals, have invested in HIEs to make it more feasible for smaller, rural providers to participate. HIEs have also created unique pricing models aimed at making it possible for smaller players to participate. Reducing or eliminating MU requirements will allow for more free capital, both for the government and for healthcare providers, to invest in HIEs, which are better suited to adapt to the constantly changing cybersecurity landscape and which also provide a viable solution to both small and large providers. Further investment at the national and state levels could be leveraged to ensure robust continued security of these HIE environments. These innovative programs are ideal candidates for evaluation, adaptation, and expansion as part of the overall strategic strategy discussed in chapters 5 and 6.

Incentivizing Cybersecurity Talent

Currently there is a large skills gap in the healthcare field. One reason driving a shortage of high-quality talent is that many healthcare organizations cannot afford to match the competitive salaries of other industries for cybersecurity professionals. Another reason is the perception that security work in healthcare will not be adequately funded, leading to uninteresting and undervalued work. This lack of qualified personnel has made it difficult for healthcare providers and insurers to adequately address cybersecurity issues. Further, the lack of overall funding reduces the likelihood that high-quality talent would be interested in the work, resulting in generally less mature security organizations. These two issues compound one another, where a lack of high-quality expertise reduces advocacy for and exacerbates the problem of insufficient funding. Lack of funding reduces the chance of hiring top-tier personnel.

To address this issue, the government should work with the private sector and higher education to support or subsidize cybersecurity professionals who choose a career path in healthcare. Such an approach is already being taken in other fields such as law, in which public service lawyers receive loan repayment assistance to offset their lower income.[58] Microsoft and Mastercard have taken a similar approach by partnering with the federal government to offset education costs for graduates who work for them after some time spent in government service. Similarly, the healthcare sector could work with the government to provide low interest loans that can be forgiven after cybersecurity professionals work in the healthcare field for some minimum time. This type of program would minimize government expenditure while also utilizing the private sector to close the skills gap in the healthcare field.

CHAPTER 8

DEFENSE

Leveraging the Dual Economies of the Defense Industrial Base

Jeffrey C. Brown, J. R. Williamson, Michael Gordon,
Michael Higgins, and Josh Higgins

The Department of Defense (DoD) and its partners have been at the forefront of cyber defense for two decades, during which time the Pentagon and prime defense contractors have established a strong model for collaboration, as formalized in 2009 in the Defense Industrial Base Framework (DIB) Agreement.[1] This agreement facilitated cyber information sharing between government and industry and established a climate for cooperation and consultations on cybersecurity. However, a relatively small percentage of the industry was able to participate in (and benefit from) the Framework Agreement process due to their lack of in-house cyber talent and the infrastructure to make use of the data being shared. Unsurprisingly, with such a small group participating, there was no noticeable decrease in the number of compromises. Therefore, the Pentagon shifted away from a collaborative approach to a compliance-based approach, with the expectation that a greater percentage of the supply base would see improved security by meeting minimum standards. Unfortunately, that expectation has been only minimally realized. The common theme in both efforts was that they are ineffective for the vast majority of the defense supply chain, which are small and medium-sized businesses (SMBs). As overall threats to information security to the DIB have increased continuously over the past few years, according to the National Defense Industrial Association's (NDIA's) 2020 report, SMBs in the DIB are in a disadvantaged position due to lack of resources to protect against emerging cyber threats.[2] In addition, the 2021 NDIA states that a changing cyber environment threatens the DIB and that the challenges of cybersecurity and economic espionage force businesses to implement costly procedures, which threatens to permanently alter the structure of the DIB.[3]

DoD did not ignore the thousands of smaller defense suppliers, but it assumed that what worked for the large system integrators would be equally effective throughout the rest of the supply chain. In hindsight, that proved to be a bad assumption. Although it would be unfair to say they did not see this problem coming, it just was not practical to redress. It is a bit of a stretch to say that the large system integrators have solved the problem, but they have invested enough in systems and in people to quite successfully avoid major incidents. The rest of the defense supply chain cannot make that claim. Now that they are the target of a much larger percentage of the attacks, the consequences are much higher. The first question to answer, then, is why strategies that worked for the largest companies in the defense industry have not worked for the bulk of the defense industry supply base.

Differing Cyber Incentive Models

The defense industrial base differs from other sectors in that it does not rely on traditional economic risk management calculations. In most industries, the loss of intellectual property from a cyberattack hurts the bottom line. Without the need to conduct research and development or recoup those costs, products produced with stolen technology appear quickly in the marketplace at lower prices. Damage to the victim's profitability is predictable.

The defense industry operates under two different economic models. Top-tier system integrators predominantly sell bespoke products to national governments that have few alternatives. Cost is a factor, but the Pentagon is unlikely to opt for a lower-cost product from a rival nation, especially if the design suspiciously resembles American-made technology as the result of an intellectual property theft. The cost of a breach in the defense industry is, therefore, seldom measured in dollars. It is more likely measured in the company's reputation or, more important, the margin of our military superiority and our warriors' safety. It may take five or ten years to manifest itself.

Despite the unique economic structure, the major defense integrators, the so-called primes, still invest in cyber out of a fundamentally patriotic sense of their responsibility to our warfighters as well as for the more pragmatic reason that strong data and network security is essential to brand credibility when doing business with the military.

But the weight of patriotic and reputational factors gets weaker farther down the supply chain where companies' mix of defense and commercial business shifts. Small- and medium-sized businesses subcontracting to primes or directly with the government have a larger proportion of commercial business. The greater the commercial component of a business, the more the traditional economic risk-assessment calculations predominate. If companies believe the damage that could occur and the likelihood of that happening are both small, then cybersecurity funding may not appear above the budgetary cut line. Financial conditions facing SMBs do not afford them the luxury of what may be uneconomic investments in cybersecurity beyond the minimum required for emerging compliance requirements, and as we discuss below, these compliance requirements do not necessarily equate to actual security because of the dynamic threat environment.

This difference in incentive structures has created a two-tiered defense ecosystem. One tier features large, well-funded system integrators. The other comprises everybody else. This dichotomy is the single most important factor that needs to be addressed in every aspect of cybersecurity. The strategies that shape our policies, our technical solutions, and our compliance requirements must account for both communities. The impact of getting this right—or wrong—dwarfs the impact of any other measures we can take. DoD has been slow to reach this conclusion. These developments only make it even more critical for industry and DoD, together, to find a strategy that will be effective for the vast majority of the DoD supply chain, much of which is represented by smaller businesses with mixed commercial-defense portfolios.

DoD and the DIB are currently in the initial stages of implementing their fourth-generation strategy, which we detail in the next sections of this chapter, but in order for the DIB sector to succeed in tamping down the growing cyber threat, there needs to be a fifth-generation strategy to accompany the previous ones: a collective defense strategy.

The First-Generation Strategy: Go It Alone

From the advent of the internet age in the late 1990s and through the emergence of the Advanced Persistent Threats (APTs), DoD and industry alike assumed every company was responsible for its own cyber defense. That may have been the only realistic strategy at the time, but the strategy nonetheless failed. Few in industry understood the scope of the threat, and none were prepared to defend against it. Most of the core applications that underpinned the internet were poorly coded and lacked any security controls, which is not surprising since it was designed for collaboration and eventually commerce, not for security. The explosion of security products we enjoy today was nowhere on the horizon. What little was known within the intelligence community was tightly held and unavailable to industry because of operational security concerns. With so much stacked against a successful defense, it is amazing that any attacks were detected or thwarted.

Moreover, the strategy did not scale downward. Only the largest companies can allocate the kind of resources required to defend against an onslaught of attacks. In the DIB, they comprise probably no more than a couple dozen of the thousands of defense contractors. For everybody else, no matter how well intentioned the companies and no matter how strict the compliance mandates, an SMB going it alone cannot afford the necessary cyber infrastructure required to be effective. Even if they could, they are unlikely to find high-quality cyber talent willing to work for small-company salaries in a very tight labor market. Absent that talent, any capital investments were wasted and only served to create a false sense of confidence.

When that bubble of unrealistic self-confidence was burst time and again by the first moderately skilled attacker to come along, the frustrations of company leadership and the DoD were only magnified. So in 2008 a consensus emerged that we needed a new strategy.

The Second-Generation Strategy: Collaboration

The collaboration strategy that appeared in 2008–9 was premised on the observation that attackers were using identical tactics and attack infrastructures against multiple companies and industries. Experience showed that if an attacker targeted fifty companies, one or two of the targets were bound to detect it. What was lacking was a mechanism to promulgate the details to the other forty-eight. Thus the new strategy reasoned that if industry and government collaborated to share information more broadly and more rapidly, we could make real progress in cybersecurity. "Information sharing" became the buzz phrase of the day. We have all heard and likely used the phrase, "It takes a village to defend . . . ," which is well aligned with this approach.

The defense community implemented the strategy in two initiatives: the DIB Framework Agreement and the Defense Security Information Exchange (DSIE), now known as the National Defense–Information Security Analysis Center (ND-ISAC).[4] The DIB Framework Agreement was a DoD-sponsored construct whereby participant companies agreed to share threat and attack information with DoD, which would then analyze it, add classified context when available, and disseminate the details anonymously to the other DIB participants.

The ND-ISAC, the new version of the DSIE, was a parallel industry-only organization founded by a dozen large primes, with the same intent as the DIB but without the bureaucratic or regulatory overhead that accompanies government involvement. It was designed to operate more quickly than the

DIB through collaboration directly among participating companies without the DoD middleman.

Despite the success of the collaboration strategy in improving industry cybersecurity for the primes, it still suffers from the same flaws that plagued the go-it-alone strategy, namely, the information still only reached a subset of defense contractors. Now instead of only one company having the information, a hundred or so participants have it. SMBs are encouraged to join, but relatively few have, compared to the thousands of suppliers in the defense industry. Most SMBs have neither the infrastructure nor the talent to put the shared information to good use, so not joining was an understandable result.

The lesson DoD took from the disappointingly moderate success of collaboration was that economic and patriotic incentives were simply not sufficient to drive cybersecurity investment all the way down DoD's supply chain. While not abandoning collaboration, DoD chose to force that investment throughout the supply chain via regulatory fiat.

The Third- and Fourth-Generation Strategy: Compliance and Maturity Models

In the shift from a collaboration strategy to a compliance strategy, there was no shortage of soul searching in both the Pentagon and industry as to why collaboration was not as successful as predicted. The conclusion of that introspection was that the benefits of collaboration did not extend to the vast majority of SMB suppliers, most of which did not have in place the foundational infrastructure and skill set to make collaboration a worthwhile endeavor. The solution then was to use compliance to compel suppliers to create that foundation, thus raising all boats and making the collaboration more broadly effective.

Compliance in DoD is implemented via contract clauses, which are blunt instruments. Unfortunately, it is the only tool DoD has. Neither the CIO nor the National Security Agency (NSA), the experts in cybersecurity, has the authority or the scalable resources to work closely with thousands of suppliers. Indeed, the Federal Advisory Committee Act (FACA) imposes significant impediments to such collaboration.[5] Thus the only practical mechanism left for DoD was to address cybersecurity in contracts, which is why compliance is embodied in the Federal Acquisition Rules by inserting compliance clauses on a contract-by-contract basis. Contract clauses are then enforced via audits, which drive the compliance environment to easily auditable controls with binary pass/fail criteria. This need to be easily auditable has had far-reaching consequences.

The compliance era in the DIB began in 2013 with the release of NIST 800-171 and the subsequent issuance of the Defense Federal Acquisition Regulation Supplement (DFARS) Rule 252.204-7012, which mandated compliance with NIST 800-171, defined Critical Unclassified Information (CUI), and established formal reporting requirements for cyber incidents involving CUI.[6] The idea was that if all companies implemented a minimum set of controls, overall cybersecurity in the industrial base had to improve. The initial rule was issued in 2013 but was updated in 2015 to allow a transition period to full compliance on December 31, 2017.

Unfortunately, what was understood was that compliance is about what you do, and security is about how well you do it. As such, nothing magical happened on January 1, 2018, despite the attestation of every defense company that they were compliant with the regulatory requirement under DFARS. Compromises still occurred with frustrating predictability. In part, the reason was that the 110 cyber controls in NIST 800-171, while all inarguably good things to do, could not possibly address every attack vector. Add to that the fact that self-attestation led to, at best, mixed accuracy. Many companies without depth in cyber talent did not understand what being compliant meant. Others implemented the technology to call themselves compliant but did not add the people and processes to make the technology effective and mature.

With Congress becoming increasingly frustrated with the continuing leakage of sensitive defense information through the supply chain, the Defense Contract Management Agency (DCMA) began to audit companies against NIST 800-171 in 2019.[7] No longer was self-attestation to meeting these controls acceptable; DCMA was looking for proof. While being audited has a way of focusing one's attention on becoming compliant, it also has a way of creating an adversarial environment and diverting scarce resources from actual security toward documenting security and preparing for the audit.

With the continued frequency of compromises despite the compliance requirements, DoD recognized a fundamental flaw in a binary compliance regime. DoD initially tried to address this issue of "just compliance" by putting an interim rule in effect for the Cybersecurity Maturity Model Certification (CMMC) program in 2021, which is now known as CMMC 1.0 The first "M" is important because it was to focus on "maturity" and address those questions of "how well" an organization was performing on their cybersecurity mission. Unfortunately, there was so much pushback from the small- and medium-sized business that make up the vast major of the DIB supply chain, that the program was revised into CMMC 2.0, which eliminated all of the maturity practices and instead focuses now just on the compliance aspects of the NIST 800-171 requirements under the DFARS 252.204.7012 regulatory clause. Even though

DoD had to give up on the attempt to bolster these programs with process and practices that led to a degree of maturity versus just compliance, all is not lost and the new CMMC program still provides value in the sense that the program does verify that claims of compliance are actually true and that the security controls expressed in NIST 800-171 are in fact evidenced in practice via a third party accreditor (very much like how the ISO 27001 program operates). At this point, CMMC should probably be re-branded as "CCMC"—for Cybersecurity Compliance Model Certification--as it does "ensure" that the suppliers who were previously *claiming* they were compliant are actually being reviewed/certified as *being* compliant. The third party accreditation will allow the program to scale across the Defense Industrial Base (DIB).

CMMC is a major step forward in two areas: prioritization of defensive measures and partnership with industry in its creation. The DoD process for creating CMMC has also been the most collaborative cyber effort in memory. From the start DoD sought out and took the advice of industry, especially the large system integrators. All of the various working groups were populated with equal representation from DoD and industry. Industry did not get everything they wanted in the CMMC, but such is the nature of a collaborative partnership. Years from now when we assess the success of CMMC, this partnership will stand out regardless of how the rest of CMMC might be judged.

However, NIST 800-171 and just about every other national or international standard suffer from the assumption that all controls are created equal. They do not tell you what you should do first or how you should spend limited resources to the greatest effect. SMBs, which are by definition resource constrained, need to know what to do next to get the greatest bang for the buck.

DoD is conducting the rulemaking process right now and will be phasing in certification requirements for the new model starting in 2023 and expects that all Defense contracts will require a CMMC Certification Level over a 5-year period. The CMMC program will define three levels of compliance. Level 1 represents the foundational or minimum baseline of controls needed to just do business with the DoD (but are not critical to national security). The individual company will be able to self-assess and report their compliance. Level 2 is needed for all companies that will be storing, processing, or transiting CUI. These controls are tied to NIST 800-171 (just as the DFARS 252.204-7012 clause requires today—but now you have to be certified at this level versus just performing your own self attestation). Level 3 will be for a very small subset of the DIB that will be performing on contracts that reflect the DoD's highest priority programs and typically contain "high valued assets" in support of the program mission and deliverables and will be based on a subset of the NIST 800-172 controls. Although "maturity" has been removed from the program, simplifying the program can be a huge benefit for the DIB as the first iteration of CMMC was perceived to be very complicated and likely too expensive to achieve. As noted later in this chapter, when it comes to collective defense, sometimes the best programs are that ones that are easiest to understand and consistently operated across the stakeholder community. CMMC implicitly aligns cybersecurity goals with economic incentives by telling companies to implement controls in a sequence embodied in the tiers. The inherent prioritization of Levels 1–3 is welcome guidance to SMBs on what to do first.

That future judgment, however, is sadly predictable. Both the original DFARS 252.204-7012 rule and CMMC are destined to disappoint for the exact same reasons the preceding go-it-alone and collaboration strategies disappointed. SMBs simply cannot afford a sufficiently robust cyber infrastructure or find the cyber talent to become secure even with the Damocles sword of compliance hanging over their heads.

A Fifth-Generation Collective Defense Model

A 2020 RAND report indicates that DoD's current approach to defending DIB firms against cyberattacks is inadequate because advanced cybersecurity requirements, which would need costly technology tools, are unaffordable to SMBs.[8] If we acknowledge the empirical evidence that there is probably no way SMBs will ever be incentivized to invest in cyber defense the same way the large defense contractors are, we must consider a radically different strategy: collective defense. In this new strategy, the ultimate, if not entirely obtainable, goal should be to make the security of a small supplier's network largely irrelevant. This modification can be used to augment the compliance strategy by collectively defending suppliers outside their networks wherever possible, thus reducing the risk of poorly implemented controls and spreading the costs out over the entire industry, much like co-op farms.

The key to any collective defense implementation is that it must be dirt cheap, easy to employ, and accessible to a much larger base of smaller defense contractors. The entire reason for collective defense is that SMBs cannot afford the investment or talent required for good defense. If the collective solution is just as expensive or complex as going it alone, we have not solved the problem.

What this implies is that whatever mechanisms we employ to collectively defend suppliers will not come from traditional vendors for whom profit margins are critical. It will more likely be run by a nonprofit or coalition of primes that are willing to break even or perhaps operate at a loss for the greater good, which is similar to the effort to create the DSIE in earlier generations. It also means whatever we do will need to be *really good where it counts but just adequate enough where it doesn't*. Metaphorically, we are looking to build a Volkswagen, not a Cadillac.

Implementing the Collective Defense Tactics

If such a structure were put in place, there are a variety of tactics that would become cost-efficient for smaller members of the DIB to employ, thus enhancing overall security. A significant payoff from the collective defense organization would be implementing a program for email screening. The overwhelming majority of attacks start with an email. The new organization should go beyond basic commercial email screening to employ bespoke screening to which we can add limited distribution of unclassified indicators closely held in the defense community. Technically this is easy. In fact, DoD tried to implement this type of service in a NSA-run pilot in 2011. It failed miserably, not because it wasn't technically successful, but rather because it was so burdened with administrative, architectural, and intelligence community restrictions that it was more trouble than it was worth. These excessive administrative issues along with resolving lawyers' concerns and companies' fear that it might be misused as a competitive edge will need to be resolved, but hopefully the community has matured in light of growing threats and this may now be possible.

Perhaps an even more valuable and definitely easier service would be a DIB domain name service (DNS). DNS is the internet protocol that turns human readable web addresses into internet routable IP addresses. Every time someone clicks on a link in an email or types a web address into a browser, a DNS request is made to look up the IP address. A DIB DNS service would be configured to return the IP address of an error page any time a participant attempted to go to a known bad address, thereby keeping them from intentionally or accidentally accessing a malicious site. The effort and knowledge required by a supplier to implement this is exactly zero. It is as simple as typing an IP address into a few network devices. This has a double benefit. It can serve to stop attacks via links embedded in email and web browsing—attacks on the way in—but should an attack succeed anyway, it can also stop many web-based command and control channels of attacks—attacks on the way out.

A third way to make supplier's networks irrelevant is to provide them with a centrally managed work environment for DoD contracts. The central authority would defend the environment. The supplier's responsibility would be limited to ensuring that multifactor authentication is used to reduce the possibility that stolen supplier credentials could still allow attacker access.

Proposals along those lines have been made in both industry and government circles for years, but little progress has been made beyond GovCloud types of services in the major cloud providers. But for a significant cross section of work conducted by SMBs it is an appealing service option.

Government or Industry?

A key question to answer in any discussion of collective defense is: Who leads the effort? Is this a service provided by DoD, or is it more of a co-op model led by industry? Both have benefits to offer.

The obvious benefit of having a service run by DoD is that there would be easier access to classified information—the exquisite 5 percent of the classified information not available to industry. That could make a huge difference in some of the most serious attacks. Add to that the probability that a government-run service would be either free to participants or at least subsidized, and you have an appealing prospect.

However, our experience with the DIB Framework Agreement and the NSA-run pilot of email screening reminds us that there are also downsides to government-led services. As discussed in chapter 5, agile management is crucial when dealing with cyber, and government-run programs are burdened by bureaucracy and legal restrictions that limit innovation, speed, and collaboration. A government-run service is also inherently less transparent as many of the indicators would be classified or closely held, making it difficult for industry to investigate any alerts or understand the nature of an attack. And if the past is any indicator, such collective defenses would also likely be limited to US companies only. With so many defense companies' supply chains increasingly extending overseas, it would leave a significant slice of industry networks undefended. Finally, justified or not, there has historically been a fear of letting the government have access to a company's data.

Industry has already taken the lessons of the four previous strategy generations to move toward collective defense. The large system integrators have established a collaborative task force to execute a collective defense strategy. Yet such an industry-led collective defense is also not without its own advantages and disadvantages. Free of the bureaucracy and most of the legal restrictions of a government-run service, an industry service would be nimbler and more responsive. It would probably also be overall cheaper to run, although there would likely have to be some sort of fee structure for participants that might be more expensive to the supplier than a subsidized government program. Given the number of suppliers involved, there will likely be competing services just to handle the volume, which will inevitably improve quality and lower costs. An industry-led collective defense could also easily serve their overseas operations and would make moot any fears of the government having access to companies' data, thus presenting fewer legal concerns for DIB firms than one run by government.

The most significant downside to an industry-run collective defense service is that access to classified and likely most closely held information will be denied. However, in exchange for losing the depth of indicators offered by access to government data, industry gains the breadth of having indicators from across the entire industry, most of which do not get reported to the government. Industry has empirical evidence of this trend when we compare what DoD provides through the DIB Framework Agreement and what industry has via the ND-ISAC. We essentially give up most of the exquisite 5 percent for a richer 95 percent. We assert that the better bang for the buck is with industry's 95 percent.

A middle ground between a government and an industry-led collective defense would be to establish a nonprofit to lead. A nonprofit, as a single central entity, would be able to establish a more collaborative relationship with DoD less encumbered by antitrust issues. It would also avoid any competitive issue that would ensure if any particular member of the DIB was providing one of the collaborative services. The nonprofit would need to have appropriate senior-level representation from the DIB-participating companies (e.g., a governing body and a planning committee) in order to ensure that the value of the provided capabilities is realized and the nonprofit is able to sustain itself over the long haul. DoD has recently put together a nonprofit organization called the Accreditation Body that will function as that "middle ground" between DoD and industry for the training and the conduct of the new CMMC program. This may well serve as a model for a collective defense organization.

Devising which model is the best fit for the nation will go a long way toward redefining what constitutes the nation's defense industrial base, which is obviously extremely critical in the ever more dangerous digital age. The proposed ODSS in the White House should make this decision a central piece of the new national digital strategy, accessing the same equivalent representation model that was used in developing CMMC.

Incentives for SMBs within Compliance and Collective Defense Strategies

The utopian goal of both the government and industry is to provide cyber incentives to SMBs that will encourage them to invest in the highest payoff cyber capabilities first. Its theory is that positive incentives, either financial, reputational or competitive, should always be more effective. Adam Smith's Invisible Hand should create a better result than a prescriptive regulatory compliance model. Indeed, for large system integrators that want to sell cyber products and services to the government, having a credible and visibly effective internal cyber defense, has been a strong positive incentive that hits all three motivations: financial, reputational, and competitive. That natural incentive is why the large system integrators were successful with the go-it-alone strategy.

Unfortunately, it has been all too obvious that those positive incentives are not as strong for SMBs. The collaboration strategy was an attempt at a positive incentive, but as noted earlier, the investment required to realize the incentive was just too great. Thus the compliance strategy emerged, and it has been anything but positive incentive. It is a comply or don't do business with the DoD incentive.

In the end, incentives for SMBs are very straightforward. SMBs are motivated by increased profit through either lower cyber and compliance costs or increased competitiveness. Even allowing for the inherent contradiction of having positive incentives within a compliance model, there are significant actions the Department of Defense could take to incentivize companies, both large and small, to invest in and prioritize the highest payoff cyber activities.

Incentivizing Adoption of Collective Defense Capabilities

Assuming we choose not to make collective defense services mandatory, how can industry and government work together to incentivize SMBs to participate? The easiest answer is to make the services dirt cheap and easy to use. That would make them so appealing that simple peer pressure and Darwinian selection of participating subcontractors by the large system integrators (i.e., competitiveness) would drive SMBs to use these services. This is also an area for the continuing conversation on US government–provided incentives for the SMBs to invest to either build or mature their cybersecurity programs.

A more flexible and transparent scoring model would create further incentives for SMBs and support more nuanced decisions by both the government and prime contractors.

Maturity Ratings as Incentives

By any measure CMMC is a major step forward compared to the original DFARS rule, but it misses an opportunity to be so much more. The cyber threat is dynamic, so the response must be as well. Despite the inclusion of the word *maturity* in the title, the process is more akin to a tiered compliance model that measures "good enough," that is, the minimum. It is not a reflection of maturity, which measures "better" along a continuous scale. But the natural desire of companies to be able to show they are better than their competitors invites a way to differentiate among the 95 percent of suppliers who will only be required to meet Level 3. This differentiation can be easily implemented by adding three features to the CMMC scoring model: Proportional Scoring, Practice Substitution, and Practice Weighting. These features would be applied in parallel with, not replace, the existing certification to a specific level. But taken together, these three changes could turn CMMC into a true maturity model that provides competitive incentives to suppliers to go beyond check-the-box compliance.

Tiered Childhood Maturity Model: A CMMC Parallel

To illustrate the fallacy of a tiered model in a continuous process, consider a tiered model that rates the maturity of children between birth and age 21. We'll use five tiers here even though CMMC 2.0 is planned to only have 3 tiers. For the purposes of the example below, we're referencing a 5-level model to demonstrate how maturity scores could be applied, even though the present CMMC 2.0 program only accounts for 3 levels—all of which are more compliance oriented against the NIST 800-171 and 800-172 standards. Level 1 would match the maturity of a 3-year-old; Level 2, a 10-year-old; Level 3, a teenager; Level 4, an 18-year-old; and Level 5, someone 21 or older.

Now consider an employer trying to hire an entry-level worker. With this model, all the employer can know is that the child is Level 3 (a teenager). As any parent knows, however, there is a huge difference between the maturity of a 13-year-old and that of an 18-year-old. But the model does not provide any additional information. No employer would accept the paucity of knowledge, and no 17-year-old prospective employee would not want to be able to show that they are a lower risk employee than the 13-year-old applicant. A tiered model simply does not convey enough information with which to make decisions.

CMMC is no different. It shows that two suppliers (or teenagers) meet a minimum Level 3 standard (i.e., at least that of a 13-year-old) but gives no supplier a chance to differentiate itself, nor does it give the contracting entity (DoD or a prime) sufficient information with which to include cyber maturity in any decision process.

Proportional Scoring

One of the major missed opportunities with CMMC stems from the fact that DoD has unintentionally relegated SMBs to second-class status by putting them in a position where they get no credit whatsoever for implementing higher-level controls unless they are among the few aspiring to Level 4 or Level 5 contracts. And even then, it's all or nothing. A company gets no credit for doing all but one of the Level 4 advanced practices even though their security is demonstrably better than someone who only did the minimum to achieve Level 3. In short, through its stair step scoring model, DoD has missed an opportunity to provide incentives for incremental improvements that would change an SMB's cost/benefit decision.

Proportional scoring solves that lack of transparency by creating a parallel scoring method that shows a proportional score towards the next level. In addition to Level 3 certification, a company would have a Maturity Score of 3.0 or 3.9, and so on, which they could voluntarily expose as a competitive differentiator to those they wish to do business with.

It would be trivially easy to create such a score. If a company has 50 percent of the practices needed to get to Level 4, they are at 3.5, 25 percent is 3.25, and so on. This allows competing SMBs to differentiate themselves,

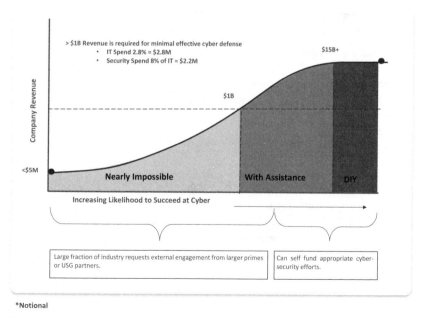

*Notional

Figure 8.1. Cyber Defense at Scale, Part 1

thus providing an incentive to improve. It also allows for peer benchmarking, which will help the security staff compete for funding. In addition, if a system integrator is considering a supplier to join its team for a proposal, but the supplier is not at the needed level, a proportional score can tell the prime how close the supplier is to getting where it needs to be. An SMB at 2.9 will be a much lower risk than another supplier at 2.0. It's a competitive advantage for the aspiring supplier and a risk reduction aid for the prime.

Such scoring would not change the assessment process in any way. Assigning the incremental score would be done post-assessment by the accreditation body, not by the assessors whose role would not change.

Practice Substitution

As much as an incentive it would be to have a proportional scoring system, CMMC could create an even greater incentive for system integrators and SMBs alike by recognizing the fact that while all CMMC practices are useful, not all practices are equal. The issue is not that all controls are not valuable. The issue is entirely about how to incentivize SMBs to do more than check the box with the easiest practice and give them credit for implementing more advanced practices.

Practice Substitution and Baseball

Consider two Cy Young Award winners—the best pitchers in baseball. There is no rule that says both of them must throw every type of pitch to be successful. One might throw mostly curveballs; the other, fastballs. Neither might throw a knuckleball. Yet both are winners by adopting different pitching strategies. Cybersecurity is the same way. You can implement a mature, successful cyber program via different paths.

Practice substitution can create an incentive for SMBs by simply changing the scoring model to a point system. Instead of each level being an all-or-nothing pass/fail step function, a point system would assign points to each practice across all levels counting as points toward a threshold. For example, today to achieve Level 3 you must complete all 130 practices. In a point system, you would require 130 points but could achieve those points by substituting higher payoff Level 4 or Level 5 practices instead of Level 3. You could specify as much as two-thirds of the practices as a mandatory threshold not eligible for substitution, but that would still leave companies a chance to innovate and substitute for the remaining 43 or so points toward Level 3.

One of the advantages of a point system is that you could add many more practices to the CMMC baseline, giving companies the option of which to choose to get the needed points for a level. This is particularly useful at Levels 4 and 5, where you could introduce emerging, innovative capabilities that show promise but are not yet proven in practice. Practice substitution thus allow companies to manage their own risk within guardrails and make choices appropriate to their own network circumstances. It is an incentive to innovate.

Weighted Scoring

The final piece of the SMB incentive triad is weighted scoring. As noted earlier, all practices are not created equal, yet in today's model each of them is weighted equally. Some Level 1 activities do not move the cybersecurity need nearly as much as Level 4 activities, but in the CMMC model they are of equal value. DoD could create a powerful incentive for SMBs to stretch to the higher payoff strategies and be more competitive than their peers by simply giving them more credit for those advanced practices. Weighting can be strategic and targeted to meet emerging threats or new technology.

This small change allows companies to trade off investment against advanced practices in the exact way both DoD and prime contractors should want. Especially as a company gets close to the next level, the incentive to leap ahead by employing an advanced, higher payoff practice would be powerful. And as an added bonus, if a new threat emerged where a low weighted practice would help, DoD could simply raise the weighting of that practice to provide an incentive for companies to implement it. The concept exactly parallels the way the government uses tax incentives today: it makes it advantageous for companies to do what the government wants them to.

All three of these proposed incentives—proportional scoring, practice substitution, and weighted scoring—can work together or independently to turn CMMC into a true maturity model that differentiates companies, incentivizes them to do more than the minimum, and provides DoD and prime contractors with more insight into the security posture of the SMB supply chain. And it requires no change to the existing CMMC process. It is an overlay.

Speaking with One Voice

As much as adopting a collective security strategy and creating incentives within CMMC would help improve the cybersecurity of the defense

industrial base, the action DoD could take that would have the most immediate impact would be to simply speak with one voice across all DoD acquisition organizations. The autonomy of the agencies and departments has
driven complexity into the system via random contact clauses. In this sense,
the DIB applauds the concepts of CMMC to have a singular set of requirements. Unfortunately, DoD has not taken a strong stance to stop agencies
and departments from issuing further "enhanced" controls that go beyond
CMMC. For industry, which operates on common systems (e-mail, collaboration tools, etc.), disparate sets of controls are impossible to implement.

The Office of the Secretary of Defense should establish a policy that
directs all acquisition organizations in the services and defense agencies to
obtain approval for any enhanced enterprise cybersecurity requirements.

The advantages of a centralized check of enhanced requirements are
numerous.

- Many of the measures proposed to date were practices that one community or another thought were good ideas but that were untethered to
  any understanding of how industry does business. A centralized review
  would allow for industry input and a broader technical feasibility check,
  hopefully eliminating much of the contentious local negotiations on
  provisions that are prohibitively expensive or based on bad assumptions.
- Individual programs would not, without some oversight, be able to
  drive costs outside their own programs. Many of the proposed requirements assume the IT systems being used to execute the program are
  dedicated to the program, so any costs would be localized. But that is
  seldom the case. To increase productivity and reduce costs, most companies will use enterprise class systems across multiple programs, so
  the cost being driven by one program would hit many other programs.
  That may be acceptable, but it should not be done without some checks
  and balances at the OSD level.
- Redundant or conflicting enhanced measures could be eliminated.
- Several enhanced measures proposed to date, such as government
  sensors on industry networks, raise legal questions that should be
  addressed up front rather than in post-award negotiations.
- By having visibility on all enhanced measures in one spot for review,
  industry would avoid today's problem of local industry program
  managers with little cyber knowledge agreeing to contract provisions
  the company cannot meet.
- If more effective or innovative cyber measures were put forward by a
  program, they could be added to CMMC for the benefit of all.

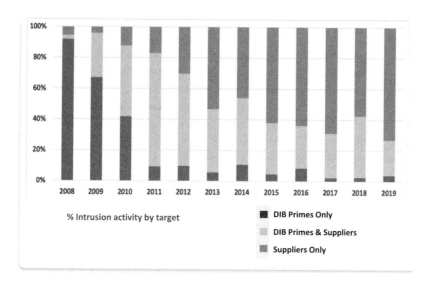

Increased Supplier Targeting +
Inability of Small-Mid Size Suppliers to Create Enduring
Cyber Programs =

Unsustainable Equation

Figure 8.2. Cyber Defense at Scale, Part 2

Perhaps most important, a centralized clearinghouse and approval authority for enhanced cybersecurity requirements would benefit the SMBs.
The SMBs, which represent the vast majority of defense suppliers by volume,
are often barely able to meet basic compliance requirements. Further bur-
dening them with enhanced requirements without a thorough review of the
trade-offs involved does more harm than good.

Conclusion

The consistent theme of cybersecurity in the defense sector is that cyber
defense processes have been successful with the large US-based prime contractors while leaving unaddressed the lack of resources of small subcontractors to address cybersecurity throughout the DIB supply chain. Existing
small suppliers are finding the status quo of DIB cyber defense untenable,
as they lack the resources necessary to comply with the stringent DoD

requirements, resulting in an exodus of valuable innovators from the defense market. Cybersecurity in the DIB must be able to address two, vastly different economies: the prime contractors (which have the time, resources, and sense of patriotic duty to implement the strongest security measures possible) and small and medium subcontractors that have limited resources to implement cybersecurity measures, and a greater share of nondefense commercial business. In order to address the threats to the DIB—from APTs to the new nation-state "independent contractors"—we must adopt new strategies that make cybersecurity as cheap and easy to implement as possible and incentivize companies to go beyond the bare minimum. That is the only way we will be able to make it viable for smaller players in the DIB to engage and implement security measures that bolster the DIB ecosystem.

CHAPTER 9

FINANCIAL SERVICES
Regulation Isn't Enough

Greg Montana, Gary McAlum, Kenneth Huh, and Tarun Krishnakumar

The US financial services sector plays a unique role as critical infrastructure for the United States and the world. Not only does the sector serve as the backbone of the US economy, but it also plays a central role in directly and indirectly supporting transnational commerce and economic activities around the globe. In addition, the sector—given its role and the services its constituents offer—handles more financial transactions and sensitive consumer information than most others. This outsized role comes with an outsized level of risk.

A 2019 report by the Boston Consulting Group found that financial services firms are "300 times" as likely as other companies to be targeted by a cyberattack.[1] Another report by HelpSystems found that a full 65 percent of large financial services companies globally were targeted by a cyberattack in 2020.[2] Similarly, Verizon's 2022 Data Breach Investigations Report found that 93 percent of cyberattacks were financially motivated and that financial and insurance remains "a favorite playground for the financially motivated organized criminal element again this year."[3] Add to this the increasingly sophisticated targeting by nation-state actors and diversifying fraud threats, and you have a potent cocktail of malicious actors targeting the sector, its constituents, and consumers as a whole.

Recognizing this, the sector has generally been acknowledged as being ahead of the curve in deploying cybersecurity to counter emerging threat vectors and ensure business continuity. Surveys also regularly place the sector as the one spending the most on cybersecurity. However, despite the sector's best efforts, cybersecurity-linked costs and losses are rising. A 2019 report by Accenture found that "the average annualized cost of cyber-crime for financial services companies globally has increased to US $18.5 million—the highest of all industries included in the study and more than

40 percent higher than the average cost of US $13 million per firm across all industries."[4] Similarly, a 2020 estimate by LexisNexis Risk Solutions suggests that for every dollar of fraud, a financial institution loses nearly four dollars ($3.78), a 12 percent increase from 2019.[5]

While firms in the sector have made substantial investments in cybersecurity (and continue to do so), several externalities have meant that the true value and potential of these investments is not being realized. The lack of a reliable digital ID framework, an overly complex cybersecurity regulatory ecosystem, and the lack of tangible progress against domestic and foreign cybercriminals are key concerns that degrade the value of cybersecurity investments and divert expertise and capacity from core functions relating to security. These three issue areas must be addressed to create a more secure and resilient financial services ecosystem in the United States. Addressing these issues will not only directly benefit the sector's cybersecurity posture but also allow sector constituents to devote more time and resources to the actual practice of security. In this context, each of these three issues, and recommendations in relation to them, is discussed in the sections that follow.

Digital Identity: The New Currency

Almost every day in this country there is another data breach that exposes the sensitive information of US consumers to the scourges of credit card fraud, identify theft, account takeover, and any number of other malicious activities. Years ago the focus of cybercriminals was obtaining credit card information that could be quickly monetized through card fraud at point-of-sale systems, among others. With the advent of stronger credit card security mechanisms like EMV (Europay, Mastercard, and Visa) chip technology, card fraud has dramatically dropped (although the threat is morphing to "card not present" transactions). Cybercriminals have steadily turned their focus to obtaining identity information that can be monetized through a variety of identity theft activities, ranging from exploiting consumer authentication systems to access accounts to filing fraudulent tax returns and obtaining consumer loans. In fact, the statistics are alarming. According to data from sources, including the FTC:

- Around 1 in 15 people experience some form of identity theft.[6]
- In 2020, there were nearly 4.8 million total reports of identity fraud in the United States, including identity theft, imposter scams, and other consumer issues.[7]

- Credit card fraud accounted for 29.7 percent of identity theft cases in 2020.[8]
- Americans are 50 percent more likely to have their identities stolen than residents of other nations.[9]
- Identity fraud accounted for $43 billion in losses for victims in 2020.[10]

It is noteworthy that despite extensive regulation and spending, US consumers are at greater risk than other areas of the world. ID theft is up to around 33 percent in the United States (double the global average).[11]

However, these statistics relate only to traditional identity theft. There is also the growing scourge of synthetic identity theft, wherein a criminal combines real and fake information to create a new identity. The real information used in this fraud is usually stolen or obtained on the dark web. This information is used to open fraudulent accounts and make fraudulent purchases. According to a recent article in *Forbes*, synthetic identity fraud is a relatively recent phenomenon that is on the rise.[12] McKinsey claims synthetic ID fraud is the fastest-growing type of financial crime in the United States. LexisNexis Risk Solutions (via Yahoo Finance) found that "61 percent of fraud losses for [large] banks stem from identity fraud [and] 20 percent of the identity fraud incurred by these larger banks is synthetic identity fraud."[13]

Ultimately, all roads lead us back to securing our digital identities. Why is this such a massive problem, and why isn't something being done? Over the years, government initiatives like the Electronic Authentication Partnership (EAP), the Trust Framework Solutions (TFS) program, and the National Strategy for Trusted Identities in Cyberspace (NSTIC) focused on trying to get the private sector to create solutions that could solve the identity conundrum. However, this identity problem uniquely requires the government to take a key leadership role since the authoritative source of legitimate identity is the government alone. There are plenty of government identity credentials in the form of paper and plastic, but it is time for the same level of government backing for digital identities. According to the Better Identity Coalition, "A patchwork system has emerged of identifiers and credentials issued by a variety of different Federal, state and local entities. . . . This patchwork has worked relatively well for in-person transactions where it was important to verify someone's identity; service providers could simply ask to see someone's credentials. However, the model has fallen apart online."[14]

To be sure, there has been some progress in the area of authentication. An increasing number of individuals, businesses, and government agencies are using multifactor authentication as opposed to knowledge-based authentication, but there are still a lot of passwords out there and a lot of "what's your favorite color?" security questions that can be easily socially engineered. The harder issue is "identity proofing," or identity verification, which is the process for verifying and authenticating the identity of legitimate customers. The COVID-19 pandemic has ushered in a new era in which customers no longer conduct business at traditional branches in face-to-face interactions; now business is conducted in digital, online transactions. According to a recent *Wall Street Journal* article, branch traffic fell more than 30 percent in April and the first three weeks of May 2020, compared to the same period in 2019, according to Novantas, a financial services research firm. Teller transactions also dropped 32 percent in March and April 2020, compared to the same period in 2019.[15] This trend has continued, as a survey by S&P found that 51 percent of customers are visiting branches less frequently and 65 percent are using mobile apps more frequently.[16] The assistant director of the FBI's Criminal Investigations Division recently warned, "The repercussions of the COVID-19 pandemic have not and will not end any time soon."

Jeremy Grant, former head of National Strategy for Trusted Identities in Cyberspace, testified that every financial institution has to solve fundamental problems related to identity. In his 2019 testimony to the US House Financial Services Committee Task Force on Artificial Intelligence, he laid out the three challenges.[17]

- First is figuring out whether someone is who they claim to be at account opening. Not surprisingly, this is one of the areas where the most work is needed. Losses from "New Account Fraud" increased 13 percent over the last year to $3.4 billion.
- Second—closely tied to the first—is synthetic identity fraud. This is when fraudsters combine a fake name with a real SSN and "trick" the financial system into thinking that an applicant's identity is real when in fact it's a "Digital Frankenstein" made up of a mix of legitimate and fake identity components.
- Third is authentication. Once an account has been created, how do you create systems that can securely log customers in to that account, in a world where passwords just do not cut it anymore?

But the sector needs to focus on solving the identity proofing problem and this is one problem that cannot be solved by either the private sector or government alone. Addressing this problem will require both sides to work together. And there are signs of hope for positive change.

In 2018, the Better Identity Coalition was launched by the Center for Cybersecurity Policy and Law, a nonprofit dedicated to working with policy makers to advance cybersecurity initiatives. Specifically, the Better Identity

Coalition is committed to working alongside policy makers to improve digital security, privacy, and convenience for everyone. The coalition brings together leading companies to promote education and collaboration on protecting identities online. In July 2018, the Coalition released policy recommendations for improving the privacy and security of digital identity solutions in "Better Identity in America: A Blueprint for Policymakers,"[18] some with multiple components.

- Prioritize the development of next-generation remote identity proofing and verification systems.
- Change the way America uses Social Security numbers.
- Promote and prioritize strong authentication.
- Pursue international coordination and standardization of identity systems.
- Educate consumers and businesses about better identity solutions.

We strongly support these recommendations and believe they are key imperatives that must be accomplished for the safety and security of our citizens. As stated in the blueprint, "At the core of our recommendations is the belief that the private sector will not be able to solve America's identity challenges on its own. We are at a juncture where the government will need to step up and play a bigger role to help address critical vulnerabilities in our "digital identity fabric."

The Better Identity Coalition's blueprint outlines several excellent action items for federal and state governments. These actions span policy, resources, innovation, and priority. Taken together, they lay out a reasonable and achievable road map. However, we believe there are five key actions that the federal government should prioritize.

1. Ensure appropriate funding for the National Institute for Standards and Technology (NIST) to develop a framework of standards and operating rules that agencies at all levels of government can leverage to deliver attribute validation services in a way that is secure, designed around the needs of consumers, and protects privacy.
2. Establish a Digital Identity Task Force focused on exploring how government policy can drive the adoption of more resilient digital identity solutions across the financial services market. A key deliverable should be a holistic identity strategy for the nation.
3. Accelerate support for a mobile driver's license (mDL). This will not solve all identity-related problems, but it will help quite a bit. The driver's license is the credential that can reliably identify the greatest

number of people at the highest level of assurance. The federal government should provide additional support to current pilot efforts to accelerate an mDL offering that is ubiquitous across all fifty states.

4. It is time to move away from using the SSN as an authentication factor and migrate to alternative solutions that can more securely authenticate consumers. The federal government should take action to ban agencies from using the SSN as an authenticator. Current efforts like the electronic Consent Based Social Security Number Verification (eCBSV) Service are only moderately helpful in the short term, and Social Security numbers remain as a primary authentication factor.

Finally, the government needs to aggressively promote the use of stronger authentication and actively enforce Executive Order 13681, which requires "all agencies making personal data accessible to citizens through digital applications [to] require the use of multiple factors of authentication and an effective identity proofing process, as appropriate."

In our increasingly connected lives, a legitimate and protected digital identity is indeed the new currency we must all have. The United States continues to fall behind the globalized economy in delivering a trusted digital identity ecosystem. In February 2020, the European Commission unveiled its new digital strategy and a suite of strategy documents. One sentence in "Shaping Europe's Digital Future" caught the attention of the identity community. It reads, "A universally accepted public electronic identity (eID) is necessary for consumers to have access to their data and securely use the products and services they want without having to use unrelated platforms to do so and unnecessarily sharing personal data with them."[19] There is a desperate need for the US government's leadership to ensure that US citizens are not left behind completely in the global digital economy.

Streamlining Cybersecurity Regulation for the Financial Services Sector

Historically, regulation in the financial services sector has been reactive rather than proactive, most often in response to financial crises or downturns.[20] The cumulative result of this trend over time is an overly complex and inefficient regulatory environment for financial sector constituents. In fact, a 2016 report by the Government Accountability Office (GAO) identified three types of issues that result from this approach. Regulatory fragmentation results where more than one federal agency is involved in the same broad area of national need and opportunities exist to improve service delivery. Overlap results when multiple agencies or programs have similar goals, engage in similar activities, or target similar beneficiaries. And duplication results when two or more agencies or programs are engaged in the same activities or provide the same services to the same beneficiaries.[21] One example of successful regulatory harmonization is the supervision of US bank service providers through the Federal Banking Agencies. The supervision regime dictated by the Federal Financial Institutions Examination Council (FFIEC) under the authority of the Bank Service Company Act, brings all of the Federal Banking Agencies together to supervise bank service providers with one regime, allowing for consistency in application of cybersecurity oversight and supervision. A model that has been in place for decades, it is an example of a program that gives regulated entities clarity on expectations and a consistent regime for cybersecurity program adherence.

In no sphere are these issues more prominent than regulation relating to cybersecurity, which is widely recognized as the most significant single issue currently confronting global financial services. Today cybersecurity regulation in the sector consists of a web of inconsistent standards and frameworks applied by an increasing number of regulators at the federal and state levels.

In practice, this translates to disproportionate amounts of cybersecurity budgets and time being spent on compliance rather than operational security. An oft-cited study estimates that some cybersecurity functions within the financial sector spend as much as 40 percent of their time on compliance.[22] And the problem does not appear to be going away any time soon. A 2017 survey by the Financial Stability Board found that all twenty-five of its member jurisdictions had issued cybersecurity regulations and that a majority were planning to issue more in the near future.[23] When added to the emergence of privacy frameworks such as the CCPA, CCPR, and GDPR (EU), there is an urgent need to review current approaches to regulation in the sector.

To be sure, the issue is not new. Several bodies, including Congress, have considered the issue and recommended more action to achieve regulatory harmonization. While some progress has been made since, there is much to be done. Present circumstances, including the COVID-19 pandemic, serve to highlight the dangers of inappropriately structured cybersecurity regulation, with financial sector constituents working with more limited resources, rising threats, and unprecedented use levels of telework and digital transaction channels. At the same time, such crises present an opportunity to review the present approach to regulating cybersecurity for the financial services sector and realign frameworks for sustainable and robust security.

Collaborative initiatives have laid the foundation for more concerted action on the issue. In 2018, the Financial Services Sector Coordinating Council (FSSCC) released the Cybersecurity Profile—a risk management tool and assessment framework that can be used by financial sector entities to evidence compliance with US and global regulatory frameworks—in other words, a "common college application for regulatory compliance."[24]

The Profile was intended to benefit both regulated entities and regulatory authorities. For the former it is meant to provide a more efficient and scalable model for cybersecurity regulatory risk management, while for regulators it is intended to facilitate more tailored and precise regulatory examinations with a common framework for examination allowing regulators to better discern systemwide issues and trends.[25]

In 2016, a report by the President's Commission on Enhancing National Cybersecurity noted the need for regulatory agencies to work toward harmonizing regulation so as to focus on risk management. Such an approach, the report noted, would help reduce "industry's cost of complying with prescriptive or conflicting regulations that may not aid cybersecurity and may unintentionally discourage rather than incentivize innovation."[26] Toward this end, the commission made several notable recommendations that may offer indicia of a way forward. For one, the commission recommended that regulatory agencies must make explicit how the requirements of their cybersecurity-related regulations map to the NIST Cybersecurity Framework. Notably, it also recommended that the Office of Management and Budget (OMB) issue a circular that makes the adoption of regulations that depart significantly from the Cybersecurity Framework explicitly subject to its regulatory impact analysis, quantifying the expected costs and benefits of proposed regulations. In this manner, an agency creating regulatory requirements departing from the benchmarks established by NIST would be required to demonstrate that the added cost of new regulatory requirements is clearly supported by a public benefit. Last, the commission recommended that state and local regulatory agencies also work to align regulatory requirements with NIST's Cybersecurity Framework.

The above examples show that substantial amounts of thought and analysis have been devoted to the issue of regulatory streamlining in cybersecurity regulation applicable to the financial services sector. What is now required is for the administration and Congress to ensure that meaningful progress is made in terms of implementing plans aimed at regulatory streamlining. As the Cybersecurity Profile and other similar initiatives have demonstrated, much groundwork has been done on the issue. Hopefully, we can turn the crisis brought on by the COVID-19 pandemic into an opportunity by taking executive and legislative action to require regulatory agencies to begin tangible harmonization and streamlining measures as a matter of law.

Previous executive action on the broad issue of regulatory streamlining has failed for several reasons, including the fact that no specific agency was designated to lead the initiative. In light of the ineffectiveness of the traditional regulatory model to substantially curb cyber breaches and the widely acknowledged inefficacy of the regulatory process, the proposed Office of Digital Security Strategy should make regulatory reform—though not necessarily deregulation in financial services—a top priority. Part of our national digital strategy should start with an executive order exclusively devoted to the regulatory streamlining of cybersecurity and which specifically designates OMB to order agencies in each sector (e.g., for Treasury in relation to the financial services sector) to require any new regulations to be certified as not inconsistent with or duplicating existing regulation. This needs to be followed up with a move away from the traditional industry-wide checklist models toward requiring financial institutions to perform empirical and economics-based cyber risk assessments following DHS SAFETY Act certified models (e.g., X-Analytics or FAIR) and establish appropriate risk appetites and create entity-specific plans to adequately provide security consistent with the risk assessment. These rigorous, entity-specific assessments could substitute for the generic checklist requirements and provide more efficient and effective enterprise cybersecurity plans and practice.

Confronting the Specter of Cybercrime

Over the past four years, the finance and insurance sectors have been the most frequently attacked industries in the world, driven by both criminal financial motives and, increasingly, nation-state-sponsored acts. From a fraud and revenue perspective, the resulting damage has been tremendous. A 2019 Accenture study, for instance, estimates that banks, insurers, and capital markets companies are expected to lose $347 billion, $305 billion, and $47 billion, respectively, over the next five years because of cybercrime.[27]

Because of the COVID-19 pandemic, threats to the financial sector have increased further. There is an old saying in risk management that you should not let a crisis go to waste, and unfortunately the criminals are living by that motto. As with any crisis, we have seen a step-up by malicious actors who seek to take advantage of the current situation. This includes increased phishing and ransomware attacks, exploiting increased remote working conditions and economic relief programs.

Phishing attacks increased 600 percent during the pandemic, with one taking place every 39 seconds, according to a United Nations estimate.[28] With an increased number of people working from home, workers increasingly conduct more business by email, raising the likelihood of an employee clicking on a malicious message they believe is from a legitimate source.

In addition to phishing campaigns, ransomware attacks are targeting many industries but especially financial technology (fintech) and healthcare. Ransomware is a type of malicious software cybercriminalss use to block you from accessing your own data. The digital extortionists encrypt the files on your system and add extensions to the attacked data to hold it "hostage" until the demanded ransom is paid.

The cost of these attacks is getting more expensive. According to the cybersecurity firm Palo Alto Networks, in 2020 the average enterprise ransom payment increased to $312,493, up from $115,123 in 2019—a staggering 171 percent increase.[29] And importantly, a study by Coveware found that the majority of ransomware attacks in the first quarter of 2021 targeted the data of corporations and other large enterprises.[30]

Recent cybercrime incidents are not limited to phishing and ransomware; they also extend to other types of malicious attacks across the threat landscape. Making the situation more difficult, many of these malicious files are using techniques like "many-to-many mapping," which can make it difficult for some firewalls to block them.

One particularly interesting and innovative criminal approach has been the use of the high unemployment numbers as a means to launch attacks. According to the IT security company Check Point Software, the number of resumes and medical leave forms hiding malware has doubled since the pandemic began.[31] In addition, they noted that a number of recently registered domains that include the word *employment* hosted malicious content.

These criminal schemes also extend opportunities created by new federal government COVID-19 relief programs—such as the Paycheck Protection Program, stimulus checks, and enhanced unemployment checks—where criminals have launched new fraud efforts aimed at diverting the funds associated with those programs into their own pockets. The assistant director of the FBI's Criminal Investigations Division recently warned, "The repercussions of the COVID-19 pandemic have not and will not end any time soon."

This enlarged attack surface has resulted in more data breaches and more overall cyberattacks. The cloud computing firm iomart reported that large-scale data breaches increased 273 percent year over year in the first quarter of 2020,[32] and the FBI has seen a dramatic increase of overall cyberattack reports. Specifically, in 2020 the FBI Internet Crime Complaint Center

(IC3) received 791,790 complaints, an increase of more than 300,000 complaints from 2019.[33]

In response, while financial firms have continued to make exponential investments in cybersecurity, the economics of cybercrime remain firmly skewed in favor of attackers. In many cases, attackers have access to an increasing array of complex tools and attack schemes. Even one success (from thousands of attempts) yields disproportionate dividends.

At the same time, attackers face limited or negligible consequences from enforcement action or prosecution. Many attacks come from geographic locations that do not consider cyberattacks criminal acts and/or do not have extradition treaties with the United States.

In this context, the costs of cybersecurity will continue to spiral unsustainably for financial sector entities as long as the costs of cybercrime for attackers remain low. There is a need for sustained policy intervention directed at improving enforcement against cybercriminals no matter where they are located.

The primary reasons for this "enforcement gap" have to do with issues of both domestic and transnational import. From a domestic perspective, it is well documented that the capacity of law enforcement to investigate complex cybercrimes is not uniform across the country. While federal agencies like the FBI and US Secret Service have developed rich expertise in investigating and prosecuting financial cybercrime, law enforcement authorities at the state and local levels often do not have the requisite training, capacity, or equipment to effectively contribute to the fight. This results in a dichotomy where high-value cases are prioritized by federal agencies while other cases are left to local law enforcement. This creates a tail-heavy scenario in which a larger number of lower-value cases may not be effectively investigated or prosecuted. From the financial sector perspective, this is harmful; both types of cases deserve attention due to their ability to undermine customer confidence and drive up costs. Even when a financial cybercrime (e.g., fraud) is actively investigated, there is no guarantee that attackers located abroad will be brought to justice.

The Misuse of the Cloud

One particularly concerning development has to do with criminals' use of the public cloud. Numerous cloud providers in the United States specialize in offering cloud computing resources while allowing the purchaser to remain anonymous (the resources are bought with digital currency), and they promise not to monitor your activities using their services. Criminals use this infrastructure with impunity to attack the financial services industry. This is very difficult to defend against because blocking these cloud providers would mean potentially blocking legitimate clients who use the same cloud provider. Further exacerbating the situation is the fact that these cloud providers allow their customers to use dynamic IP addresses, so when a financial institution blocks one attacking IP, the perpetrators simply continue from another.

The Way Forward

The growth in cyberattacks against the financial services sector justifies the need for policy countermeasures, including greater law enforcement cooperation, public-private partnership, and stronger policies to eliminate the incentive of criminals to attack. The World Economic Forum (WEF) recently highlighted a "stunning enforcement gap for cybercrime, citing that even in the United States, the likelihood of successfully prosecuting a cybercrime is estimated at 0.05 percent, far below the 46 percent rate of prosecution for violent crime."[34]

Following its November 2019 meeting on cybersecurity in Geneva, the WEF pointed out the many barriers to cooperation in fighting cybercrime. They included "privacy challenges, cultural differences, a lack of shared standards around evidence collection, fear of losing competitive advantage, lack of clear frameworks or standards for public-private cooperation and liability and anti-trust concerns."[35]

Surely these barriers are imposing, but the WEF's recommendations are encouraging. For governments and industry to consider leveraging platforms such as those provided by WEF and the Cyber Threat Alliance "to create a neutral and impartial environment in which to foster public-private cooperation on cyber investigations" has merit.[36] Those recommendations make sense and should be explored. However, the time and impetus to expedite this cooperation needs government leadership.

To that end, the US government has an opportunity to take a global leadership role in proposing an international standard and cooperation agreement for civil cyber defense, including investigations and prosecution. The model already exists in military defense: the North Atlantic Treaty Organization, born from the need for nations to collectively defend against the threat posed by the former Soviet Union. A new treaty is needed for cooperation that sets the standards and policy for synchronization of global law against cybercrime and the mechanisms for cyber law enforcement investigation and cooperation. This cyber-NATO defense agreement could not be more necessary or timely.

As the human factor is a key element in the success of an attack, the government should incentivize the private sector to offer cutting-edge training and capacity-building programs to counter emerging threats in cybersecurity. The incentive need not be cash based. For instance, a company that trains all its employees using a particular curriculum or certification standard may receive a presumption that it took reasonable employee training initiatives in relation to any legal claims that may result.

Alternatively, companies investing in cybersecurity training and awareness should be permitted to deduct some of their costs or given a tax credit. After all, the benefits of improvements to cyber hygiene are systemic and far-reaching.

Domestically, the federal government should require all cloud providers to know their clients, similar to the requirements of financial institutions. Requiring due diligence, including an OFAC sanctions check of clients and regular ongoing customer due diligence and monitoring of client activities, would be a giant step forward in reducing criminals' use of the cloud.

Internationally, the United States must redouble diplomatic efforts to iron out legal and practical obstacles that impede the investigation and prosecution of transnational cybercrime. The United States is in a cyber cold war with a number of state actors that may never end. Cyber war efforts are less evident but more nefarious in their effect on the nation. To this end, the United States should devote additional resources to bringing states like Russia and China into global regimes aimed at countering cybercrime. [37] Similarly, mutual legal assistance treaties and arrangements must be renegotiated to ensure adequate coverage of emerging issues in cybercrime. Where foreign states are noncooperative, the US administration—with support from Congress—should consider developing new and effective means, including the prospect of economic sanctions.[38] This includes raising cybercrime issues as a key part of new or renegotiated trade agreements where many other digital trade topics are already being raised. Only with the application of new ideas to an age-old problem can transnational cybercrime be effectively countered.

One option to reduce the growth and combat the pernicious scourge of ransomware is to eliminate the financial incentive for criminals. Currently the only legal barrier to paying a ransom is the risk of inadvertently paying an entity in violation of OFAC and sanctions. Pending Federal and State legislation directly forbidding payment for extortion could help to remove the underlying incentive for criminals to launch ransomware attacks in the first place. Critics say that paying ransom is just part of the new world order, but would the US government stand for it if these criminals came into a bank branch or a hospital and stole hardware and held it for ransom or kidnapped and ransomed a teller? Would we accept the media saying the victim should have had more security?

Beyond these efforts, more can be done to improve the defensive posture of the financial sector. A long-standing complaint of industry has been the lack of robust, timely, and specific threat intelligence from the government. The administration should look to study gaps in threat-intelligence reporting for the financial sector and implement measures to provide more specific, contextualized, and actionable inputs. In chapter 5, we advocated developing an office to evaluate a national strategy for cybersecurity, and we reiterate here that adding such an office would help ensure that these issues receive the highest levels of visibility and attention by the federal government.

Greater government action to protect the US financial service sector is clearly needed and warranted. The above steps, including public-private training, international cooperation in prevention, investigation and prosecution of criminals and governments that aid and abet them, outlawing of ransom, and information sharing can and will make a positive impact in protecting the financial services industry as a most vital critical infrastructure sector to the nation and the globe.

CHAPTER 10

ENERGY

Protecting the Smart Grid

Ryan Boulais and Jamison Gardner

Advancements in technology have been dramatically changing the energy sector over the past decade. Technology has made energy production, transmission, and consumption more efficient and cost-effective. At the same time, it has empowered the consumer. While the business model of the energy producers, especially utilities, has resembled that of a monopoly for quite some time, a shift in how energy is produced, delivered, and consumed is causing this model to be disrupted. More and more energy companies are being forced to adapt to the changing landscape in order to remain viable. However, with the increased adoption of high-tech solutions comes significant and consequential cybersecurity challenges in the industry. The MIT Energy Initiative's report "Utility of the Future" recognized that with advanced technologies deployed in "widespread connection of distributed energy resources and smart appliances," the industry should heighten cybersecurity posture with emphasis on resilience building and business continuity.[1] Accordingly, addressing the growing cyber threats, risks, and vulnerabilities of the "smart grid" is a resource-intensive endeavor that will require the cooperation of the private and public sectors to achieve.

The US electric grid consists of thousands of power plants and substations along with millions of miles of electrical lines.[2] It is perhaps the world's "largest interconnected machine," on which hundreds of millions of people rely for power.[3] Traditionally, there has been a simple producer-consumer dynamic that existed between utilities and their customers. Utilities have historically operated as government-sanctioned monopolies with heavy federal and state oversight and limited competition.[4] However, the advent of the smart grid is fundamentally changing how consumers and producers interact in the energy sector.

165

"Smart grid" is the name that has been given to the electric grid in the United States, which is becoming increasingly capable of two-way, digital communication between consumers and producers.[5] Historically, the energy grid has been operated by thousands of analog machines with a one-way flow of power and information between producers and consumers. However, the smart grid is opening the door to new opportunities for providers and con- sumers alike by introducing new connected technology to the grid. Consum- ers can now utilize smart devices, like smart meters and thermostats, that are digitally connected to the grid.[6] These IoT (Internet of Things) devices allow for the instantaneous two-way flow of information between consumers and producers. Smart devices also allow consumers to make more informed decisions about how and when they use power.[7] For instance, consumers can now monitor their power usage in real time and decide what level of par- ticipation they will have with the grid. At the same time, this technological renovation of the grid brings new ways for producers to manage the grid and respond to customer demand.

In addition, consumers can now also be producers of electricity. Con- sumers with solar panels, or other production methods, can sell excess energy directly back to the grid.[8] This is a relatively new dynamic that is changing the way many interact with the grid. More and more consumers are becoming less reliant on utilities as they invest in their own methods of clean energy production. Even more consequential is the addition of new players in the electricity game that are introducing more competition to an industry traditionally devoid of it.[9] A growing number of consumers are now presented with options for power outside their local utility, and more consumers are choosing to pursue clean energy options from third parties.[10] Thus the traditional relationship between consumers and producers in the energy sector is rapidly changing.

The smart grid and the evolution of the energy market in the United States present two key challenges for utilities. First, the smart grid, despite the numerous benefits and efficiencies it provides, is making cybersecurity more difficult for energy companies. Second, meeting the challenges of securing the smart grid is extremely resource intensive and is not economi- cally feasible for many energy companies.

For example, the thousands of devices now digitally connected to the grid present a key challenge. Each of these devices can potentially act as an access point for cybercriminals into the larger web of devices, which could allow them to attack systems critical to power delivery and management.[11] What adds to the difficulty is the sheer size and complexity of the smart grid network. The smart grid has an estimated size of between one hundred and one thousand times larger than the internet.[12] An increasing number of homes and businesses are now equipped with IoT devices that are linked to the grid, and more devices are being employed every year to manage the grid. Monitoring such a massive network requires extensive resources and advanced technology, which are often not economically viable for many companies. Thus the interconnected nature of the smart grid will continue to offer significant advantages to producers and consumers but will also pose a significant challenge for utilities and other companies for the foreseeable future.

The more interconnected nature of the smart grid also exacerbates the effects of cyberattacks on the system as a whole. Even if only a small utility is targeted, the effects of the attack can ripple outward and affect the system in a larger way. It was recently discovered that the SolarWinds attack affected around 25 percent of power utilities.[13] Officials at the North American Electric Reliability Corp. (NERC) released this information on April 15, 2021. It was reported that a much smaller number of utilities' operational technology (OT) and industrial control systems were also affected. While there has been no subsequent activity by the hackers after the initial breach, security experts warned that there could be SolarWinds impacts and vulnerabilities that have yet to be discovered. It is not known if there has been persistent access to these networks and systems, and the ongoing effects could be felt for years to come.

Threats to the electric grid, however, have become more concerning after the SolarWinds breach. As tensions have escalated between Russia and Ukraine, US cyber officials have been planning for the worst-case scenario if Russia mounted a cyberattack on the US electric grid. The Biden administration has issued a joint advisory to the utilities and energy sector about Russian-sponsored hackers' increased interest in targeting US critical infrastructure.[14] Furthermore, the FBI has amplified messaging from utility sector leaders urging the energy sector to shore up its cyber defenses amid growing threats.[15]

Oldsmar Water Treatment Plant Attack

While securing the smart grid and keeping up with advancing technology is vitally important for utility companies, many are not even properly secured against amateur attacks. The attack against a water treatment plant in Oldsmar, Florida, in February 2021 illustrates the importance of implementing simple security measures. According to a Massachusetts cybersecurity advisory for public water suppliers, the attackers used the remote access software TeamViewer to access the plant's SCADA controls. This software was installed on one of the computers used by water treatment plant personnel to conduct system status checks. Furthermore, every computer used by plant personnel was connected to the SCADA system, and all used the Windows 7 operating system. Microsoft ended support for Windows 7 in January 2020, meaning that they will no longer update the software's security.[16] Last, it was ascertained that all computers used the same password for remote access, and all were connected directly to the internet without any type of firewall protection installed.[17]

While the attack was thwarted by plant personnel before the attackers had affected the water supply, it demonstrates the importance of having security measures in place, like two-factor authentication, firewall protection, and a secure operating system. If utilities are struggling to protect themselves against simple attacks like the one in Oldsmar, they will be overwhelmed by the need to protect advanced technology as the smart grid grows. In an interview about the attack, Jerry Ray, chief operating officer at the cybersecurity company SecureAge, noted that while the attack was simple and clumsy from the IT side, it was more complicated from the water treatment side: "If it was a nation-state, anyone who was trained, with significant funding, we would never have known about it."[18]

According to the 2020 Cyberspace Solarium Commission report, there are three issues imperiling the cybersecurity of the country's water infrastructure: "Codifying SSA responsibilities, ensuring that SSA's such as the EPA conduct their risk management assignments effectively, and better enabling state and local governments are all critical steps toward improving the capacity of water utilities to prevent and mitigate the growing threats they face from cyberspace."[19]

To address the growing concerns of water utilities, the White House launched a hundred-day pilot program with the Cybersecurity and Infrastructure Security Agency and the EPA focused on helping water system operators install threat monitoring technology.[20] Federal officials will use the program to inform cybersecurity recommendations and training for the entire water sector. The two challenges to this effort are that water utilities are limited by city budgets and that the EPA's regulatory authority on cyber is in flux.

Another, newer challenge that has been introduced with the advent of the smart grid is the challenge of securing customer data. Traditionally, data protection has been focused on protecting a few closed systems with minimal touchpoints. However, with the increasing use of devices such as smart power meters collecting and transmitting massive amounts of data, the issue of data protection has been brought to the forefront of the cybersecurity discussion in the energy sector.[21] The Institute for Electric Innovation estimated nearly 115 million smart meters were installed in homes and businesses in the United States by the end of 2021, with 107 million smart meters installed in 2020.[22] Smart meters are particularly concerning because they record and transmit data about consumers' power usage in frequent, constant intervals.[23] The National Institute of Standards and Technology stated that "such detailed information about appliance use can also reveal whether a building is occupied or vacant, show residency patterns over time, and reflect intimate details of people's lives and their habits and preferences inside their homes."[24]

While this data is valuable to producers and consumers alike, securing it presents formidable obstacles both technologically and financially. The energy sector must now not only be concerned about attacks aimed at crippling the smart grid; they must also prioritize the security of large amounts of customer data.

Economics are at the heart of the challenges the smart grid faces. The potential "payoff" for a cybercriminal or nation-state targeting the US grid is quite high, while the chances of prosecution and the costs of launching an attack can be relatively low. Unlike many other types of cyberattacks, an attack against the grid would likely be politically motivated as opposed to financially motivated.[25] However, the political and strategic payoff of crippling part of America's power grid for a rival nation would be massive. Attacks on the power grid are prime examples of the sorts of the growing systemic cyber risk discussed in chapter 3.

Unfortunately, the economics of cybersecurity in the energy sector are less favorable for utilities than for other companies. The evolution of the energy market in the United States has started to strain many utilities financially as increased competition and changing consumer preferences reduce revenues. At the same time, new technology like the virtual cloud has required extensive investment by many in the energy sector.[26] This increased investment in technology coupled with aged physical assets and legacy systems have left many utilities in a difficult financial position.

For most utilities, the benefits of heavy investment in cybersecurity are not substantial enough to justify the costs.[27] Although the implications of successful cyberattacks on the grid are dire, to date the US grid has been relatively unscathed. Utilities therefore are likely to focus their limited resources on maximizing revenues instead of investing more heavily in expensive cybersecurity technology or personnel.[28] The benefits of significant cybersecurity investments can be hard to perceive. As mentioned earlier in this book, private companies invest in security at a commercial level that makes financial sense. Thus expecting all of the more than three thousand interconnected utilities to expend the resources necessary to completely secure their systems against sophisticated cyberattacks from nation-states is unsustainable and unrealistic, as the cost to do so cannot be managed on a long-term basis funded by ratepayers, and, lacking economic justification, shareholder investment is liable to dry up.

Mitigating or preventing successful cyberattacks on the grid is a goal shared by the private sector and the government across all industries of the economy. However, the case for government involvement in securing the electrical grid is particularly compelling considering what is at stake and those who are likely to launch cyberattacks on the grid.[29] A successful cyberattack on the US grid could leave tens of millions of people without power for extended periods of time. At the same time, critical services like hospitals could be disabled, denying citizens' needed care and services.[30] Damage estimates range from $240 billion in losses all the way to loss of human life in the worst-case scenarios.[31] Although the US grid has been relatively free from disruptive attacks so far, the writing on the wall is clear. Just a year ago the first disruptive cyberattack against the US power grid was carried out by an unknown attacker.[32] It is likely that this attack was carried out by a simple "automated bot . . . scanning the internet for vulnerable devices" or by an unskilled hacker.[33] In 2015, an unknown group of sophisticated cybercriminals was able to infiltrate Ukraine's grid, which resulted in over 200,000 people losing power.[34] The control system that was attacked in Ukraine was found to have been more secure at the time of attack than some similar systems in the United States.[35] The successful attack against Ukraine's grid crystallized the message of many of those who were warning about the cyber vulnerability of critical infrastructure, like the grid, in the United States. As of now, it has not been determined who exactly was responsible for these events or what motivated them. However, these recent attacks show that those with a desire to target the grid can do so with little fear of retaliation and can potentially cause "catastrophic damage to portions of the US power grid."[36]

Furthermore, it is likely that an attack aimed at crippling the grid would come from a rival nation or a group of sophisticated cybercriminals, as was the case in the Ukraine attack. It is no secret that nations often strategically target the critical infrastructure of their opponents. The United States has been rather open about launching targeted attacks against the Russian grid as a proverbial shot across the bow.[37] Recently, it was discovered that Iran has been secretly targeting critical infrastructure, like telecommunications, in several different regions, including North America.[38] In addition, according to a DHS advisory, Russia has been carving its way into the US grid and targeting critical infrastructure.[39] Strategic targeting of the US grid by foreign nations is unlikely to stop any time soon. As seen with the SolarWinds attack, foreign nationals are becoming bolder, and attacks are focused on a wide range of targets, which makes them even more damaging.

These nation-states have vast resources and highly skilled personnel who have the ability to launch sophisticated attacks against the grid that span across several years. With the increased level of vulnerability that the smart grid has introduced to the energy sector and the countless Americans who depend on the grid for their well-being, the need for the government to work with private industry to secure the grid is at an all-time high. It would be naive to assume that any significant portion of the 3,330 utilities would be able to adequately defend their systems from such a sophisticated attack by a rival nation. Furthermore, the high level of systemic risk present in the interconnected smart grid means that one weak link could compromise huge portions of the electric grid. Thus it is imperative that the government work with the private sector to address these vulnerabilities and protect Americans from the potential fallout of a successful cyberattack on the grid.

Public-private partnerships (PPP) are not a new concept. Government has partnered with industry several times to tackle particularly challenging cybersecurity problems.[40] Information Sharing and Analysis Organizations (ISAOs) currently facilitate the sharing of information and threat analysis among a broad range of private companies and DHS.[41] The Obama administration was a strong supporter of these collaborative organizations and issued an executive order aimed at promoting their greater utilization.[42] Before that, Information Sharing and Analysis Centers (ISACs) were established for each key sector of the economy. ISACs are less inclusive than ISAOs but functioned in a similar way to "collect, analyze and disseminate actionable threat information . . . and provide members tools to mitigate risks and enhance resiliency."[43]

More recently, an information sharing program among key players in the financial sector and the government was initiated. Project Indigo was launched in 2017 and involved direct coordination between eight major banks and US Cyber Command.[44] The program allowed Cyber Command to receive valuable information from private banks that allowed them to analyze, understand, and work to mitigate the risk of cyberattacks on financial institutions.[45] Project Indigo was not highly publicized or well known, but it provided the groundwork for the Pathfinder Program in the financial sector. The Pathfinder Program took Project Indigo to a new level by involving coordination among multiple government agencies, like DoD, NSA, and DHS, and key players in the private sector.[46] This collaboration allowed the multiple government agencies to work hand in hand with the private sector to address the growing cybersecurity challenges facing some of the largest financial intuitions in the world.

The success of the Pathfinder Program in the financial sector led to the same program being rolled out for the energy sector in early 2020. The energy sector program brought together DoD, DHS, NSA, and the Department of Energy with private sector players to "advance information sharing, improve training and education to understand systemic risks, and develop joint operational preparedness and response activities to cybersecurity threats."[47] Cyber Command will also be involved with the energy sector's Pathfinder Program by sharing threat and risk information.[48] The Pathfinder Program is a step in the right direction because it facilitates not only collaboration among key government agencies but also partnership with industry. In its March 2020 report, the Cyberspace Solarium Commission referred to the Pathfinder initiative(s) as "a key proof of concept of collaboration between the private sector and critical infrastructure in support of the US cyber defense and security mission."[49] In that same report, the commission identifies rich participation by the DoD in these collaborative programs as a key to success.[50]

We recommend that collaborative cybersecurity programs, such as the Pathfinder Program, be prioritized in the energy sector (as well as analyzed and potentially adapted for other sectors through the ODSS). Utilities in particular can benefit from the resources and expertise that DoD and other agencies bring to the table. Conversely, government agencies can benefit greatly from the private sector sharing information about security needs and strategies to address key vulnerabilities. The ODSS should also carry out assessment of these existing collaborative programs to determine how they can be strengthened and what needs to be done to ensure long-term participation by both government agencies and the private sector.[51] There is a pressing need for an institutionalized process to make sure these collaborations are successful and effective. Far too many commissions and task forces have set forth seemingly strong solutions to cybersecurity problems but with no way to ensure their implementation or long-term adoption and success. The creation of an Office of Digital Security Strategy, as recommended in chapter 5, would take these innovative but disparate programs and institutionalize their systematic review and ongoing refinement.

As mentioned earlier, information sharing programs like Pathfinder are, by themselves, inadequate to achieve security. Putting too much emphasis on information sharing to solve cybersecurity vulnerabilities in the energy sector is akin to "focusing on what neighborhood kids are throwing rocks at our houses, instead of fixing our houses," according to Matthew Green, a research professor at the Johns Hopkins Information Security Institute.[52] Instead, collaboration between the government and private sector must include the joint development of solutions to key problems currently facing the energy sector.

For example, the Pathfinder Program should include the collaborative development of government-backed economic solutions to allow for greater investment in cybersecurity in the energy sector to counter sophisticated threats. Revenues for utilities continue to decrease and nation-states are increasing their efforts to disrupt critical infrastructure in the United States. At some point, the government has to stop simply sharing threat information and then mandating that utilities figure out on their own how to finance cybersecurity for the grid. While a few of the top utilities may have the personnel and resources to maintain robust cybersecurity, it is unrealistic to expect the majority of utilities in the United States to be able to invest in cybersecurity at the level needed to defend against sophisticated attacks from rival nations. Economic solutions to assist the energy sector with their cybersecurity programs could include a mix of economic incentives such as tax credits, direct investment by the government, and reduction of regulations that work to increase the cost of energy.

The economics of robust cybersecurity in the energy sector are especially pertinent to smaller electric utilities. Just like many of the smaller players in other sectors of the economy, smaller electric utilities struggle to maintain high levels of security due primarily to budgetary constraints. In early 2019, a "hacking campaign" targeted several small and midsized utilities that are relatively unknown but that are crucial to critical functions of the economy.[53] Because the motivations for attacking the grid are largely strategic and political, smaller utilities with less money and less robust security are likely to be targeted. For example, one of the smaller utilities targeted in the 2019 attack is critical to the operation of a major shipping route in the United States.[54] Cybercriminals can likely achieve their goals without dealing with the more sophisticated defenses of a larger company.

Smaller utilities often struggle with cybersecurity; they lack the cybersecurity tools and personnel to maintain robust security.[55] The vulnerabilities of smaller utilities should be a concern of the entire industry because the ever-increasing connectivity of the smart grid presents high levels of systemic risk. Accordingly, the government and industry partners in the Pathfinder Program should focus on solutions that help address the needs of smaller and midsize utilities. A stable entity within the government focused on this sort of cross-sector technique sharing may be necessary to secure the entire grid.

As discussed in chapter 6, a resource sharing platform suggested by the RAND Corporation would encourage the government and larger firms to help provide critical tools and resources to smaller firms. These tools and information are shared using a cloud-based platform at a significantly reduced cost in exchange for participation in collaborative programs. A similar model could be adapted for the energy sector wherein larger utilities partner with the government to provide access to sophisticated cybersecurity tools and resources to smaller and midsize utilities through a private cloud. Participation in the Pathfinder Program should be a prerequisite to accessing these resources and would allow for greater flow of information and education between the government and the private sector. This type of resource sharing, coupled with targeted economic incentives and information sharing, would work to directly address the key challenges to securing the smart grid in the United States.

CHAPTER 11

RETAIL

Serving Consumers
and Keeping Them Secure

Andy Kirkland and Alexander T. Green

For decades the retail sector has been one of the cornerstone industries of the US economy. It provides the largest share—10 percent—of employment in the workforce and supports one in four US jobs, accounting for 42 million Americans.[1] In 2021, retail sales were an estimated $4.4 trillion, a growth rate of between 10.5 and 13.5 percent as the economy continues to recover from the COVID-19 pandemic.[2] A lot of the gains that have been seen in the retail sector over the past several decades are a result of the advancements in automation and technology.[3] Roughly $601 billion of the $5.5 trillion sales for 2019 were spent through online merchants, up 15 percent from the previous year.[4] In 2020, e-commerce in the United States grew 32.4 percent.[5] But with growing advancements and dependence on the internet and technology come cybersecurity challenges that retail firms are having to confront.

An estimated 80 to 90 percent of all people who log into a retailer's e-commerce website are hackers using stolen personal information.[6] Like cybercrime in most sectors, the economics of the problem favors the attackers. Cybercriminals are mounting the attacks and reaping the rewards. Financial gains are the primary motives driving hackers to attack retailers, accounting for 99 percent of all retail cyberattacks.[7] Moreover, a recent study found that it takes the retail sector an average of 228 days to identify a breach and another 83 days to contain it.[8] That is more than 300 days that a hacker is taking advantage of retailers' systems and maintaining the stolen personal information. The breaches cost retailers $30 billion a year.[9]

Data Breach Statistics

Type of Data Compromised:[10]
- 49% Personal
- 47% Payment

- 27% Credentials
- 25% Other

Motives of Actor:[11]
- 99% Financial
- 1% Espionage

Actors:[12]
- 75% External
- 25% Internal
- 1% Partner

Average Cost of a Breach:[13] $2.01 million

Average Cost per Record:[14] $119

Days to Identify and Contain a Breach:[15]
- Identify: 288 days
- Contain: 83 days

Digital Transformation and Underinvestment in Cybersecurity

Like many businesses, retail firms are rapidly going through their own digital transformation and becoming increasingly dependent on technology, particularly with the growth of automation and artificial intelligence (AI). AI technologies have allowed firms to make tremendous gains in business. AI has offered retailers the opportunity to predict and adjust prices, assist in supply chain prediction and management, aid customers in visual searching, provide virtual fitting rooms, and predict consumer behaviors.[16] Companies such as Levi's and Gap have seen increased sales in areas where they have installed a virtual fitting kiosk that measures 200,000 points of one's body in 20 seconds and provides one with a "perfectly matched" outfit.[17] However, this increased use of technology comes with downfalls in the area of cybersecurity. Creating more access points for hackers to take advantage of increases the risk that the retailer's enormous amount of information is being compromised.

Retailers have been so enthusiastic about how digital transformation can enhance their business models that many of them have not focused on the negative repercussions that come from it, poor security being one of them. Operating in an intensely competitive market with low profit margins, retailers are driven to provide the customer with a positive experience at the expense of applications for security.[18]

These market forces driving an underinvestment in security are reinforced by typical consumer behavior. The customer turnover rate is the rate that a customer is willing to take their business elsewhere because of a data breach. The turnover rate in retail is only 2.4 percent.[19] That is roughly one-third the turnover rate in the healthcare sector (7 percent) and less than half the turnover rate in financial services (5.9 percent).[20]

This means that customers in the retail sector are less likely to stop shopping at retail firms when they are made aware of a security breach, further incentivizing retailers to provide lower costs for customers and better customer experience instead of improved cybersecurity. As long as retailers are continuing to see economic gains by applying new technological tools and not losing customers even when they are breached, they will likely continue to be underprepared for a highly probable cyberattack.

It is not surprising, then, that retailers underestimate the significance of the security threat. Retailers estimate the probability of a breach at 45 percent, when in actuality the probability is 72 percent. As a result, only one-third of retailers have a large enough budget to provide proper cybersecurity. In a study assessing which industry sector planned to increase spending on cybersecurity last year, the retail industry came in 13th of 13 sectors. That study also found that retail ranked 11th of 13 sectors in terms of the percentage of companies that used leading cybersecurity practices, 10th in terms of using advanced methods, and 12th in terms of using stress tests for cybersecurity.[21] On average only 27 percent of automated retail cybersecurity is being fully deployed, which is up from 15 percent in 2019.[22]

We identify two main issues that must be addressed to create a more secure and resilient retail space to defend against cybercrime. The first issue is the cybersecurity risks associated with increased access to digital platforms. With the growth of technology, more people than ever have access to the systems that modern retailers use, and most retailers are unaware of the best ways to protect themselves. The second issue concerns collecting, handling, and defending the information stored on retailers' servers. There are different definitions across country and state lines as to what personal information is, as well as who owns it, who has control of it, and how to protect it. The lack of clarity the government provides on this front makes it difficult for firms to adequately assure security.

Retail is quickly becoming one of the biggest targets for cybercrime. Mandiant's 2021 Special Report labeled the retail industry the second most targeted industry by cybercriminals in 2020, up nine places from ranking eleventh, where it had ranked since 2015.[23] The pandemic has emboldened cybercriminals as the cost of malware has decreased and retailers have not kept pace with the cyber threat. Retailers are targeted because of the large amount of personal data they have, and criminals are further incentivized because there is little stopping them. The websites of the largest retailers are especially inviting to criminals because they have such a large attack surface.[24] As retailers focus more on user experience (UX), they make their platforms harder to defend. This problem will only get worse as e-commerce continues to grow.

The COVID-19 pandemic greatly increased people's use of online merchants in 2020 and 2021, and this is expected to continue in the future. The number of US consumers using online retailers for select product categories has increased across the board, from consumer electronics, which saw a 6 percent increase, to accessories and jewelry, which both saw a 15 percent increase.[25] With more people shopping online, the risk to personal data and retailers' security increases, as the rewards for attackers become even greater. A report by Digital Commerce 360 said that consumers spent $861.12 billion online with US merchants in 2020, an increase of 44 percent year over year.[26] This is nearly triple the 15.1 percent jump in 2019. Overall, online spending represented 21.3 percent of total retail sales in 2020, which is a 7 percent increase from 2018. This is the largest year over year increase for e-commerce penetration ever recorded.

Risks Associated with Increased Reliance on Advanced Technologies

Modern retailers are providing digital platforms and services that are being accessed by people within and outside the firms and at various stages in the supply chain. The large number of people who have access to these platforms has left a lot of room for hackers to infiltrate and take advantage of the systems and customers' personal data. There are four distinct issues that arise from this extended access to information.

- How the web and mobile platforms are being used.
- How the personal information they store is used.
- Behavior of the employees of the firms.
- Third-party access.

Platform Risk

Today practically every retailer has its own specific web and mobile application that customers can log into. Consumers have come to expect this type of modality, which, in turn, makes it essentially a competitive necessity. These platforms typically can be accessed at any time of the day, just about anywhere in the world. They help customers find store locations, order products, earn points, and gain rewards. This has allowed firms to reach new audiences and increase profits, often while cutting costs. However, it also broadens the competitive playing field as more retailers can now compete in markets previously unreachable due to geography, thus adding competitive pressure on the retailer. Unfortunately, with advancements come security problems. According to a recent Verizon Data Breach Investigations Report, web applications account for most breaches.[27] And 75 percent of those were external in nature. Vulnerabilities in these platforms create risks for employees, suppliers, and customers. Almost all these players are using systems with limited authentication requirements, thus increasing the chances of a compromise. However, increasing the authentication requirements can delay sales, which frustrates customers and drives them to other retail outlets.[28] With security undermined by competitive market forces, hackers are increasingly able to slide into the holes of inefficiently protected, easily accessible applications.

Data Risk

By holding large amounts of data, retailers become increasingly attractive targets for hackers. Lillian Hardy, partner and cybersecurity specialist at the law firm Hogan Lovells, noted that although retailers want to acquire as much consumer data as they can to better serve their customers and gain a competitive edge, collecting this data means they will need to be more responsible about how this data is protected.[29] When criminals hack into a system, they are able to collect large banks of credit card numbers and personal information to carry out fraud operations and make hundreds of illegal purchases before the banks are able to notice and stop it.[30] There have been a number of high-profile breaches like this. One example is the Target breach that affected up to 70 million people and cost the company $18.5 million.[31] When broken down individually, the average costs to a business per stolen record is from $145 to $158.[32] Collectively, the more information a company obtains, the more attractive the company is to hackers and the more risk the company takes.[33]

Though information sharing models are sometimes inefficient, there have been a few success stories. A major retailer detected conduct involving a brand-new Java Script Remote Access Tool (RAT). The retailer was able to track it to a specific recent phishing email and another similar attempt they received the week before. They then shared the information about this threat in direct dialogue with at least three other major retailers. Those other retailers checked within their own companies and told the first retailer that they were able to spot the same malware and avoid harm because of the information that had been shared. The major retailer also shared the information with one of its ISACs. That ISAC's research then identified as many as thirty retailers that had been targeted.

Employee Risk

Employees raise a significant security concern for retail companies. Linda Priebe, partner specializing in security at the law firm Culhane Meadows Haughian & Walsh, noted that employees can be a cause of data breaches because they sometimes send sensitive material over email, steal confidential information, or just simply need more cybersecurity training.[34] A Ponemon Institute study found that 91 percent of retailers believed they had insufficient personnel to handle cybersecurity.[35] The problem is amplified with the greater trend to work from home.[36] Statistics show that of these employees working remotely, 77 percent use unmanaged personal devices to gain access to the company's system.[37] The more people who have access to the system, the greater chance of compromise.

Supply Chain/Third-Party Risk

A further security issue is the risk in the retail supply chain and other third parties. Retailers often rely on third parties to conduct business, such as web and mobile application providers, cloud providers, and point of sale providers. This presents a challenge because they cannot always control how their supply chain partners perform cybersecurity. Cybercriminals are aware of these deficiencies in the supply chain and take advantage of them to gain access to the larger, more profitable company. According to a report by the Ponemon Institute, the highest-rated cybersecurity concern was third-party risk.[38] This concern is warranted. Between 2018 and 2019 records exposed due to third-party breaches increased by 273 percent to 4.8 billion records, averaging 13 million records exposed in each third-party breach.[39] The lack of integrated cybersecurity among the participants in the supply chain due to access of the systems makes it difficult for retail firms to effectively operate and to protect against malicious intrusions.

Collecting, Handling, and Protecting Personal Information

As discussed earlier, retailers are tasked with storing incredibly large amounts of data, particularly customers' personal information. The average company holds over 500,000 files that contain sensitive information.[40] In 2018, US companies alone spent over $19 billion on obtaining and analyzing this consumer information.[41] The process of protecting the information stored is not made easy for retailers, and the government has not made it any easier. They face difficulties in determining what personal data is and how to protect it and the differences in rules and regulations across jurisdictions on how to handle these difficulties.

What Is Personal Data?

Cybersecurity and data privacy are basically two sides of the same coin. Protecting privacy and personal information from data breaches requires adequate cybersecurity. According to Verizon's 2021 Data Breach Report, personal information is the second-largest type of data being compromised, accounting for nearly 50 percent of breaches.[42] To better defend against cyberattacks companies need to better understand what the attackers are targeting. Though what legally defines personally identifiable information (PII) varies across states, for the most part they consider some mixture of first or last name, social security number, driver's license or passport, and financial account information.[43] There is no baseline definition that is applicable to all the states, and even in a given state definitions are fluid. The Federal Trade Commission (FTC), which has often taken the lead in defining the term, continues to expand its definition as to what is worthy of protection. Former director of the FTC's Bureau of Consumer Protection, Jessica Rich, noted, "In many cases, persistent identifiers, such as device identifiers, MAC addresses, static IP addresses, and retail loyalty card numbers meet this test."[44] The continually changing guidance from the FTC leaves little clarity that has been passed into law, leaving individuals and companies uncertain about what information they need to protect. Even if interpreted appropriately, these regulatory redundancies, complexities, and inconsistencies are costing firms substantial amounts of money that should be spent elsewhere, specifically, on cybersecurity.

Data Privacy versus Cybersecurity

There is a common misconception that "data privacy" and "cybersecurity" are the same when it comes to protecting information. In reality, they are strikingly different. From a broad perspective, cybersecurity is protection against unauthorized access to systems.[45] On the other side, privacy is the control of what and when there is authorized access to certain data.[46] It is often said that "you can't have privacy without security, but you can have security without privacy."[47]

This illustrates that in order to have privacy, there needs to be security to protect it, but just because you have security, that does not mean the information will not be compromised by someone who has access to the system. Individuals may abuse their privilege to secure systems and leak or misuse the information; this is not a fault of the technically secure system. To have privacy, there needs to be security, and for companies to protect private information, they need to create securely protected systems.

Jurisdictional Problems

Retailers face jurisdictional issues when it comes to making transactions in and across state and international borders.[48] Currently the United States has no up-to-date federal cybersecurity privacy law. As of 2021 three states have enacted dedicated privacy laws covering consumers, nineteen other states are debating new privacy laws, and the remaining twenty-eight only have the traditional breach notification and security laws.[49] Ten percent of US companies are in the process of trying to adhere to fifty or more information privacy laws.[50] California, one of the three states that enacted a dedicated privacy law (California Consumer Privacy Act), allows consumers to have more control over the personal information that is collected from them.[51] According to a report by the Office of the California Attorney General, assuring compliance with this new law is expected to cost the state approximately $55 billion (almost 2 percent of California's gross state product). Just to meet compliance requirements, costs for firms are expected to range anywhere from $467 million to $16 billion over the next decade.[52]

These varying and inconsistent laws across borders also make it difficult for retail firms to effectively provide cybersecurity protection for the data that they have been entrusted to protect. Some of these laws have different and incompatible terms in regard to what counts as personal information deserving to be protected, what party is covered, and even what constitutes a breach.[53] When notifying customers that there has been a breach of their login credentials, states vary on how stringent the method of notice is. Illinois gives retail firms the option to provide notice to customers affected "in electronic or other form" advising them to change their login credentials to protect their affected accounts. On the other hand, Nebraska considers login credentials the same as all other types of personal information and mandates a written hard copy notice sent to the customer and to the Nebraska attorney general.[54] In the digital era, when retailers routinely operate across state lines, having multiple state laws is confusing and inefficient. The incompatible definitions and regulations across states unnecessarily increases costs and redirects the already scarce security personnel to redundant compliance activities. As a result, the incongruity between states undermines security without appreciable added benefit for consumers.

Congress has the constitutional authority to "regulate" commerce among the states. The baseline federal rule would likely not solve all the issues retailers have to handle regarding cybersecurity. However, as noted in the earlier chapters of this book, it would help clear up some of the confusion between states. The Obama administration attempted to provide a "Consumer Privacy Bill of Rights." Its goal was to "provide a baseline of clear protections for consumers and greater certainty for businesses."[55] Unfortunately, the bill ended up losing traction due to poor timing.[56] This work if revitalized could provide the basis for a uniform federal law. Retailers, as well as many other businesses, are willing to comply with whatever regulations are determined appropriate by the policy makers. However, having to serve multiple masters hurts both the businesses and the consumers. Uniformity, at whatever level, would be the wise security policy.

The Path Forward

To resolve the issues mentioned above will require both creative and practical solutions to better manage and protect the enormous amount of valuable information retailers interact with on a daily basis. If we continue to use current methods and regulations, corporations will continue to be hacked and damaged. It is up to the private sector and government to work together and make these solutions become a functional part of reality. Many retailers are small companies (SMBs) whose access to adequate cybersecurity expertise is scarce even if they had the resources. A 2018 joint industry-DHS White Paper on Collective Defense noted:

> SMBs that are part of the critical infrastructure supply chain are frequently at more of a disadvantage to cyberspace attackers than their larger counterparts for a variety of reasons including limited budgets, access to timely, relevant and actionable information, technical expertise, and time to devote to comprehensive cybersecurity solutions. Given the importance of these SMBs to the Nation and their unique cybersecurity challenges, the government should pursue and sustain a collaborative process with industry and the SMB community to develop a comprehensive strategy to increase their overall cybersecurity.[57]

To date, no such cyber strategy has been developed. However, this would be an excellent role for the Office of Strategic Cyber Defense advocated in chapter 5. Such a plan could leverage several other ideas suggested in that chapter.

For example, several of the larger sectors such as defense and financial services have developed a range of collaborative programs that the strategy proposed in chapter 5 would call on for analysis and testing to determine how to adapt these strategies to similar problems that exist in less cyber mature sectors. In addition, the ideas for joint infrastructure sharing between prime defense companies and their smaller supply chain partners could be tested and then uniquely adapted to small retailers with modifications. The retail sector, like the DIB, is characterized by a few major entities (e.g., Walmart, Amazon) that might be able to share more aggressively to support the entirety of the retail ecosystem. The White Paper on Collective Defense specifically notes that "a joint policy statement on the sharing of cybersecurity information from the Federal Trade Commission (FTC) and DOJ suggests that properly designed cyber threat information sharing is not likely to raise antitrust concerns. This current guidance could be actively explored through a focus on collaborating with and supporting SMBs."[58]

That same white paper also noted that many small and medium-sized businesses are still unaware of the NIST Cybersecurity Framework (NIST CSF) and that others find that it could be more user-friendly and may not have expertise to implement the Framework or struggle with expense involved in implementation."

The NIST CSF as developed nearly a decade ago has grown immensely, with a wide variety of associated refences now attached to it. It was always a challenge for small companies to use this framework, and now it is more daunting, which may explain the low growth in utility documented earlier. If the government would simply perform cost/benefit analysis on elements of the framework in respect to smaller companies they could provide the metrics industry can use to determine which "uses" of the framework will be of most utility to them. The joint Industry-DHS Policy Leadership Working Group endorsed this notion in its 2018 report: "The USG [US government] should work on measuring the NIST Framework's impact and cost effectiveness when it is adopted by an organization."[59]

A National Data Breach Bill

Baseline regulatory and legislative mandates and compliance frameworks that address personal information across jurisdictions must be consolidated and streamlined. This would include defining what constitutes personal identification, how to properly protect it, and how to respond in the wake of a breach.

To do this, the government should, as mentioned in chapter 6, create a federal data privacy and security law that preempts state law and allows firms to consistently operate their businesses without the regulatory inefficiencies. This law needs to properly define what companies need to protect, as well as the baseline protections that they need to implement. These definitions should consolidate and fill the gaps left open by the varying state laws to provide a minimum framework that addresses the issue.

Another area this law should cover is baseline requirements on how retailers, both large and small scale, should properly vet third-party supply chain members and how to protect against third-party intrusions. If retailers become better educated at spotting third-party inefficiencies, cybercriminals would be less incentivized to attempt to hack a company using a third party.

By clearly defining and streamlining these rules and definitions, firms will save money that would have otherwise been spent on compliance while also better protecting them from the constant threat of cybercriminals.

Improving Authentication Requirements for Digital Systems

Congress should set new voluntary standards on retailers' authentication requirements for their systems. The standards should be analyzed and set appropriately, depending on the level of access, such as customer, employee, third-party supply chain, or executive. To incentivize firms to participate, there should be tax breaks, beginning with the baseline protections and increasing with each increased standard of protection. A model for this sort of maturity-based system is outlined in chapter 8. This could be modified through the ODSS, with increasing levels of security tied to greater tax credits. The smaller companies, which typically may not be able to afford baseline authentication standards and need to worry more about making a profit and staying competitive, would now be able to justify spending more money on cybersecurity. Further, as the largest sector employer in the United States, this tax break would help keep small businesses safe and free up money to increase innovation and maintain or increase job growth. Larger companies, which may have more information to protect, may already have authentication processes in place but would now be further incentivized to enhance their requirements with the benefit of an added tax break. ODSS can evaluate the use of authentication and set the incentives for use on a sliding scale.

These authentication requirements should have a sunset date and be reevaluated and updated every few years. For example, Nordstrom has a five-year plan that calls for reviewing cybersecurity with its vendors and tech partners to make sure that their systems remain up to date.[60] Such guidelines and standards provided by ODSS would help get companies that would not have otherwise been thinking about updating their cybersecurity thinking in that way. This model would help retail firms know where to prioritize their cybersecurity investments and educate them about where their next dollar would be best spent to be able to move up a level and receive an increased tax break.

Conclusion

The consistent theme in retail cybersecurity is determining how to protect data that is being collected on platforms that are accessed by people over whom companies have little to no control. The platforms that are being used are vulnerable, and the government is not helping protect them with its varying laws and increased compliance costs. Government and industry must revisit existing laws and procedures to better utilize the resources and information that have been given.

CHAPTER 12

TELECOMMUNICATIONS

Managing International Risk in a Post-COVID-19 World

Richard Spearman

As the economy goes digital, manufacturing gets more automated, and big data, analytics, and artificial intelligence become essential business enablers, the telecommunications (telco) sector moves ever closer to center stage as Critical National Infrastructure (CNI). Increasingly seen as the sector of sectors—or the cardiovascular system of the future economy—telco is under intense scrutiny from businesses, consumers, and from governments, all of whom recognize their increasing dependence on the services it provides. This dependence is only going to increase. There has never been a more demanding time for the sector.

As with all sectors identified by governments as CNI, telco is subject to government oversight and a degree of regulation. Operating licenses, licensing of spectrum usage, stringent coverage, and service and resilience obligations are just some examples of the way in which government has an active role in how the sector is managed. More recently there has been increasing government focus on the protection of customer data and an active debate on the complex question of where responsibility lies for managing potentially harmful content. This in turn has fed through into debates on the use of encryption—a vital tool in protecting data but also a means by which bad actors and criminals can hide illegal or damaging activity on service providers' networks.

Customers of telco and communications companies are seeking deeper assurance about how exactly the services they receive are built and managed—reflecting their awareness of the level of their dependency on the services and the quantities and potential sensitivity of their data passing across these networks. In this context, cybersecurity is an absolutely critical issue for the sector, customers, and governments because the risks are very real and the consequences of a significant cybersecurity incident are potentially enormous. Regulatory penalties for incidents where the service provider is found to be responsible for data breaches or for business losses resulting from service interruptions continue to rise. For example, the maximum penalty for a breach of the European General Directive Privacy Regulation (GDPR) is 4 percent of a company's global revenue.[1] Governments, companies, and consumers are all demanding an acceleration in the pace of digitization; secure networks are an essential prerequisite.

The COVID-19 pandemic only served to underline the importance of the telco and communication sector to the economy and also offered a glimpse of the untapped potential of "going digital." As the world dealt with the health consequences of the disease, social distancing and lockdown dramatically increased societies' dependence on communications networks, which is expected to continue despite improvements throughout the pandemic.

COVID-19 presented significant challenges for the sector. There were very rapid and significant changes in the patterns, types, and volumes of traffic on the networks as populations faced huge changes in their private and work lives. Network service providers moved rapidly to facilitate the mass rollout of working from home for millions, thereby protecting the economy from even greater damage. They were also a critical enabler of the lockdowns that proved so effective in slowing and managing the spread of the disease in many countries. They supported the dramatic expansion of access to e-learning when schools and universities closed and enabled video calls for those in isolation or with those who fell ill and could not be visited. The use of telco data for tracking and tracing positive cases and their contacts and the provision of entertainment, internet access, and gaming for the hundreds of millions of people confined to their homes for weeks at a time were all significant in facilitating and enabling the governmental and societal response to the pandemic.

The urgency of the requirement for as many people as possible to work from home drove both innovation in new ways of working and significant expansion in global network capacity. In commenting on the Cybersecurity and Infrastructure Security Agency's (CISA's) own move to 93 percent remote working, former DHS director, Chris Krebs, commented that telecom networks "have absolutely performed as intended, kudos to the telecom operators."[2]

These immediate benefits delivered by the sector in responding to COVID-19 provide important pointers for the future. As the pandemic has eased, it has become clear that for many companies there will be no return to pre-COVID-19 conditions. Business leaders and workforces are sifting through the lessons and the possibilities opened up as a result of what for many people were rapid and radical changes to their normal routines. As people have gotten used to working from home and have pushed the limits, and their skills in exploiting digital connectivity have improved, a broader range of possible options for how work could be organized in the future have been opened up. COVID-19 forced companies to be bold; for example, faced with the stark choice of having no call center consumer support or allowing call center staff to work remotely, many companies chose the latter. A combination of rapid innovation, network capacity expansion, and IT changes (to both allow remote working and enhance the protections and controls on data being worked remotely) led to a dramatic shift in what was considered possible. In some instances, the new ways of working meant new risks were identified, and these had to be mitigated or managed. Temporary changes in local government regulations were agreed on in many countries to facilitate the changes. Some of the changes in work practices may prove temporary but not all. Such innovation at speed has underlined the potential for "digital" to enable "different." While the debate continues as to exactly how the future will be shaped, the ability to significantly change the way work is organized, under pressure, and within a period of four months, has changed perceptions of what is possible.

Telco Sector Challenges

The potential for these changes to become mainstream and to continue to drive change in how work is organized in the future underlines the importance of the sector and the huge potential it offers for supporting economic recovery and future growth. The requirement for the sector to deliver existing and new services flexibly, quickly, resiliently, and, above all, securely has never been greater. The ability of the sector to manage the significant challenges of COVID-19 shows its ability to adapt to new responsibilities and opportunities. At the same time, and reflecting its increasingly critical role in society and the economy, the sector faces significant challenges.

The Increasing Politicization of the Telco Supply Chain

This is a complex and politically charged issue with a long history, which is set to have a very significant impact on the future development of the telco sector globally. The telco supply chain issue mixes sovereign national security judgments with commercial decisions on equipment choices. The extent to which governments decide they need to intervene for political reasons in this process is shaking up the current supply chain dramatically.

Over the past decade two Chinese companies, Huawei and ZTE, have grown to the point where they constitute around 50 percent of global production of key telecommunications network equipment.[3] There are two other global-scale producers: Ericsson and Nokia. While Samsung is also a scale producer of this equipment, the company has traditionally focused on Far Eastern markets. In markets outside the United States, Huawei and ZTE have gained a very significant share of the network equipment business in 2G, 3G, and 4G, and based on the scale of Chinese domestic demand, they are also leading China's rapid expansion into 5G.

In the United States, the presence of Huawei amounts to no more than 7 percent of the total network infrastructure, and this is predominantly in the networks of smaller rural providers. Contrast this with figures of over 30 percent in many European countries and higher figures still in many African countries. Huawei and ZTE also contribute very significantly to the global supply of handsets, so the debate about their significance to the supply chain is not just about network equipment. It is also important to register the importance of China as an offshore manufacturer for many US and European companies, including Ericsson, Nokia, CISCO, Apple, and many more. There is significant interdependency. The current sharp deterioration in US-China relations—accompanied by a broader reassessment in Europe and elsewhere of relations with China—poses very specific and significant challenges to the telco sector.[4]

Sectors designated as CNI are used to being the focus of special attention by governments in calculations of national security risk. The concentration of supply in China—a country recognized as a serious state actor and adversary in cyberspace—has generated an international debate on the wisdom of using Chinese-supplied equipment in such an important sector. The issue is part of the wider growing tension between the United States and China over trade, foreign policy, future technology dominance, and human rights. The US decision to focus on Huawei as a provider that poses a particular threat has created a very complex political and commercial environment for governments and telco companies across the globe to navigate.

The United States has moved to the position of banning Huawei equipment from domestic networks, and with the relatively small volume of equipment currently deployed, the task and cost of enforcing this will be relatively modest. This is not the case elsewhere. National political decisions regarding the use of Huawei (from significant reduction to total ban) could have very serious implications for operators. There is a very real risk of slowing down the rollout of 5G, delaying other network upgrades, and—where political decisions require significant changes to the network—introducing potentially very significant additional cost that operators or governments will need to meet. Any effective ban on the use of Chinese equipment by telco companies will leave an effective choice between only two suppliers—not enough to ensure effective competition, innovation, and supply chain resilience. It is reasonable to make a decision on a national security basis, but the practical management of the second order consequences need to be worked through in detail. Failure to do so represents a serious risk to the sector for the medium and long term.

If politically driven changes do not attract financial compensation from governments, the telco sector outside the United States—where return on capital expenditure is in many cases already very low—will be further financially stressed. The market capitalization of telcos has significantly declined. This is not a good outcome from a government and societal perspective for a CNI sector that has been central to both COVID-19 management and economic recovery and future development.

Cybersecurity Threat Landscape

It is a statement of the obvious that telco networks are established targets for both state and non-state actors and are constantly being attacked. State and non-state actors target operators and their customers for system information and data that they can exploit. As the volumes of data exchanged over global communications networks continue to rise, especially with the sharp increase due to COVID-19, communications companies become an ever more attractive target. Attackers are interested in penetrating providers both in their own right and as the vector to facilitate attacks on the company's customers. None of this is new, but the pandemic sharply increased the transition to reliance on virtual communications. If businesses continue to conduct a portion of operations remotely, communications might continue to be a target of cyberattacks. The threats are complex and fast evolving, and the increasing interconnectedness of everything provides an ever expanding potential attack surface for attackers.

Communications companies are at the heart of this new interconnectivity and are on the front line both in defending their networks and in working with their customers and in partnership with government to develop effective defenses beyond their boundaries. This requires significant and sustained investment and constant innovation in skills and new technologies. While recognizing that no cyber defense system will be universally effective against all threats all the time, it is essential that the communications sector consistently meet reasonable standards in deterring, detecting, and responding to attacks consistent with their business plan. Additional security, beyond what is commercially required and reaching to broad national defense requirements, needs to be augmented by government. This is at the core of the business and central to maintaining customer (including the government's) confidence. It is only by developing and maintaining trust that communications service providers will persuade customers to stay with them and to start using the services of the future that will be crucial to economic growth. Many of these new services—automation, autonomous transport, e-medicine—will critically depend on consumer confidence in the provider and in particular in the ability to protect data and services from cyberattack. Good security will be central to this.

Government Intervention in the Sector

As discussed in chapters 5 and 6, there is a legitimate need for governments to regulate the sector. Licensing to ensure operator suitability and guarantee levels of service and the allocation of spectrum are necessary. There is a difference between individual operator resilience and national resilience, and governments need to have the powers to orchestrate where required to ensure that national security requirements are met. In addition, governments also act to ensure fair competition. Further, as CNI there are increasingly demanding government-mandated cybersecurity, data protection, and service requirements, which is understandable but not without cost and complexity. Governments have taken a close and in many cases interventionist approach to pricing—connectivity as an essential requirement for all—restricting companies' room to maneuver and depressing profits, shareholder value, and return on capital.

Just at the time telcos need to be investing even more in their network resilience as well as in the future—5G, IoT, AI, and Big Data—many of them are under serious financial pressure. However, as detailed earlier, the regulatory models need to evolve just as the technology and business realities and nature of the cyber threat have evolved. As the former chair of the Federal Communications Commission, Tom Wheeler, has written, the traditional regulatory model is ill-suited to face these twenty-first-century realities and in need of renovation, as we proposed in chapter 5.

The Way Forward

The COVID-19 pandemic has placed the telco sector under considerable financial strain while also demonstrating its criticality of connectivity to the functioning of economies and societies worldwide. Addressing the following issues would make a real difference to the overall health of the sector as well as contribute to the best possible outcomes in cybersecurity.

Creating a Much Deeper Partnership with Government

A new public-private partnership between telco and government is urgently needed. It is not an exaggeration to say that getting this right will be key to future economic success and has been a key component of post-COVID recovery efforts. Governments need to rethink how they regulate telco; some regulation is inevitable, but it needs to be smarter in supporting the economic health of the sector. The new partnership between telco and government needs to be more about collaboration: the two must work together to deliver on shared objectives such as increasing fiber rollout and faster internet speeds. Working constructively together to maintain the security of connectivity while also serving economic needs is but one example of the broad benefits that would stem from a new partnership between telco and government.

A developed partnership between telco and government would support an improvement in the financial health of the sector, a particular issue in Europe. The current regulatory framework governing telco in Europe is rendering the return on investment unsustainable and reduces the scope for necessary investment, including in cybersecurity.

Governments have traditionally prioritized customer pricing and low price entry over investment in infrastructure. Delivering common standards and rules to apply fairly, including establishing a level playing field between telco and internet companies, would make a significant difference. The system of spectrum allocation and the structure of the auctions need to be radically overhauled. Governments squeeze revenue out of the sector through inefficient and overpriced spectrum auctions. This is not in the longer-term interests of the telco sector or of governments as it affects the financial health of the industry and the ability to make the investments that both would like to see.

Giving telcos fiscal headroom will ultimately enable much greater capital expenditure, including on cybersecurity. From investing in new technologies, in network resilience, and in cybersecurity, the financial well-being of the telco sector and the security of networks are inextricably linked.

There has been much work done on improving information sharing both within the sector and between the sector and government, but this needs to improve and develop significantly going forward. The increasing sophistication of the threat actors and the criticality of the networks mean that governments are going to have to assist in the defense of networks and in the deterrence and disruption of attackers—well beyond current information sharing. This is already the case with preventive information sharing and post-incident assistance in certain cases, but it needs flagging as a critical capability. Government has a legitimate role in regulating industry—particularly in CNI—but it also needs to be an active collaborator. These different roles can generate reluctance on both sides, but this is too important for both sides not to get it right.

Building a Significantly Diversified Supply Chain

The technical, security, and risk discussion about the telco supply chain security—including the use of "high-risk vendors"—is now inextricably linked with the geopolitical tensions between the United States and China. This linkage may have been inevitable, but it also distracts from and risks distorting the discussion on how we build a diverse, resilient, and secure supply chain. And how can this be done when globalization has been the direction of travel for so long? "Uncoupling" might sound attractive, but it is fiendishly difficult to achieve without risking significant disruption, additional expense, and possible reduction of resilience and performance of networks in the short term. There is broad agreement between telcos and governments that there is insufficient choice and there is a need for greater competition. Governments need to take action to diversify the supply chain by providing the conditions required for new market entrants. A diverse supply chain will lead to healthy competition, will drive down costs, and will ensure that the supply chain is fundamentally more secure.

One key part of achieving this is the development of OpenRAN. OpenRAN standardizes network architecture in the radio access network (RAN) and provides open interfaces to enable the components of different suppliers to be fully interoperable. This reduces vendor lock-in and lowers the barriers to entry for new vendors, including small start-ups, as multiple vendors can contribute to elements of the OpenRAN architecture.[5] Multivendor interoperability can only work if the right policy framework is in place.

Government support will be essential if this is to move forward at pace. The traditional RAN vendor market has shrunk because vendor profitability decreased to the point that many former providers withdrew from the market.

OpenRAN has seen the creation of many small companies that are developing software and applications, but they will need support if they are to grow and scale up. Governments need to step in with significant financial support to assist this process. Telcos need to commit to future orders as a means of helping the start-ups attract the right investment in order to scale up.

Government can also help with standards setting. There is a need for common global standards for OpenRAN to succeed. This will prevent fragmentation and deliver OpenRAN solutions that can then be integrated at a global scale.

Patent licensing will also require reform for OpenRAN to work. Currently, patents are held by (and cross-licensed between) the traditional vendors in the 5G supply chain. Greater transparency on what patents are needed to implement standardized functionality is therefore essential. The standard essential patent (SEP) market will need to be opened up to determine whether licenses are fair, reasonable, and nondiscriminatory. SEP license fees will ultimately need to be capped; SEP royalties must reflect the contribution of the patent innovation. Regulated patent pools could support the delivery of an aggregated cap.

While OpenRAN's success is contingent on the availability of public funding, the development of global standards, and reform to SEP licensing, the delivery of multi-vendor interoperability will require winning partnerships. Cooperation between incumbent vendors and new market entrants is vital as interoperability requires uninhibited interaction, collaboration, and trust among all parties. Incumbent vendors must play a role in the OpenRAN architecture while also allowing other parts to be offered to new suppliers. Such cooperation will enhance the health of 5G ecosystems globally and support the global economic recovery through the protection of incumbent vendor business coupled with the opportunity for new market entrants.

CHAPTER 13

INFORMATION TECHNOLOGY

Defining How to Govern IT

Larry Clinton, Carter (Yingzhou) Zheng, and Tarun Krishnakumar

The twenty-first century has been the era of IT, although it is unassailable that the information technology industry became dominant in many respects at the turn of the century. During the past few decades "high-tech" has become immensely popular. Cell phones begat smartphones, desktop computers begat tablets, broadband begat YouTube, all carrying virtually instantaneous access to services, education, culture, and economy. In the digital era, some people have come to believe that access to these devices qualifies as a necessity for modern life.

One empirical measure of the dominance of the technology industry is the stock market. On August 20, 2020—in the midst of the COVID-19 pandemic—the *Washington Post* reported that the largest measure of stock market performance, the S&P 500, had reached a record high.[1] However, virtually all the rise in the index was powered by six tech stocks that had gained 70 percent during the year, while the rest of the index was down 4 percent.

The pandemic only served to highlight the centrality of tech companies. The extreme increase in stock value was due to multiple factors, including consumers relying on Amazon to deliver almost anything through its online portal, Netflix providing the entertainment to fill all the empty hours for hundreds of millions of stay-at-home workers, and Google and Facebook being the go-to centers for information on almost anything. Certainly, living through the pandemic would have been very different had it hit in 1990.

However, like a long-term infatuation turning into a troubled marriage, the warm feelings the populace, and many in government, had for the techies when they were young have cooled and become tenuous. The shift in perspectives is evident in recent studies. For example, the Pew Research Center reveals several notable trends about public perceptions of large technology companies, especially those in the social media space that they interact with daily. For instance, a majority of Americans—72 percent across party lines—believe that social media companies have "too much power and influence in politics."[2] At least half of Americans support more government regulation of "big tech companies," while nearly three-quarters of Americans express "little or no confidence" in the abilities of technology companies (i.e., social media) to prevent misuse of their platforms to influence the 2020 presidential election.[3] In the same survey, 78 percent believed that these companies had a responsibility to prevent such misuse.

In a similar vein, studies show that a majority of Americans feel that they have little control over data collected about them by private entities as well as the government—with 79 percent expressing some level of concern over how such data would be used.[4] Overall, these trends showcase, at the very least, some level of concern or dissatisfaction with the manner in which Americans interact with modern technology. In most instances, these concerns revolve around issues such as personal privacy, government surveillance, and the misuse of social media.

While these matters are a concern in their own right, the above trends hold relevance for the broader issues canvassed in this volume. The atmosphere for policy making on "marquee" issues receiving intense public glare can also set the tone for more general policies, affecting trust and regulation in general. In the case of the big tech companies, public concern or outrage over hot button issues, including social media manipulation, unlawful online content, privacy, and security, can play a crucial role in shaping legislative and regulatory priorities. Trust deficits in these areas may permeate into other (unrelated) sectors of the digital economy and come to characterize broader government–private sector interactions.

A key distinctive characteristic of the IT sector, particularly in comparison to other designated critical sectors such as energy and telecommunications, is that IT has grown and flourished in a generally unregulated environment. The culture of the IT industry embraces innovation, risk, new ideas, and the desire to create disruptive products and services that are antithetical to the centrally managed structures governing sectors that are more traditional.

The overwhelming consensus of the industry's major players is that this unregulated environment has been an essential feature, and primary driver, of the historic growth and productivity that the sector has achieved. For many years, the popularity and profitability of the tech companies shielded them from virtually all government regulation. But that may be about to change.

Actions have already been taken, especially surrounding the issue of "big techs" and antitrust concerns. Debate over the issue has been ongoing for the past few years, but 2020 marks a turning point as countries around the globe are making efforts to tackle the issue. Google and Facebook are facing multiple antitrust lawsuits brought by the US government, which is the first action by the government since the case against Microsoft in 1998. Alibaba is facing antitrust investigation by the Chinese government, and the EU has proposed new laws to regulate big techs and prevent them from impeding competition in the EU market.[5]

Further, given the interrelated nature of many of these issues, eye-catching controversies that often play out in the public sphere can distort or skew attention away from more nuanced issues or sectoral perspectives on issues such as privacy and cybersecurity. In other words, it is often difficult to address more nuanced questions of cybersecurity policy without first addressing its most controversial or newsworthy ones. Among the issues that face the IT industry today are

- how to balance legitimate law enforcement issues with personal privacy;
- how, or if, major technology companies should be regulated; and
- how government and industry can work better together on IT issues in the era of digital transformation.

Making Progress in the Privacy and Encryption Debate

Despite intensive efforts, government and the private sector continue to remain apart on finding holistic solutions to balance privacy and law enforcement interests. As information technology has evolved to become more personally relevant in the lives of the populace, it has brought with it contradictions in terms of what values it embraces and how the technology should be configured to reflect societal versus personal values.

Within this domain, a key point of controversy has been the debate about modern encryption technology allowing threats and actors to go dark. "Going dark" is a phrase used to describe the "widening gap between law enforcement's legal privilege to intercept electronic communications and its practical ability to actually intercept those communications."[6] Concerned with the capacity of modern digital devices to compromise personal privacy, many consumers, and policy makers, have campaigned for devices to be built with increased security for personal data. In response, the tech companies have pioneered strong encryption and embedded it in the technology. However, the proliferation of advanced encryption technology also acts as a barrier for law enforcement seeking information in connection with investigations, despite having obtained a lawful warrant. The effectively encrypted

technologies can be used by vicious criminals and terrorists to shield themselves when obviously contravening societal interests in public safety.

This tension is not new. A key report by Harvard University's Berkman
Center for Internet & Society found: "Often recounted as the 'crypto wars,'
government access to encrypted communications has been the subject
of hot debate and restrictive policy since the 1970s, with the government
ultimately relaxing many export-control restrictions on software containing
strong cryptographic algorithms in 2000."[7]

While the tension between privacy and law enforcement access was best
characterized by the Apple-FBI litigation, the debate has reemerged in new
and more complex forms since. However, the key question remains the same:
Should law enforcement be permitted to access encrypted data? If so, to what
extent must the private sector be compelled to cooperate to achieve this end?

From the perspective of the Department of Justice (DOJ), the issue is
characterized in the following terms:

> Service providers, device manufacturers, and application developers
> are deploying products and services with encryption that can only
> be decrypted by the end user or customer. Because of warrant-proof
> encryption, the government often cannot obtain the electronic evi-
> dence and intelligence necessary to investigate and prosecute threats
> to public safety and national security, even with a warrant or court
> order. This provides a "lawless space" that criminals, terrorists, and
> other bad actors can exploit for their nefarious ends.[8]

While recognizing the security-linked benefits of encryption, DOJ
highlights the increasing strength of modern protocols and algorithms as
obstructing critical national security and law enforcement investigations—
in relation to both "data at rest" and "data in transit." Taking note of contemporary developments, DOJ also points to the effect of the COVID-19
pandemic on the issue—highlighting that the increased presence of children
online may put them at greater risk of encountering online child predators,
many of whom may rely on anonymity and end-to-end encryption.

On the other hand, consumer advocates note that encryption significantly enhances privacy and cybersecurity at a time when data collection is
reaching new heights in scale as well as sensitivity. The emergence of more
invasive technology and investigative techniques has led to rising concerns
about the massive amounts of data collection. This includes the increasing
proliferation of facial recognition algorithms and law enforcement use of geo-
fenced warrants. The imperfect technology underlying the former has led to

cases of misidentification, discrimination, and mass data collection, while the latter relies on collecting a haystack of information to identify a needle of an investigative lead.[9] At the time of this writing, various approaches to contact tracing for COVID-19 exposure have also raised concerns related to mass data collection.[10]

The IT industry notes that the industry provides broad societal and economic benefits built on its record of customer service. Art Coviello, former CEO and chair of one of the most prominent cybersecurity firms, RSA, points out:

> Not only is the IT sector one of our most successful industries but it also enjoys one of our largest favorable trade balances. The sector earned this position through continuous innovation and trust in the quality of its products. Sustaining it depends on keeping its reputation. Even so, for years the IT industry has been accused of not doing enough to make its products secure. There is now serious discussion in policy circles of deliberately weakening those same products through encryption backdoors meant to make it easier for the intelligence community and law enforcement to do their jobs.[11]

Coviello goes on to note that "revelations of pervasive Internet surveillance conducted by the National Security Agency in the Snowden case significantly damaged foreign sales. If the United States is not careful, we could be saying goodbye to that favorable balance of trade and America's preeminent position in IT."

Moreover, the industry points out that accommodating backdoor proposals would not accomplish the stated national security objectives. The Internet Security Alliance found, "Adversarial nations, criminals, hacktivists, and terrorists would simply obtain encryption applications from abroad. Open source versions of encryption tool kits (the algorithms in software necessary to build or embed encryption applications) have been available for decades. They have been used to create applications that encrypt voice or data communications and stored data."[12]

Finally, the industry argues that rather than impeding law enforcement digital technology has actually been a boon for law enforcement. Despite the proliferation of warrant-proof encryption, general trends in technological change will create as many opportunities to gather data as are lost. This means that even where data is encrypted, other avenues may exist to gather the same information or evidence. For example, numerous technology-related ways to gather evidence were either unavailable or only modestly available ten years ago, including location information from mobile devices, information about contacts and confederates, and an array of databases that create "digital dossiers" about individuals. Technology, far from causing law enforcement to go dark, as they claim (largely because of encryption), is instead digitally capturing activities that until recently went unrecorded. Much of this information is data about data—metadata—and has significantly fewer legal protections than so-called content data, such as the substance of electronic messages.

In reality, it is often not even necessary to know what people say in an e-mail or voice call to accomplish law enforcement aims; tracking and location, in combination with other law enforcement tactics, can be sufficient. Increasingly, metadata generated by mobile devices is stored in the cloud and accessible by lawful court order. New enabling capabilities for the Internet of Things and advances in computer power and storage capacity for big data applications using metadata can be used by law enforcement and the defense and intelligence communities in lawful ways to assist them in their missions. From this perspective law enforcement can enhance its goals by adjusting their investigative techniques to this new digital world rather than fight the inevitable continued use of encryption.

Balancing Privacy and Public Safety

The growing tensions regarding technology's dual role in society strains public trust in both the private sector and government. These debates are now a simmering pot waiting to boil over with the emergence of the latest controversy. Still, being pragmatic, it is helpful to realize that the digital age will not disappear any time soon. It is difficult to see how the encryption genie can be placed back in the bottle.

It is also helpful to appreciate that the debate is not binary. The relationship between privacy and security is not linear. No reasonable person disputes that law enforcement access to data for lawful investigative purposes is essential. However, concerns arise when the same access comes at the cost of long-term undermining of personal privacy or cybersecurity. Similarly, there is little dispute that encryption is an important element of cybersecurity, and undermining encryption, for any purpose, may itself constitute a threat to the national security.

The United States needs to accommodate immediate security needs without undermining the progress the IT sector has made in enhancing individuals' lives and protecting their rights to privacy. One path to address end-to-end encryption is for law enforcement to aim for accessing communications without breaking or undermining the protocol itself. As the Berkman Center's "Going Dark" report concluded:

> The increased availability of encryption technologies certainly impedes government surveillance under certain circumstances, and in this sense, the government is losing some surveillance opportunities. However, we concluded that the combination of technological developments and market forces is likely to fill some of these gaps and, more broadly, to ensure that the government will gain new opportunities to gather critical information from surveillance.[13]

Most important, where law enforcement agencies can procure a lawful warrant to access information, they must be able to execute it, and where private sector entities receive such a warrant, they must be required to do everything within their power to execute it. Progress lies in creating clear guidelines so that these controversies can be settled in a manner that does not undermine broader cybersecurity. This includes disputes intermediated by a trusted third party, here the judiciary, and the creation of clear guidelines that prohibit law enforcement from seeking remedies that may have impacts on cybersecurity beyond the investigation at hand. For instance, where law enforcement is repeatedly frustrated by a particular security feature or encryption technique, the solution must not be to ban or prohibit such technology. Instead, law enforcement must be permitted to seek active assistance from the concerned entity to circumvent such protections—without necessarily breaking them.

Either executive action or legislation must ensure that investigative agencies do not force private companies to undermine or break cybersecurity in its entirety. This requires broader consultations, accountability, and transparency. The former deputy attorney general Jeffrey Rosen's remarks at the DOJ's Lawful Access Summit in 2019 provide an indication of the balance to be arrived at, but to be effective they must be given the force of law.

> I am not for a moment suggesting that we should "weaken" encryption. As we confront the problem of "warrant-proof" encryption, nobody is calling for secret "back doors" to communications systems, even though that is often how the issue is misreported. As FBI Director Wray said this morning, law enforcement seeks a front door—that is, access through a transparent and publicly acknowledged system, and only once we have secured the authorization of a court. And we

don't want the keys to that door. The companies that develop these platforms should keep the keys, maintaining their users' trust by providing access to content only when a judge has ordered it.[14]

Such an approach ensures that the broader contours of systemwide cybersecurity are not determined in what is essentially a dispute between two stakeholders. Further, DOJ must develop internal guidance under which law enforcement—prior to seeking a particularly invasive solution—must be required to periodically consult with broader cybersecurity community constituents to determine if modifications or actions required by an investigative demand may leave Americans more vulnerable to cyber threats.

Similarly, if law enforcement identifies or uses a vulnerability (such as a zero-day exploit) to obtain encrypted information, it must be required to share this vulnerability with affected parties, who may then patch it. In other words, existing approaches and frameworks in the area must be dismantled and replaced by constituent elements that operate to improve overall stakeholder trust and cooperation rather than set up periodic flash points or clashes that have the opposite effect in the long run.

However, only so much can be done by executive and DOJ action. Congressional intervention is required to address existing stalemates. For instance, private entities that receive a lawful warrant must execute the same—or face penalties. At the same time, Congress may include safeguards within a reformed framework that ensures that law enforcement consult regularly with the cybersecurity community and refrain from employing techniques that may have adverse implications for the cybersecurity ecosystem as a whole.

Reimagining Intermediary Liability

In May 2020 President Donald Trump issued an executive order accusing social media companies of engaging in arbitrary conduct, political bias, and "invoking inconsistent, irrational, and groundless justifications to censor or otherwise restrict Americans' speech here at home."[15] According to the order:

Online platforms are engaging in selective censorship that is harming our national discourse. Tens of thousands of Americans have reported, among other troubling behaviors, online platforms "flagging" content as inappropriate, even though it does not violate any stated terms of service; making unannounced and unexplained changes to company policies that have the effect of disfavoring certain viewpoints; and deleting content and entire accounts with no warning, no rationale, and no recourse.

Lawmakers' scrutiny of tech companies has only expanded during the Biden administration and the Democratic-controlled Congress. For example, the congressional committee charged with investigating the January 6, 2021, attack on the US Capitol subpoenaed Facebook's parent company, Meta, as well as Google, Twitter, and Reddit to testify about how tech companies have addressed misinformation and violent extremism on their platforms. The only other issue in technology policy that comes close to the privacy-security debate in its intensity and frequency of flare-up is the debate over unlawful or harmful content proliferated on social media. At the core of this debate is the immunity granted to online intermediaries from liability for user content in the form of Section 230 of the Communications Decency Act (CDA): "No provider or user of an interactive computer service shall be treated as the publisher or speaker of any information provided by another information content provider."[16]

The breadth of this immunity has often proven to be an obstacle to ensuring that social media and other technology companies act expeditiously to remove or disable access to content identified to be harmful or unlawful. However, as history shows, this is the opposite of the effect the provision originally intended.

Sometimes referred to as the "twenty-six words which created the internet,"[17] CDA 230 was originally intended to encourage internet service providers to remove harmful content without fear of being held liable as publishers of such content. The protection was enacted in response to court decisions in the 1990s that seemed to suggest that online service providers could mitigate liability by adopting a "hands-off" approach to user content moderation.[18] In other words, the exercise of editorial control or content moderation by online service providers led to a greater likelihood that they would be found to be publishers for the purposes of liability stemming from unlawful content (rather than simply pipes for distribution of content). Like the telephone companies that are deemed common carriers or "mere conduits," the online platforms, to the extent that they primarily carried other's content, would not be liable.

However, in the years since CDA 230's enactment, courts have interpreted the provisions to confer extremely broad protections to online service providers.[19] This trend has created tensions between the entities that benefit from broad protections and other stakeholders seeking to limit the spread of certain types of harmful content. According to one expert, CDA 230 has fostered an open and diverse internet—but one where "others have suffered real and serious harms."[20] In the words of the same expert, CDA 230 has protected portals with less than laudable goals such as "a gossip website that encourages users to submit 'the dirt' and selects which submissions to post and highlight" and "social media platforms used by terrorists, even when the platform's algorithms helped make that user content visible."[21]

On the one hand, large technology companies claim that their very existence would be in doubt without the broad exemptions of CDA 230. In a *New York Times* interview, Facebook CEO Mark Zuckerberg argued that tech companies like his needed this protection to grow and provide a critical counterbalance to the growing tech companies being subsidized by China. "If we adopt a stance" he argued, "which is that 'okay, we're going to, as a country decide that we want to clip the wings of companies and make it harder for them to operate,' there are plenty of other companies who will do the work we do, and they don't have our values." On the other hand, opponents—from across the political spectrum—claim that the provision grants too much immunity and does not do enough to ensure that content that is (in their respective eyes) unlawful or harmful is removed from these platforms. To Democrats, this often means hate speech and disinformation, while to colleagues across the aisle, the provision shields intermediaries from liability for "censoring Conservative voices."[22] While the specific issues of concern differ, broad consensus exists that the provision is ripe for review.

The debate over the distinction between publishers and platforms centers on whether social media companies like Twitter and Facebook are liable for the material they publish or immune, like telecommunication platforms, from incoming and outgoing messages. While publishers are generally liable for their voices and the material they publish, platforms are immune from information transmitted by users regardless of whether the material could cause harm. Social media companies like Twitter and Facebook are much like a bookstore in that they maintain third-party materials without censoring the content and have the right to remove some materials according to company policies.

As Twitter and Facebook banned former President Trump's account after the January 6 Capitol insurrection, concerns over social media companies' measures taken under company policy and politicized decision making due to CDA 230's lack of clarity have escalated ever since. Policy makers and federal agencies have also studied CDA 230 reform for years. DOJ's 2020 report provided recommendations to reform CDA 230 in four pillars: incentivizing online platforms to address illicit content, clarifying federal government civil enforcement capabilities, promoting competition, and promoting open discourse and greater transparency. The suggestions aim to "incentivize online platforms to police responsibly content that is illegal and exploitive while continuing to encourage a vibrant, open, and competitive internet."[23]

At its core, the dispute surrounding CDA 230 presents another stark example of the systemic disunity that a hot button policy issue can bring to the fore. To improve trust between stakeholders in the digital ecosystem, it is another issue that must be urgently and decisively addressed.

Balancing Free Speech and Reputations

As discussed above, for various reasons broad consensus exists on the need to reform or at the very least conduct a detailed review of the desirability of CDA 230 in its current form. This consensus is helped by the realization that the modern digital ecosystem has evolved far past what was contemplated at the time CDA 230 was enacted. As Jeff Kosseff testified before the Senate Commerce Committee, "We are in a very different world than 1996, when 40 million people worldwide had Internet access, and being suspended from Prodigy was unlikely to have significant consequences to one's livelihood. Suspension from a large social media platform in 2020, on the other hand, has a much greater impact."[24]

However, wholesale repeal of CDA 230, according to experts, would result in instability and unpredictable outcomes—perhaps even to online service providers opting not to moderate any content for fear of legal liability as publishers. Similarly, some platforms may choose to eliminate user content in its entirety. Both these outcomes may have net negative implications for the diverse and free nature of speech on the internet.

Others, however, argue that online service providers must not be given a free pass where their conduct is consistently in bad faith—or where they demonstrate willful blindness to unlawful or harmful content on their platforms. The immediate need is for balanced outcomes that continue to uphold the internet as a diverse space for speech and expression but that, simultaneously, incentivize good moderation while providing clear and well-enshrined remedies for affected parties. Along with this, social media entities must be required to take decisive steps to remove harmful or unlawful content and develop best practices in transparency and accountability.

Several of these principles have found their way into proposed legislation, such as the Platform Accountability and Consumer Transparency (PACT)

Act. The PACT Act approach has been widely praised by a broad variety of stakeholders and is likely to result in a workable blueprint approach going forward.

Emphasizing transparency and accountability for social media content moderation practices, the proposal requires covered entities to explain their moderation practices, publish quarterly reports, and promote sharing of best practices through an NIST-administered voluntary platform.[25] The PACT Act also aims to provide streamlined processes for content-related complaints and requires entities to remove content that is determined by a court to be illegal. Importantly, the PACT Act creates carve-outs for smaller entities that may not have the content moderation resources of a large social media company. While the PACT Act is only one such proposal, it represents a robust strategy for the way ahead. Proposals that aim to enhance net trust among stakeholders in the digital ecosystem must be prioritized.

At the same time, the law must not protect companies that act in bad faith or become willfully blind to illegal conduct or content on their platforms. In this context, one possible model mirrors the approach prescribed under the Digital Millennium Copyright Act (DMCA). Under the DMCA, for online service providers to obtain immunity in relation to copyright claims, they must ensure that they adopt and implement a repeat infringer policy—that is, a system for termination of the accounts of users who commit repeated acts of infringement. In other words, an entity that ignores repeated acts of infringement is no longer eligible to receive "safe harbor" protection under the DMCA. There is no reason a similar approach cannot be taken in relation to CDA 230: entities that refuse to act against unlawful content should not be entitled to immunities. Where a platform becomes a haven for unlawful content on a recurring basis, the law must permit action against the entity. Such an approach will ensure that bad actors do not reap the benefits that CDA 230 is meant to grant to entities that improve the diversity of content online.

However, as in the case with the privacy and security debate, more groundwork may be needed before legislative intervention. As some experts have suggested, given the controversial nature of the issue and the wildly varying reasons to recommend its reform, further fact-finding may be needed.

A Systematic Process for Integrating Tech into Modern Public Policy

The issues highlighted above illustrate clearly that in the digital age policies cannot be effectively managed within a disparate and uncoordinated government structure. There needs to be a conscious, comprehensive, and deliberate digital strategy established and run from the White House. We have proposed an Office of Digital Security Strategy to move toward this enlightened and contemporary structure. Our leading private organizations are adopting these digital transformation strategies, and our most intense adversaries have long since adapted and implemented similar methods, much to our current disadvantage.

There is an old adage in IT and security: "You can't secure what you can't manage, and you can't manage what you can't secure." In the civilian agencies, the lack of organizational tenure; the lack of sufficient resources, human and financial; the decentralized nature of overall operational and governance responsibility; and an IT environment that requires agility and scalable operating discipline that does not exist make the task of securing government systems virtually insurmountable.

Given the importance of digital technology in the running of our government, the need to manage and secure critical infrastructure, and the ongoing productivity benefits of continued innovation, a project on this scale needs to be one of the highest priorities for the highest levels of government. Shouldn't the responsibility for digital and IT infrastructure warrant a cabinet level–like position, with full authority and funding? While it has been noted that there is skepticism in Congress about "IT Projects," there really is no alternative to getting this done. Historically, Americans have shown time and time again an ability to achieve anything we set our minds to.

It is time to bring the digital infrastructure of the federal government into the twenty-first century. The government can and should be reaping more of the productivity and operational benefits of the digital age. Whether it is tax collection, healthcare.gov, or background investigation data, there is far too much at stake to not do a better job of protecting government infrastructures. Cybersecurity is an issue that cuts across individual departments and all sectors of the economy, an issue that is everywhere but is treated as if it is nowhere, since it lacks a bureaucratic power base.

CONCLUSION

Larry Clinton

The Internet Security Alliance undertook the research for this book before the Russian and Chinese systemic cyberattacks of 2020 and 2021, bearing out the premise that the cybersecurity of the United States must be reconceptualized. What have we learned from this exercise of rethinking the issue, and how can we do better? To these questions we offer five summary observations.

Cybersecurity Is Not Simple

Digital technology is remarkably deceptive. As a personal example, my son, who will soon turn thirty, is severely autistic. Despite two and a half decades of daily therapy and education, he cannot add two and three. But give him an iPad, and with very limited instruction, he can surf the Web, find music and videos, and entertain himself for hours.

It is perhaps because of the deceptively simple operation of digital technology that one may assume that there must be a fairly simple—and inexpensive—way to secure it. What we have seen is a parade of simple prescriptions such as "all one needs to do is practice good 'hygiene' or comply with sensible regulation, or responsibly share information." Very often the simple prescribed steps are for others to take: if only industry would create "secure" devices, if only government would set clear standards and regulations or establish adequate liability, if only industry behaved responsibly, and so on.

However, in reality, digital technology is extremely intricate and complicated. The internet is not a single network; it is composed of networks that consist of millions and millions of lines of code interwoven together, absent any grand plan as to how it ought to be used and by whom. Its original intent was not to be the guardian of information but to be the gateway to information. This information is tremendously valuable and as such creates a uniquely large motive for attack.

Because of its complexity, a sustainably secure system will demand, at the outset, an appreciation of the full context of the issue. Moreover, as demonstrated throughout this book, a sustainable program will thoughtfully integrate the technical, economic, and public policy dimensions in such a way as to maintain the viability and benefits of the digital age while developing a more realistic process for managing security at an acceptable level. As illustrated in several chapters in part 2 of this book, the context of a practical security system may vary considerably even with respect to critical industry sectors. For example, the functional economics in the defense sector are dramatically different from the economics that govern the healthcare sector. In addition, digitization may in itself fundamentally alter the context of a sector, as demonstrated in the utility and telecommunications sectors, and thus demand policies that are inappropriate in other sectors like IT or retail.

We believe that constructing a viable public policy is both necessary and possible. Several of the "simple" solutions noted above, as well as the steps suggested in part 1, might well be integrated into such a system of systems. There is one thing of which we can be certain: this will not be simple.

Beware of Fighting the Last War

Another irony in light of the successful Russian SolarWinds and Microsoft server attacks of 2020 is that they were recognized just a few weeks after the widely praised work of the Department of Homeland Security's Cybersecurity and Infrastructure Security Agency in securing the 2020 presidential election, called the most secure election in US history. This feat was especially noteworthy as all eighteen intelligence agencies of the federal government found that the Russian government had compromised the previous, 2016, presidential election.

This juxtaposition of successful attacks by Russia and China on the United States is reminiscent of the creation of the Maginot Line by France following World War I. The Maginot Line was a set of fortifications on the France-Germany border designed to protect France from German invasion and was quickly and easily compromised by Germany at the outset of World War II largely because it was built on the assumption that World War II would look much like World War I. The Maginot Line has now become one of military history's most famous reminders that one should never assume the next conflict will look like the last. It is a mistake to focus on the previous war.

Some have suggested that CISA was guilty of fighting the previous war because it focused on election security when there were greater threats—as it turned out—from Russia and China. Such a claim is dramatically misguided. CISA was not designed, and certainly not resourced and enabled, to fend off an attack such as the one on the SolarWinds and Microsoft servers, or the ransomware and other cybercriminal activities that we have documented. Former CISA director, Chris Krebs, and his team did a terrific job handling an extremely complicated task: coordinating the security of more than fifty different electoral systems in a highly charged political climate. But sadly, we need to do more, and we cannot expect either government or the private sector to be solely responsible.

The more appropriate cyber analogy to the Maginot Line comes from the still largely prevalent focus on cybersecurity in entity-specific terms, with an emphasis on technical/operational security. As we discussed in chapters 1 and 3, in particular, these are inadequate conceptualizations of the digital issue.

In order for the United States to effectively compete in the digital era, it will need to look forward and develop new structures and understandings of how the digital age has changed the world in which we live. As discussed in chapter 13, digitalization has altered how our economy functions. It has created an asymmetric battlefield of cyber weaponry that has altered our notions of national defense. As almost any parent of a Millennial or Gen-Zer has observed, it has changed our notions of what privacy is. There is virtually no segment of American life—apart from government structures—that has not changed radically in response to the digital era.

Moreover, as detailed in chapter 4, relying on the traditional methods and structures to address the complexity of the still-evolving digital threat is doomed to failure. In contrast, as illustrated in chapter 2, China, which had the "benefit" of essentially starting anew with its reopening in the late 1970s and 1980s (the dawn of the digital era), has understood and embraced digitalization in a much more integrated and holistic fashion that has generated significant pragmatic advancements from the Chinese government's perspective.

Government will need to embrace change to a far greater degree than it has to date, including a much more fulsome and novel partnership with the private sector if the United States is to catch up with many of its adversaries and once again achieve a true leadership role in the digital century. Some suggestions in that direction are articulated in chapter 6.

We Are in This Together

Starting with the National Strategy to Secure Cyberspace issued by the Bush administration in the wake of the 9/11 attacks, the philosophy guiding cybersecurity in the United States has been one of partnership between the public and private sectors. Of course, in many respects, in a democracy where government is empowered and serves at the pleasure of the governed—the private sector—there is always a partnership between the two. Unfortunately, the nature of the relationship between the public and private sectors does not seem to have matured in the twenty years since the initial National Cyber Strategy was articulated.

There is broad consensus, which the authors of this volume share, that a robust public-private partnership is required to create a reasonably and suitably secure digital environment. Unfortunately, that has not developed. The supposed innovation of a modernized partnership is largely rhetorical. A new digitally sensitive partnership model that recognizes the aligned but differing perspectives and needs of each party created by the fact that they are using, and in fact are dependent on, the same technological system has not emerged. In most cases, the partnership suggested in the initial strategy and successive iterations of it is essentially no different from the partnership between the public and private sectors of the postwar industrial era.

When very young children are brought together on their initial play dates parents often will observe that they are not actually playing *with* each other. They are simply playing *next to* each other—a phenomenon termed "parallel play." That phenomenon is an apt metaphor for the actual public-private partnership between industry and government as it relates to cybersecurity.

In reality, both the public and private sectors design, fund, and operate various initiatives to manage the security of their systems, but to a large degree they stand next to each to other and do not form a common or collective defense, which, as we have demonstrated repeatedly, has not worked. Even when a project, such as information sharing, is established and repeatedly trumpeted as a priority, the reality, as we document extensively in chapter 4, is that it generally does not receive sufficient government support or participation. Government does share with government and industry shares with industry—parallel play—but the barriers to effective collaboration, which range from lack of trust to poorly adapted structures to inadequate funding, persist nearly a quarter century after they were originally promulgated.

To be fair, there have been efforts, mostly conceptual, to modernize and enliven the partnership model. One of the most sophisticated of these efforts is the National Infrastructure Protection Plan (NIPP), discussed in chapter 6. The NIPP correctly observes that it is the private sector that owns and operates the vast majority of critical infrastructure and hence has an obligation to secure it. However, the NIPP also recognizes that security is not an absolute state. There are levels of security, and the public and private sectors have different levels of security based legitimately on their own missions and needs. The public sector, which legitimately assesses security on a commercial level as required to maintain their mission, has a higher risk tolerance than does the federal government, which has economic as well as a range of noneconomic security needs.

This legitimate difference in risk assessment cuts to the core of difference between the public and private sectors: although security is a concern for both public and private entities, they each, for legitimate reasons, assess risk differently and hence fund security on a different basis. This reasonable but problematic gap between commercial-level security and national-level security has been recognized and articulated for years. However, like the issues plaguing information sharing, government has not taken the steps to address the gap. Many in government instead choose to point fingers at the private sector, asserting that reasonable security by the private sector ought to be based on government needs irrespective of the nature of the threats, which include attacks on private systems by nation-states, or the cost of adequate national-level security and its suitability based on traditional business models.

What all this points to is an immature appreciation of the nature of the public-private relationship in the digital age. To address this there will need to be renewed and sincere commitment coupled with structural changes, several of which are suggested in chapter 6.

Embrace Digital Transition

As someone who has worked in and with government in Washington, DC, for over thirty-five years, I have learned that the most powerful force in government is not partisanship. It is not money. It is not policy. It is turf.

As we have analyzed the nature of the cybersecurity issue in this volume, a constant theme has been the existence of traditional structures and methods that have been unsuitable fits for the uniqueness of the digital security issue. Several decades into the digital age there is virtually no significant entity in government that is charged specifically with conceptualizing how to address the issues raised by the dominant technology, which is the nervous system of virtually every aspect of modern life. Instead, there is a disembodied series of structures and agencies, sometimes working at cross purposes, that bring their own narrow perspectives and agendas to what needs to be a broad and coherent strategy. This is the case with the public sector and private, local, and federal law enforcement, the military, and nation-states—even those who are at least ostensibly friends and partners.

Obviously, breaking down these barriers will be difficult, but it can be done, and it certainly can be initiated. In fact, there are multiple organizations around the world—from governments from China to Estonia to all manner of private entities that have gone through a conscientious process of digital transformation.

As outlined in chapter 6, corporate leaders around the world have developed a set of principles for the most senior leaders to follow in engaging in this transformative process, beginning with looking at digital issues through a strategic, as opposed to an operational, lens. Management processes have evolved to bring agile structures into action, which are more suited to the fast-changing digital environment. Key to many of these modern structures is the use of clear goals and objectives that are readily evaluated and modified to improve effectiveness or the discontinuing of programs that are less successful than anticipated. These structures can be adapted and adopted by government.

These modern processes, together with a more egalitarian process that brings the public and private sectors into a more operative partnership, are at the heart of the proposed new White House office of digital strategy and security discussed in chapter 5. As noted, these features could fairly easily, and at minimal cost, be integrated into the new Office of the National Cybersecurity Director established in the 2020 National Defense Authorization Act.

Money, Money, Money

As virtually every chapter in this book demonstrates, it is all but inconceivable that the United States can secure its cyber systems with investment at anything like its current relatively minimal levels, notwithstanding the "downpayments" proposed by the Biden administration. However, it is also true that the amount of money required to make substantial improvements in cybersecurity pale in comparison to many other national objectives. Even a fivefold increase in the FBI's budget to fight cybercrime would be less than the proposed cost of a new FBI building.

Similar increases in education funding for cybersecurity programs, perhaps coupled with aggressive recruitment programs such as for our armed forces and generous scholarships (even free tuition) in return for government employment for targeted communities are, in the grand scheme, a minuscule portion of the federal budget. Making the proposed enhancements of the Cyber Director position inclusive of the sorts of studies of cyber programs and adaptation and expansion of effective programs would be less than a billion dollars. Even tax breaks to small companies that certify use of the cyber programs the government has demonstrated are effective would be a paltry piece of the federal budget.

Moreover, direct federal outlays might not even be necessary in some respects. Simply demonstrating empirically the effectiveness of various cyber standards and practices as cost-effective would likely stimulate broad voluntary adoption at virtually no cost to government. Finding and adapting market incentive programs in various sectors and applying them to the digital world could similarly generate substantial improvements without substantial government expenditures.

Given the enormous costs of our current inadequate cybersecurity, the price of implementing a thoughtful, pro-market, and adequately supported digital strategy would be one of the most sensible investments government can make in its own self-interests and the interests of its citizens. We have seen this before, for example, when the government established NASA during the Space Race, and we can and should do it again for cybersecurity.

NOTES

FOREWORD

1. Richard Powers, *The Overstory: A Novel* (New York: Norton, 2018), 72.
2. Joel Wallenstrom, "The Consequences of Choosing Speed over Security," *Forbes*, February 26, 2021, www.forbes.com/sites/forbestechcouncil/2021/02/26/the-consequences -of-choosing-speed-over-security/?sh=2db0dd6a411a.

INTRODUCTION

1. Kimberly Mlitz, "Cybersecurity Spending Worldwide 2021," March 29, 2021, www .statista.com/statistics/991304/worldwide-cybersecurity-spending/.
2. Press Briefing by Press Secretary Jen Psaki and Deputy National Security Advisor for Cyber and Emerging Technology Anne Neuberger, February 17, 2021, www.whitehouse .gov/briefing-room/press-briefings/2021/02/17/press-briefing-by-press-secretary-jen -psaki-and-deputy-national-security-advisor-for-cyber-and-emerging-technology-anne -neuberger-february-17-2021/.
3. Press Briefing.
4. Zolan Kanno-Youngs and David E. Sanger, "U.S. Accuses China of Hacking Microsoft," *New York Times,* July 19, 2021, updated August 26, 2021, www.nytimes.com/2021/07/19 /us/politics/microsoft-hacking-china-biden.html.
5. Kanno-Youngs and Sanger.
6. Matt Egan, "Colonial Pipeline Is Restarting but the Gas Crisis Isn't Over," CNN, May 13, 2021, www.cnn.com/2021/05/13/business/gas-shortage-colonial-pipeline/index.html.
7. Verizon, "2021 Data Breach Investigations Report," 2021, www.verizon.com/business /resources/reports/dbir/2021/results-and-analysis/.
8. International Data Corporation, "2021 Ransomware Study: Where You Are Matters!," July 2021, www.idc.com/getdoc.jsp?containerId=US48093721.
9. FBI, "Ransomware Awareness for Holidays and Weekends," September 2, 2021, www.cisa .gov/uscert/ncas/alerts/aa21-243a.
10. Trevor Hunnicutt, Arshad Mohammed, and Andrew Osborn, "U.S. Imposes Wide Array of Sanctions on Russia for 'Malign' Actions," Reuters, April 15, 2021, www.reuters.com /world/middle-east/us-imposes-wide-array-sanctions-russia-malign-actions-2021 -04-15/.

11. C. Biesecker, "White House Attributes SolarWinds Hack to Russian Agency," *Defense Daily*, April 15, 2021, www.defensedaily.com/white-house-attributes-solarwinds-hack -russian-agency/cyber/.

12. Jim Himes, "Himes Calls for Stronger Cyber Response from Biden Administration," April 15, 2021, https://himes.house.gov/media-center/press-releases/himes-calls-stronger -cyber-response-biden-administration.

13. "The Way Forward on Homeland Security: House Committee on Homeland Security," House Homeland Security Committee, March 17, 2021, https://homeland.house.gov /activities/hearings/the-way-forward-on-homeland-security.

14. "Understanding and Responding to the SolarWinds Supply Chain Attack: The Federal Perspective," Homeland Security & Governmental Affairs Committee, March 18, 2021, www.hsgac.senate.gov/understanding-and-responding-to-the-solarwinds-supply-chain -attack-the-federal-perspective.

15. "Cyberspace Solarium Commission CO-CHAIRS Issue Statement on Colonial PIPE- LINE CYBERATTACK," May 10, 2021, www.king.senate.gov/newsroom/press-releases /cyberspace-solarium-commission-co-chairs-issue-statement-on-colonial-pipeline -cyberattack.

16. "Leaders of House Homeland, Transportation Panels Seek Details on Interagency Efforts after Pipeline Hack," May 12, 2021, https://insidecybersecurity.com/daily-news/leaders -house-homeland-transportation-panels-seek-details-interagency-efforts-after?s=na.

17. "Executive Order on Improving the Nation's Cybersecurity," White House, May 12, 2021, www.whitehouse.gov/briefing-room/presidential-actions/2021/05/12/executive-order -on-improving-the-nations-cybersecurity/.

18. "Munich Cyber Security Conference 2021," Security Network Munich, 2021, www.the haguesecuritydelta.com/events/event/2592-munich-cyber-security-conference-2021 -2021-04-29.

CHAPTER 1. THE ECONOMICS OF CYBERSECURITY

1. Troels Oerting Presentation, G-20 Digital Security Working Group, February 4, 2020, Riyadh, Saudi Arabia.

2. Steve Morgan, "Cybercrime to Cost the World $10.5 Trillion Annually by 2025," *Cyber- crime Magazine*, November 13, 2020, https://cybersecurityventures.com/cybercrime -damage-costs-10-trillion-by-2025/.

3. M. Szmigiera, "G20: GDP by Country 2019 and 2025," Statista, April 1, 2021, www .statista.com/statistics/722944/g20-country-gdp-levels/.

4. Luis Martinez, "Intel Heads Now Fear Cyber Attack More than Terror," *ABC News*, March 13, 2013, https://abcnews.go.com/Blotter/intel-heads-now-fear-cyber-attack -terror/story?id=18719593.

5. Dan C. Coats, Statement for the Record, Worldwide Threat Assessment of the US Intelli- gence Community, Senate Select Committee on Intelligence, Director of National Intel- ligence, May 11, 2017, www.dni.gov/files/documents/Newsroom/Testimonies/SSCI %20Unclassified%20SFR%20-%20Final.pdf.

6. Julian E. Barnes, "Russia Continues to Meddle in US Elections to Help Trump, US Intel- ligence Says," *New York Times*, August 8, 2020, www.nytimes.com/2020/08/07/us /politics/russia-china-trump-biden-election-interference.html.

7. Marcus Aurelius, *Mediations: A New Translation, with an Introduction, by Gregory Hays* (New York: Modern Library, 2002).

8. Verizon, "Verizon Data Breach Investigations Report (2021)," 7, www.verizon.com /business/resources/reports/2021-data-breach-investigations-report.pdf.

9. See chapters 9, 11, 7, 8, and 10, respectively.

10. Internet Security Alliance and National Association of Corporate Directors, "Cyber-Risk Oversight Director's Handbook Series," NACD, 2014, www.nacdonline.org/files/NACD %20Cyber-Risk%20Oversight%20Executive%20Summary.pdf.

11. Steve Morgan, "Cybercrime to Cost the World $10.5 Trillion Annually by 2025," *Cybercrime Magazine*, January 22, 2021, https://cybersecurityventures.com/cybercrime-damage -costs-10-trillion-by-2025/.

12. Michael Daniel, Cybersecurity Coordinator, Obama administration, comment during meeting with Internet Security Alliance Board of Directors, October 29, 2013.

13. Adam Janofsky, "Companies Struggle to Stay on Top of Security Patches," *Wall Street Journal*, May 29, 2018, www.wsj.com/articles/companies-struggle-to-stay-on-top-of-security -patches-1527645840.

14. Stephen Streng, "Adulterating More than Food: The Cyber Risk to Food Processing and Manufacturing," Food Protection and Defense Institute, September 2019, 6, https:// foodprotection.dl8.umn.edu/sites/foodprotection.umn.edu/files/2020-06/fpdi-food -ics-cybersecurity-white-paper.pdf.

15. McAfee, "Economic Impact of Cyber Crime: No Slowing Down," February 2018, 4, www.mcafee.com/enterprise/en-us/assets/reports/restricted/rp-economic-impact -cybercrime.pdf.

16. Casey Crane, "42 Cyber Attack Statistics by Year: A Look at the Last Decade," Infosec Insights, November 20, 2020, https://sectigostore.com/blog/42-cyber-attack-statistics -by-year-a-look-at-the-last-decade/.

17. Microsoft, "Ghost in the Shell: Investigating Web Shell Attacks," February 4, 2020, www .microsoft.com/security/blog/2020/02/04/ghost-in-the-shell-investigating-web-shell -attacks/.

18. Risk Based Security, "2019 Year End Data Breach QuickView Report," February 2020, 4, https://pages.riskbasedsecurity.com/hubfs/Reports/2019/2019%20Year%20End %20Data%20Breach%20QuickView%20Report.pdf.

19. Patrick Flesch, "Five Biggest Cyberattacks of 2019 and Lessons Learned," Gordon Flesch Company, November 7, 2019, www.gflesch.com/elevity-it-blog/biggest-cyberattacks-2019.

20. Ross Anderson and Tyler Moore, "The Economics of Information Security," University of Cambridge, Computer Laboratory, November 2006, 2, www.researchgate.net /publication/216757755_The_Economics_of_Information_Security/link/549b102 f0cf2d6581ab2e132/download.

21. Sarah Li Cain, "What Happens If Your Bank Account Is Hacked?," *Consumerism Commentary*, July 15, 2020, https://www.consumerismcommentary.com/what-happens-if-your -bank-account-is-hacked/.

22. Anderson and Moore, "Economics of Information Security," 3.

23. Melissa Hathaway, "Patching Our Digital Future Is Unsustainable and Dangerous," Center for International and Governance Innovation, www.cigionline.org/articles/patching -our-digital-future-unsustainable-and-dangerous.

24. Andrea Bonime-Blanc, *The Reputation Risk Handbook: Surviving and Thriving in the Age of Hyper-Transparency* (New York: Routledge, 2014), 35.

25. Ivan Levingston and Jenny Surane, "Equifax Breach a Year Later: Record Profits, Share Revival," *Chicago Tribune*, December 12, 2018, www.chicagotribune.com/business/ct -biz-equifax-data-breach-20180907-story.html.

26. Hathaway, "Patching Our Digital Future."

27. "The Dark Web: DDoS Attacks Sell for as Low as $10 per Hour," The Realtime Report, August 26, 2020, www.missioncriticalmagazine.com/articles/93185-the-dark-web-ddos -attacks-sell-for-as-low-as-10-per-hour#:~:text=A%20basic%20targeted%20malware %20attack,to%20weapon%20for%20online%20extortion.

28. Miguel Gomez, "Dark Web Price Index 2020: Check All 2020 Dark Web Prices," PrivacyAffairs, February 25, 2021, www.privacyaffairs.com/dark-web-price-index -2020/.

29. Lauren McCamy, "7 Things You Can Hire a Hacker to Do and How Much It Will (Generally) Cost," *Business Insider*, November 27, 2018, www.businessinsider.com/things-hire -hacker-to-do-how-much-it-costs-2018-11.

30. "The Dark Web: DDoS Attacks Sell for As Low As $10 Per Hour."

31. Digital Shadows, "The Ecosystem of Phishing: From Minnows to Marlins," February 20, 2020, https://www.digitalshadows.com/blog-and-research/the-ecosystem-of-phishing/.

32. McAfee, "Economic Impact of Cybercrime, 3.

33. "Only 1% of Cybercrimes Prosecuted," Information Security Buzz, May 29, 2019, www .informationsecuritybuzz.com/expert-comments/only-1-of-cybercrimes-prosecuted /#:~:text=A%20recent%20report%20from%20Richard,of%20computer%20hacking %20last%20year.

34. McAfee, "Economic Impact of Cybercrime—No Slowing Down," CSIS, February 3–4, 2018, https://csis-website-prod.s3.amazonaws.com/s3fs-public/publication/economic -impact-cybercrime.pdf.

35. "Coronavirus in the U.S.: Latest Map and Case Count," *New York Times*, March 3, 2020, www.nytimes.com/interactive/2020/us/coronavirus-us-cases.html.

36. McKinsey, "The Future of Work after COVID-19," February 18, 2021, www.mckinsey .com/featured-insights/future-of-work/the-future-of-work-after-covid-19.

37. Aamer Baig, Bryce Hall, Paul Jenkins, Eric Lamarre, and Brian McCarthy, "The COVID-19 Recovery Will Be Digital: A Plan for the First 90 Days," McKinsey Digital, May 14, 2020, www.mckinsey.com/business-functions/mckinsey-digital/our-insights/the-covid-19 -recovery-will-be-digital-a-plan-for-the-first-90-days.

38. Michael Sentones, "Global Survey: The Cybersecurity Reality of the COVID-19 Remote Workforce," Crowdstrike, May 11, 2020, www.crowdstrike.com/blog/global-survey-the -cybersecurity-reality-of-the-covid-19-remote-workforce/.

39. Catherine Stupp and James Rundle, "Companies Battle Another Pandemic: Skyrocketing Hacking Attempts," *Wall Street Journal*, August 24, 2020, www.wsj.com/articles /companies-battle-another-pandemic-skyrocketing-hacking-attempts-11598068863 ?mod=djemCybersecruityPro&tpl=cy.

40. Jessica Davis, "Report: Rise in COVID-19 Vaccine Social Engineering, BEC, Phishing," HealthITSecurity, January 21, 2021, https://healthitsecurity.com/news/report-rise-in -covid-19-vaccine-social-engineering-bec-phishing.

41. "New Research Shows Significant Increase in Phishing Attacks since the Pandemic Began Straining Corporate IT Security Teams," *Security Magazine RSS*, August 28, 2020, www .securitymagazine.com/articles/93194-new-research-shows-significant-increase-in -phishing-attacks-since-the-pandemic-began-straining-corporate-it-security-teams.

42. "VMware Carbon Black Global Threat Report," VMware, July 2020, 5, www.carbonblack
    .com/wp-content/uploads/VMWCB-Report-GTR-Extended-Enterprise-Under-Threat
    -Global.pdf.

43. Sentones, "Global Survey."

44. Anderson and Moore, "Economics of Information Security."

45. "Social contract, in political philosophy, an actual or hypothetical compact, or agreement,
    between the ruled and their rulers, defining the rights and duties of each. In primeval
    times, according to the theory, individuals were born into an anarchic state of nature,
    which was happy or unhappy according to the particular version. They then, by exercising
    natural reason, formed a society (and a government) by means of a contract among them-
    selves." *Encyclopedia Britannica*, www.britannica.com/topic/social-contract.

46. Richard A. Clarke and Robert K. Knake, *The Fifth Domain: Defending Our Country, Our
    Companies, and Ourselves in the Age of Cyber Threats* (Hoboken, NJ: Wiley, 2019), 9.

47. Clarke and Knake, 10.

48. Internet Security Alliance, "Internet Security Alliance: The Advanced Persistent Threat:
    Practical Controls That Small and Medium-Sized Business Leaders Should Consider
    Implementing," June 6, 2013, http://isalliance.org/publications/2013-06-06-ISA_APT
    _Paper-Practical_Controls_for_SMBs.pdf?_hstc=216482249.e7c0af0efdd41a653140
    fecad23cdf89.1452124800044.1452124800045.1452124800046.1&_hssc=216482249
    .1.1452124800047&_hsfp=3972014050.

CHAPTER 2. DANGEROUS AND EFFECTIVE

1. Sun Tzu and Samuel B. Griffith, *The Art of War* (Oxford: Clarendon Press, 1964).

2. Hong Shen, "Building a Digital Silk Road? Situating the Internet in China's Belt and Road
   Initiative," *International Journal of Communication* 12 (2018), https://ijoc.org/index.php
   /ijoc/article/view/8405.

3. US Department of the Treasury, Major Foreign Holders of Treasury Securities, updated
   January 18, 2022, https://ticdata.treasury.gov/Publish/mfh.txt.

4. Paul Mozur and Steven Lee Myers, "Xi's Gambit: China Plans for a World without
   American Technology," *New York Times*, July 19, 2021, www.nytimes.com/2021/03/10
   /business/china-us-tech-rivalry.html.

5. Dic Lo and Mei Wu, "The State and Industrial Policy in Chinese Economic Development," International Labor Organization, May 5, 2014, www.ilo.org/global/publications
   /books/WCMS_315676/lang--en/index.htm.

6. Jane Perlez and Yufan Huang, "Behind China's $1 Trillion Plan to Shake Up the Economic
   Order," *New York Times*, May 13, 2017, www.nytimes.com/2017/05/13/business/china
   -railway-one-belt-one-road-1-trillion-plan.html.

7. James Lewis, "Section 301 Investigation: China's Acts, Policies and Practices Related
   to Technology Transfer, Intellectual Property, and Innovation," Center for Strategic
   and International Studies, April 2020, 3, https://csis-website-prod.s3.amazonaws.com
   /s3fs-public/publication/200422_Lewis_Investigation_v4.pdf?vRNUKyco1phYotvBN
   qET9kuz2GjKNAsL.

8. Kara Frederick, "The 5G Future Is Not Just about Huawei," *Foreign Policy*, May 3, 2019,
   https://foreignpolicy.com/2019/05/03/the-5g-future-is-not-just-about-huawei/.

9. Shen, "Building a Digital Silk Road?"

10. See https://energyandcleanair.org/publications/costs-of-air-pollution-from-fossil-fuels/.

11. Jonathan Kaiman, "China's Toxic Air Pollution Resembles Nuclear Winter, Say Scientists," *The Guardian*, February 24, 2014, www.theguardian.com/world/2014/feb/25/china-toxic-air-pollution-nuclear-winter-scientists.

12. Congressional Research Service, "China's Economic Rise: History, Trends, Challenges, and Implications for the United States," June 25, 2019, 2, https://fas.org/sgp/crs/row/RL33534.pdf.

13. Congressional Research Service.

14. Andrew Chatzky and James McBride, "China's Massive Belt and Road Initiative," Council on Foreign Relations, January 28, 2020, www.cfr.org/backgrounder/chinas-massive-belt-and-road-initiative.

15. Dic Lo and Mei Wu, "The State and Industrial Policy."

16. Dic Lo and Mei Wu.

17. Dic Lo and Mei Wu.

18. Zhuang Rongwen, "In-Depth Study and Implementation of President Xi's Important Thoughts on Cyber Power," Cyberspace Administration of China, May 4, 2020, www.cidf.net/n1/2020/0504/c429159-31696813.html.

19. Perlez and Huang, "Behind China's $1 Trillion Plan."

20. Lewis, "Section 301 Investigation."

21. Tanner Brown, "Five Things to Know about China's Promised Crackdown on Intellectual-Property Theft," MarketWatch, November 25, 2019, www.marketwatch.com/story/five-things-to-know-about-chinas-promised-crackdown-on-intellectual-property-theft-2019-11-25.

22. Handong Wu, "The Construction of Intellectual Property Culture in Contemporary Chinese," China National Intellectual Property Administration, August 26, 2009, http://ip.people.com.cn/n/2014/1229/c391950-26295092.html.

23. United States Trade Representative, "2016 Report to Congress on China's WTO Compliance," January 17, 2017, www.andi.com.co/Uploads/2016-China-Report-to-Congress_636536196041366302.pdf.

24. "Findings of the Investigation into China's Acts, Policies, and Practices Related to Technology Transfer, Intellectual Property, and Innovation under Section 301 of the Trade Act of 1974," USTR Report to Congress, March 22, 2018, 23, https://ustr.gov/sites/default/files/Section%20301%20FINAL.PDF.

25. "How China's Economic Aggression Threatens the Technologies and Intellectual Property of the United States and the World," White House Office of Trade and Manufacturing Policy, June 2018, 4, https://china.usc.edu/sites/default/files/article/attachments/white-house-china-threatens-us-intellectual-property-2018-06.pdf.

26. Remarks, General Keith Alexander, Director, NSA, on Cyber Espionage and the Theft of U.S. Intellectual Property and Technology, Hearing Before the Subcommittee on Oversight and Investigations of the Committee on Energy and Commerce House of Representatives, July 9, 2013.

27. John C. Mallery, Brian David A. Mussington, and Jonathan P. Gill, "Defending Our Economic Future against Cyber Threats to Innovation," Institute for Defense Analyses, July 14, 2016, 3, www.jstor.org/stable/pdf/resrep22679.pdf.

28. Lewis, "Section 301 Investigation."

29. Shen, "Building a Digital Silk Road?"

30. Christopher Ashley Ford, "Huawei and Its Siblings, the Chinese Tech Giants: National Security and Foreign Policy Implications," Multilateral Action on Sensitive Technologies (MAST)

Conference, US Department of State, September 11, 2019, www.state.gov/huawei-and-its
-siblings-the-chinese-tech-giants-national-security-and-foreign-policy-implications/.

31. Chuin-Wei Yap, "State Support Helped Fuel Huawei's Global Rise," *Wall Street Journal*, December 25, 2019, www.wsj.com/articles/state-support-helped-fuel-huaweis-global -rise-11577280736.

32. Chuin-Wei Yap, "State Support."

33. Stefan Halper, "China: The Three Warfares," Prepared for Andy Marshall, Director, Office of Net Assessment Office of the Secretary of Defense, Washington, DC, May 2013, 11, https://cryptome.org/2014/06/prc-three-wars.pdf.

34. Seradettin Yilmaz and Liu Changming, "China's Belt and Road Strategy in Eurasia and Euro-Atlanticism," *Europe and Asia Studies* 70, no. 2 (2018): 270–71, www.tandfonline .com/doi/abs/10.1080/09668136.2018.1435777.

35. Chuin-Wei Yap, "State Support."

36. Chuin-Wei Yap.

37. Paul Triolo, Kevin Allison, Clarise Brown, and Kelsey Broderick, "The Digital Silk Road: Expanding China's Digital Footprint," Eurasia Group, April 2020, www.eurasiagroup.net /files/upload/Digital-Silk-Road-Expanding-China-Digital-Footprint.pdf.

38. Triolo et al.

39. Chuin-Wei Yap, "State Support."

40. Jonathan E. Hillman, "A 'China Model?' Beijing's Promotion of Alternative Global Norms and Standards," Center for Strategic and International Studies, Statement before U.S.-China Economic and Security Review Commission, March 13, 2020, www.csis.org /analysis/china-model-beijings-promotion-alternative-global-norms-and-standards.

41. Ngaire Woods, "Whose Aid? Whose Influence? China, Emerging Donors and the Silent Revolution in Development Assistance," *International Affairs* 84, no. 6 (2018): 1205–21, https://doi.org/10.1111/j.1468-2346.2008.00765.

42. Woods, "Whose Aid?"

43. Robert Menendez, "The New Big Brother: China and Digital Authoritarianism," Democratic Staff Report Prepared for the Use of the Committee on Foreign Relations, United States Senate, July 21, 2020, www.foreign.senate.gov/press/ranking/release/ranking -member-menendez-publishes-new-minority-report-the-new-big-brother_china-and -digital-authoritarianism-.

44. Shen, "Building a Digital Silk Road?"

45. Gurmeet Kanwal, "Pakistan's Gwadar Port: A New Naval Base in China's String of Pearls in the Indo-Pacific," Center for Strategic and International Studies, April 2, 2018, www .csis.org/analysis/pakistans-gwadar-port-new-naval-base-chinas-string-pearls-indo -pacific.

46. Kanwal.

47. Kirk Semple, "China Extends Reach in the Caribbean, Unsettling the US," *New York Times*, November 8, 2020, www.nytimes.com/2020/11/08/world/americas/china-caribbean .html.

48. Ernesto Londono and Leticia Casado, "Brazil Needs Vaccines; China Is Benefiting," *New York Times*, March 15, 2021, www.nytimes.com/2021/03/15/world/americas/brazil -vaccine-china.html.

49. Ted Piccone, "China's Long Game on Human Rights at the United Nations," Brookings Institution, September 2018, www.brookings.edu/wp-content/uploads/2018/09/FP _20181009_china_human_rights.pdf.

50. Erik Brattberg, "China's Relations with U.S. Allies and Partners in Europe," Carnegie Endowment for Peace, April 5, 2018, https://carnegieendowment.org/2018/04/05/china-s-relations-with-u.s.-allies-and-partners-in-europe-pub-75977.

51. Chuin-Wei Yap, "State Support."

52. Chuin-Wei Yap.

53. Lindsay Maizland and Andrew Chatzky, "Huawei: China's Controversial Tech Giant," Council on Foreign Relations, August 6, 2020, www.cfr.org/backgrounder/huawei-chinas-controversial-tech-giant.

54. Arjun Kharpal, "Huawei Pivots to Software with Google-like Ambitions as U.S. Sanctions Hit Hardware Business," updated April 26, 2021, CNBC, www.cnbc.com/2021/04/26/huawei-focuses-on-software-as-us-sanctions-hurt-hardware-business.html.

55. Kharpal.

56. Triolo et al., "The Digital Silk Road."

57. Joakim Reiter, "5G After COVID," Lawfare, April 16, 2020, www.lawfareblog.com/5g-after-covid-19.

58. Reiter.

59. Reiter.

60. Triolo et al., "The Digital Silk Road."

61. Gery Shih, "A Lion or a Porcupine, Insecurity Drives China's Xi to Take on the World," Washington Post, August 7, 2020, www.washingtonpost.com/world/asia_pacific/china-trump-xi-cold-war-asia-conflict-huawei-tiktok-communist-party/2020/08/07/5a6531c4-cc91-11ea-99b0-8426e26d203b_story.html.

62. Triolo et al., "The Digital Silk Road."

63. Semple, "China Extends Reach."

64. Triolo et al., "The Digital Silk Road."

65. Ford, "Huawei and Its Siblings."

66. Ford.

67. Peter H. Diamandis, "China's BAT: Baidu, Alibaba, and Tencent," Diamandis Blog, August 12, 2018, www.diamandis.com/blog/baidu-alibaba-tencent.

68. Coco Feng, "China's 'Two Sessions': First Mention of Blockchain in Five-Year Plan Boosts Still-Nascent Industry," South China Morning Post, March 12, 2021, www.scmp.com/tech/policy/article/3125020/chinas-two-sessions-first-mention-blockchain-five-year-plan-boosts.

69. Sangeet Paul Choudary, "China's Country-as-Platform Strategy for Global Influence," Brookings Institution, November 19, 2020, www.brookings.edu/techstream/chinas-country-as-platform-strategy-for-global-influence/.

70. "The 13th Five-Year Plan for Economic and Social Development of the People's Republic of China (2016–2020)," chap. 50, sec. 3, Compilation and Translation Bureau, Central Committee of the Communist Party of China, https://en.ndrc.gov.cn/policies/202105/P020210527785800103339.pdf.

71. Lefen Lin and Shaonan Wang, "Construction of the Belt and Road Initiative and the Internationalization of the RMB," International Political Economy 15 (2015).

72. David Olsson and Andrew Fei, "Why International Use of RMB Is about to Be Propelled," King & Wood Mallesons, April 5, 2018, www.lexology.com/library/detail.aspx?g=dfc8d439-8791-4d1d-9729-e34184940430.

73. Menendez, "The New Big Brother."

74. Triolo et al., "The Digital Silk Road."

75. Paul Triolo and Robert Greene, "Will China Control the Global Internet via Its Digital Silk Road?," Carnegie Endowment for International Peace, May 8, 2020, https://carnegie endowment.org/2020/05/08/will-china-control-global-internet-via-its-digital-silk-road -pub-81857.

76. Shibani Mahtani, "The Future of the Internet Could Be Chinese and Authoritarian, a Senate Foreign Relations Report Warns," *Washington Post*, July 21, 2020, www.washington post.com/world/asia_pacific/the-future-of-the-internet-could-be-chinese-and -authoritarian-warns-senate-foreign-relations-report/2020/07/21/e6b5092c-ca4a-11ea -99b0-8426e26d203b_story.html.

77. Menendez, "The New Big Brother."

CHAPTER 3. THE SOLAR WINDS OF CHANGE

1. "Advanced Persistent Threat Compromise of Government Agencies, Critical Infrastructure, and Private Sector Organizations," U.S. Cybersecurity and Infrastructure Security Agency, December 17, 2020, https://us-cert.cisa.gov/ncas/alerts/aa20-352a; SolarWinds Corporation, Form 8-K, December 14, 2020, www.sec.gov/ix?doc=/Archives/edgar/data /1739942/000162828020017451/swi-20201214.htm.

2. Internet Archive, SolarWinds' Customers, https://web.archive.org/web/20201214065 036/; www.solarwinds.com/company/customers.

3. "HAFNIUM Targeting Exchange Servers with 0-Day Exploits," Microsoft Threat Intelligence Center, March 16, 2021, www.microsoft.com/security/blog/2021/03/02/hafnium -targeting-exchange-servers/.

4. Steven Morgan, "Cybercrime to Cost the World $10.5 Trillion Annually by 2025," *Cybercrime Magazine*, November 13, 2020, https://cybersecurityventures.com/cybercrime -damage-costs-10-trillion-by-2025/.

5. Jessica Davis, "Ransomware Shuts Down Colorado Hospital IT Network Amid COVID-19," Health IT Security, April 28, 2020, https://healthitsecurity.com/news /ransomware-shuts-down-colorado-hospital-it-network-amid-covid-19.

6. Zack Whittaker, "Garmin Confirms Ransomware Attack Took Down Services," TechCrunch, July 27, 2020, https://techcrunch.com/2020/07/27/garmin-confirms-ransom ware-attack-outage/.

7. "Ransomware Impacting Pipeline Operations," Cybersecurity and Infrastructure Security Agency, updated October 24, 2020, https://us-cert.cisa.gov/ncas/alerts/aa20-049a.

8. We recognize recent updates to the NIST framework version 1.1 that aim to incorporate "cyber supply chain risks." However, little guidance is given about methods for doing so, and greater guidance is needed.

9. Howard Marks, "Risk Revisited Again," Oaktree Capital Management, June 8, 2015, www .oaktreecapital.com/docs/default-source/memos/2015-06-08-risk-revisited-again.pdf ?sfvrsn=2.

10. "Election Security Spotlight—CIA Triad," EI-ISAC, Center for Internet Security, www .cisecurity.org/spotlight/ei-isac-cybersecurity-spotlight-cia-triad/.

11. "Cyber Supply Chain Risk Management," National Institute of Standards and Technology, accessed April 28, 2021, https://csrc.nist.gov/projects/cyber-supply-chain-risk -management; "News Report: Ripples Across the Risk Surface," RiskRecon, accessed April 28, 2021, https://www.riskrecon.com/ripples-across-the-risk-surface.

12. "Advanced Persistent Threat Compromise of Government Agencies, Critical Infrastructure, and Private Sector Organizations," U.S. Cybersecurity and Infrastructure Security Agency, April 15, 2021, https://us-cert.cisa.gov/ncas/alerts/aa20-352a.

13. "Identifying Cyber Threats with FSARC," JP Morgan, October 9, 2018, https://www.jpmorgan.com/commercial-banking/insights/cyber-threats-fsarc#:~:text=To%20help%20identify%20potential%20risks,nearly%20two%20dozen%20cyber%20scenarios.

14. Jon Boyens et al., "Key Practices in Cyber Supply Chain Risk Management: Observations from Industry," National Institute of Standards and Technology, February 2021, https://nvlpubs.nist.gov/nistpubs/ir/2021/NIST.IR.8276.pdf.

15. Dave Lewis, "The DDoS Attack against Dyn One Year Later," *Forbes*, October 23, 2017, https://www.forbes.com/sites/davelewis/2017/10/23/the-ddos-attack-against-dyn-one-year-later/#227609061ae9.

16. White House, "Press Briefing on the Attribution of the WannaCry Malware Attack to North Korea," December 19, 2017, https://kr.usembassy.gov/121917-press-briefing-attribution-wannacry-malware-attack-north-korea/.

17. Andy Greenberg, "The Untold Story of NotPetya, the Most Devastating Cyberattack in History," *Wired*, August 22, 2018, an excerpt from his book, *Sandworm: A New Era of Cyberwar and the Hunt for the Kremlin's Most Dangerous Hackers* (New York: Doubleday, 2019), www.wired.com/story/notpetya-cyberattack-ukraine-russia-code-crashed-the-world/.

18. Greenberg, "The Untold Story."

19. "24.4M Patients, 21 Companies Now Say They Were Affected by AMCA Data Breach," Advisory Board, August 13, 2019, www.advisory.com/daily-briefing/2019/08/13/data-breach.

20. Steven Wilamowsky and Aaron M. Krieger, "Declaration of Russell H. Fuchs Pursuant to Local Bankruptcy Rule 10072 and in Support of 'First Day' Motions," US Bankruptcy Court Southern District of New York, June 17, 2019, https://krebsonsecurity.com/wp-content/uploads/2019/06/RMCB-bank.pdf.

21. Manny Fernandez, Mihir Zaveri, and Emily S. Rueb, "Ransomware Attack Hits 22 Texas Towns, Authorities Say," *New York Times*, August 20, 2019, www.nytimes.com/2019/08/20/us/texas-ransomware.html.

22. Renee Dudley, "The New Target That Enables Ransomware Hackers to Paralyze Dozens of Towns and Businesses at Once," ProPublica, September 12, 2019, www.propublica.org/article/the-new-target-that-enables-ransomware-hackers-to-paralyze-dozens-of-towns-and-businesses-at-once.

23. "Highly Evasive Attacker Leverages SolarWinds Supply Chain to Compromise Multiple Global Victims with SUNBURST Backdoor," FireEye, December 13, 2020, www.mandiant.com/resources/evasive-attacker-leverages-solarwinds-supply-chain-compromises-with-sunburst-backdoor.

24. Jon Porter, "White House Now Says 100 Companies Hit by SolarWinds Hack, but More May Be Impacted," *The Verge*, February 18, 2021, www.theverge.com/2021/2/18/22288961/solarwinds-hack-100-companies-9-federal-agencies.

25. Gopal Ratnam, "Cleaning Up SolarWinds Hack May Cost as Much as $100 Billion," *Roll Call*, January 11, 2021, www.rollcall.com/2021/01/11/cleaning-up-solarwinds-hack-may-cost-as-much-as-100-billion/.

26. "HAFNIUM Targeting Exchange Servers with 0-Day Exploits," Microsoft Threat Intelligence Center, March 16, 2021, https://www.microsoft.com/security/blog/2021/03/02/hafnium-targeting-exchange-servers/.

27. "At Least 30,000 U.S. Organizations Newly Hacked Via Holes in Microsoft's Email Software," Krebs on Security, March 5, 2021, https://krebsonsecurity.com/2021/03/at-least-30000-u-s-organizations-newly-hacked-via-holes-in-microsofts-email-software/.

28. "Ripples Across the Risk Surface," Cyentia Cybersecurity Research Library, June 10, 2020, https://library.cyentia.com/report/report_003839.html.

29. "Systemic Cyber Risk Reduction Venture," Cybersecurity and Infrastructure Security Agency, https://www.cisa.gov/systemic-cyber-risk-reduction.

30. "National Critical Functions Set," Cybersecurity and Infrastructure Security Agency, https://www.cisa.gov/national-critical-functions-set.

31. Shalanda D. Young, Letter to Senate Committee on Appropriations, April 9, 2021, www.whitehouse.gov/wp-content/uploads/2021/04/FY2022-Discretionary-Request.pdf.

32. Robert M. Sapolsky, *Behave: The Biology of Humans at Our Best and Worst* (New York: Penguin, 2017), 6.

33. Donella H. Meadows, *Thinking in Systems: A Primer* (London: Earthscan, 2009), 95.

34. Meadows.

35. Nassim Taleb, *The Black Swan: The Impact of the Highly Improbable* (New York: Random House, 2007), 16.

36. "Energy: Understanding Our Oil Supply Chain," American Petroleum Institute, www.api.org/-/media/Files/Policy/Safety/API-Oil-Supply-Chain.pdf.

37. Greenberg, "The Untold Story."

38. Jeffrey Burt, "Despite BlueKeep Warnings, Many Organizations Fail to Patch," Bank Information Security, July 18, 2019, www.bankinfosecurity.com/despite-bluekeep-warnings-many-organizations-fail-to-patch-a-12795.

39. Yonathan Klijnsma, "Spray and Pray Magecart Group Breaches Websites via Misconfigured Amazon S3 Buckets," RiskIQ, July 11, 2019, www.riskiq.com/blog/labs/magecart-amazon-s3-buckets/; "22,900 MongoDB Databases Affected in Ransomware Attack," Dark Reading, July 3, 2020, www.darkreading.com/cloud/22900-mongodb-databases-affected-in-ransomware-attack/d/d-id/1338271.

40. "What Is FAIR?," FAIR Institute, accessed April 26, 2021, www.fairinstitute.org/what-is-fair; "About Us," X-Analytics, accessed May 5, 2021, www.x-analytics.com/aboutus.

41. Manos Antonakakis et al., "Understanding the Mirai Botnet," 26th USENIX Security Symposium, August 16, 2017, https://elie.net/static/files/understanding-the-mirai-botnet/understanding-the-mirai-botnet-paper.pdf.

42. Kapil Raina, "Zero Trust Security Explained: Principles of the Zero Trust Model," CrowdStrike, May 6, 2021, https://www.crowdstrike.com/cybersecurity-101/zero-trust-security/.

43. "Zero Trust Architecture," National Institute for Standards and Technology, August 2020, https://nvlpubs.nist.gov/nistpubs/SpecialPublications/NIST.SP.800-207.pdf.

44. "Cyber Resource Hub," Cybersecurity and Infrastructure Security Agency, www.cisa.gov/cyber-resource-hub.

45. "Cyber Supply Chain Risk Management Practices for Systems and Organizations (2nd Draft)," National Institute for Standards and Technology, October 28, 2021, https://csrc.nist.gov/publications/detail/sp/800-161/rev-1/draft.

46. Eric Geller, "$2 Trillion Can Build a Lot of Infrastructure. But Can the U.S. Secure It?," Politico, April 26, 2021, https://www.politico.com/news/2021/04/26/cybersecurity-hole-biden-infrastructure-plan-484640; White House, "Fact Sheet: The American Jobs Plan," March 31, 2021, https://www.whitehouse.gov/briefing-room/statements-releases/2021/03/31/fact-sheet-the-american-jobs-plan/.

47. Howard Marks, "Risk Revisited Again," Oaktree Capital Management, June 8, 2015, www .oaktreecapital.com/docs/default-source/memos/2015-06-08-risk-revisited-again.pdf ?sfvrsn=2.

CHAPTER 4. OUTDATED AND INEFFECTIVE

1. Richard A. Clarke and Robert K. Knake, *The Fifth Domain: Defending Our Country, Our Companies, and Ourselves in the Age of Cyber Threats* (New York: Penguin, 2019), 11.
2. James E. Lee, "Cybersecurity Problems Won't be Solved by Regulation," Security Info-watch, April 20, 2018, www.securityinfowatch.com/cybersecurity/information-security /computer-and-network-security-software/article/12408872/all-the-regulations-in-the -world-cant-solve-cybersecuritys-problems.
3. Clarke and Knake, *The Fifth Domain*, 113.
4. Robin Singh, "Top 10 Regulatory Challenges in the Healthcare Environment?" Nav-tex Global, October 29, 2018, www.navexglobal.com/blog/article/top-10-regulatory -challenges-in-the-healthcare-environment/.
5. "Top Cyber Security Experts Report: 4,000 Cyber Attacks a Day Since COVID-19 Pandemic," PR Newswire, August 11, 2020, https://www.prnewswire.com/news-releases /top-cyber-security-experts-report-4-000-cyber-attacks-a-day-since-covid-19-pandemic -301110157.html; "HIPPA Compliance and Cybersecurity: How the Two Work Together," Security Boulevard, July 2, 2019, https://securityboulevard.com/2019/07 /hipaa-compliance-and-cybersecurity-how-the-two-work-together/.
6. Verizon, "Verizon Data Breach Investigations Report (2020)," 54–56, January 28, 2022, https://enterprise.verizon.com/resources/reports/2020/2020-data-breach-investigations -report.pdf.
7. Jessica Davis, "Healthcare Needs More than HIPAA, Legislation to Improve Security," Health IT Security, August 13, 2019, https://healthitsecurity.com/news/healthcare -needs-more-than-hipaa-legislation-to-improve-security.
8. ESI ThoughtLab, "Driving Cybersecurity Performance," January 28, 2022, https:// econsultsolutions.com/esi-thoughtlab/driving-cybersecurity-performance/. The information in the rest of this paragraph and the following two paragraphs comes from this report.
9. Tom Wheeler and David Simpson, "Why 5G Requires New Approaches to Cyber-security: Racing to Protect the Most Important Network of the 21st Century," Brookings Institution, September 3, 2019, www.brookings.edu/research/why-5g-requires-new -approaches-to-cybersecurity/.
10. NIST Cybersecurity Framework, January 28, 2022, www.nist.gov/cyberframework.
11. President Barack Obama, "Executive Order—Improving Critical Infrastructure Cyberse-curity," February 12, 2013, https://obamawhitehouse.archives.gov/the-press-office/2013 /02/12/executive-order-improving-critical-infrastructure-cybersecurity.
12. ESI ThoughtLab, "Driving Cybersecurity Performance," 9.
13. ESI ThoughtLab, 15.
14. Sean Atkins and Chappell Lawson, "Regulation or Integration? Cybersecurity for Critical Infrastructure and Its Implication for Business-Government Relations," Massachusetts Institute of Technology, December 2020.
15. Douglas W. Hubbard and Richard Seierson, *How to Measure Anything in Cybersecurity Risk* (Hoboken, NJ: John Wiley & Sons, 2016), 85.

16. Atkins and Lawson, "Regulation or Integration?"
17. For example, Steve Morgan, "Cybersecurity Jobs Report: 3.5 Million Openings in 2025," *Cybercrime Magazine*, November 9, 2021, https://cybersecurityventures.com/jobs/.
18. Christopher C. Krebs, "Closing a Critical Gap in Cybersecurity," *Lawfare*, December 16, 2019, www.lawfareblog.com/closing-critical-gap-cybersecurity.
19. "Cybersecurity: DOD Needs to Take Decisive Actions to Improve Cyber Hygiene," US Government Accountability Office, April 2020, https://assets.documentcloud.org /documents/6838199/GAO-Cyber.pdf.
20. "Federal Cybersecurity: America's Data at Risk," Staff Report, US Senate Committee on Homeland Security and Governmental Affairs, 2019, www.hsgac.senate.gov/imo/media /doc/2019-06-25%20PSI%20Staff%20Report%20-%20Federal%20Cybersecurity %20Updated.pdf.
21. "High-Risk Series: Substantial Efforts Needed to Achieve Greater Progress on High-Risk Areas," US Government Accountability Office, March 2019, 179, www.gao.gov/assets /700/697245.pdf.
22. "High Risk Series: Dedicated Leadership Needed to Address Limited Progress in Most High-Risk Areas," US Government Accountability Office, March 2, 2021, 173, www.gao .gov/assets/gao-21-119sp.pdf.
23. "Reflections of a Longtime Government IT Auditor before He Steps Down," Federal News Network, February 28, 2020, https://federalnewsnetwork com/cybersecurity/2020/02 /reflections-of-a-longtime-government-it-auditor-before-he-steps-down/.
24. Michael Daniel, Tal Goldstein, Amy Hogan-Burney, and Derek Manky, "Partnership against Cybercrime Insight Report," World Economic Forum, November 2020, 9, www3 .weforum.org/docs/WEF_Partnership_against_Cybercrime_report_2020.pdf; William Dixon, "Fighting Cybercrime: What Happens to the Law When the Law Cannot be Enforced?," World Economic Forum, February 19, 2019, www.weforum.org/agenda /2019/02/fighting-cybercrime-what-happens-to-the-law-when-the-law-cannot-be -enforced/.
25. Richard and Anthony Shuker, "Why Is It So Hard to Catch Cybercriminals?," *Technology Means Business*, January 6, 2020, https://blog.tmb.co.uk/why-is-it-so-hard-to-catch -cyber-criminals.
26. International Association of Chiefs of Police (IACP), "Understanding Digital Evidence," January 28, 2022, www.iacpcybercenter.org/investigators/digital-evidence /understanding-digital-evidence/.
27. IACP.
28. Anthony, "Why Is It So Hard to Catch Cybercriminals?"
29. Brandon Gaskew, "Reader's Guide to Understanding the US Cyber Enforcement Architecture and Budget," Third Way, February 21, 2019, www.thirdway.org/memo/readers -guide-to-understanding-the-us-cyber-enforcement-architecture-and-budget.
30. Maggie Miller, "FBI asks Congress for $40M to Help Combat Wave of Ransomware Attacks," *The Hill*, June 2021, https://thehill.com/policy/cybersecurity/559947-fbi-asks -congress-for-40-million-to-help-combat-wave-of-ransomware.
31. Jamie Dimon, Letter to Shareholders, April 2019, JP Morgan Chase, 35, www.jpmorgan chase.com/corporate/investor-relations/document/ceo-letter-to-shareholders-2018.pdf.
32. Johannes Deichmann, Benjamin Klein, Gundbert Scherf, and Rupert Stutzle, "The Race for Cybersecurity: Protecting the Connected Car in the Era of New Regulation," McKinsey and Company, October 1, 2019, www.mckinsey.com/~/media/McKinsey

/Industries/Automotive%20and%20Assembly/Our%20Insights/The%20race%20for
%20cybersecurity%20Protecting%20the%20connected%20car%20in%20the%20era
%20of%20new%20regulation/The-race-for-cybersecurity-Protecting-the-connected-car
-in-the-era-of-new-regulation.pdf.

33. Steve Tengler, "The Top Twenty Unspoken Automotive Cybersecurity Questions and
Their Risks," *Forbes*, September 1, 2020, www.forbes.com/sites/stevetengler/2020/09
/01/the-top-twenty-unspoken-automotive-cybersecurity-questions-and-their-risks/?sh
=7e39bcb0457d.

34. US Department of Homeland Security, FY 2021 Budget in Brief, www.dhs.gov/sites
/default/files/publications/fy_2021_dhs_bib_web_version.pdf.

35. Ondrej Burkacky, Johannes Deichmann, Benjamin Klein, Klaus Pototzky, and Gundbert
Scherf, "Cybersecurity in Automotive: Mastering the Challenge," McKinsey and Company, June 22, 2020, https://www.mckinsey.com/industries/automotive-and-assembly
/our-insights/cybersecurity-in-automotive-mastering-the-challenge#; Derek B. Johnson,
"Budget Request Emphasizes Cyber, Network Security Efforts," *FCW*, February 10, 2020,
https://fcw.com/articles/2020/02/10/budget-request-cyber-johnson.aspx.

36. Salim Hasham, Shoan Joshi, and Daniel Mikkelsen, "Financial Crime and Fraud in
the Age of Cybersecurity," McKinsey and Company, October 1, 2019, www.mckinsey
.com/business-functions/risk/our-insights/financial-crime-and-fraud-in-the-age-of
-cybersecurity.

37. Gaskew, "Reader's Guide."

38. Michael Daly, "Law Enforcement Has to Get Serious about Cyber Crime," VentureBeat,
May 26, 2018, https://venturebeat.com/2018/05/26/law-enforcement-has-to-get-serious
-about-cyber-crime/.

39. Gaskew, "Reader's Guide"; Michael Garcia and Mieke Eoyang, "A Road Map for Tackling
Cybercrime," *Lawfare*, December 10, 2020, www.lawfareblog.com/road-map-tackling
-cybercrime.

40. US DOJ, "Assistant Attorney General Brian A. Benczkowski Delivers Remarks at the
'Justice in Cyberspace' Symposium," February 5, 2020, www.justice.gov/opa/speech
/assistant-attorney-general-brian-benczkowski-delivers-remarks-justice-cyberspace.

41. US DOJ.

42. Maggie Miller, "Russia Arrests Hacker in Colonial Pipeline Attack, U.S. Says," Politico
Pro, January 2022, www.politico.com/news/2022/01/14/russia-colonial-pipeline-arrest
-527166.

43. Council of Europe, "Implementation of the Budapest Convention on Cybercrime,"
December 2016, www.oas.org/juridico/PDFs/cyb9_coe_cyb_oas_Dec16_v1.pdf.

44. White House, "Fact Sheet: President Xi Jinping's State Visit to the United States," September 25, 2015, https://obamawhitehouse.archives.gov/the-press-office/2015/09/25/fact
-sheet-president-xi-jinpings-state-visit-united-states.

45. White House, "Remarks by President Obama and President Xi of the People's Republic of
China in Joint Press Conference," September 25, 2015, https://obamawhitehouse.archives
.gov/the-press-office/2015/09/25/remarks-president-obama-and-president-xi-peoples
-republic-china-joint.

46. Asia Pacific Regional Security Assessment 2019, "Chapter Five: China's Cyber Power
in a New Era," IISS, May 2019, www.iiss.org/publications/strategic-dossiers/asiapacific
-regional-security-assessment-2019/rsa19-07-chapter-5.

47. Asia Pacific Regional Security Assessment 2019.
48. Office of the US Trade Representative, "Findings of the Investigation into China's Acts, Policies, and Practices Related to Technology Transfer, Intellectual Property, and Innovation Under Section 301 of the Trade Act of 1974," March 22, 2018, 154, https://ustr.gov/sites/default/files/Section%20301%20FINAL.PDF.
49. Brian Krebs, "At Least 30,000 U.S. Organizations Newly Hacked via Holes in Microsoft's Email Software," Krebs on Security, March 5, 2021, https://krebsonsecurity.com/2021/03/at-least-30000-u-s-organizations-newly-hacked-via-holes-in-microsofts-email-software/.
50. Chris Bing, "Trump Administration Says China Broke Obama-Xi Hacking Agreement," CyberScoop, May 22, 2018, https://www.cyberscoop.com/trump-china-hacking-obama-xi-agreement/; Jack Goldsmith and Robert D. Williams, "The Failure of the United States' Chinese-Hacking Indictment Strategy," *Lawfare*, December 28, 2018, www.lawfareblog.com/failure-united-states-chinese-hacking-indictment-strategy.
51. Jack Goldsmith and Stuart Russell, "Strengths Become Vulnerabilities," Hoover Institution, 2018, 13, www.hoover.org/sites/default/files/research/docs/381100534-strengths-become-vulnerabilities.pdf.
52. Jason Healey, "The Cyber Budget Shows What the U.S. Values—And It Isn't Defense," *Lawfare*, June 1, 2020, hwww.lawfareblog.com/cyber-budget-shows-what-us-values%E2%80%94and-it-isnt-defense.
53. Council on Foreign Relations, "U.S. Relations with China, 1949–2020," accessed January 28, 2022, www.cfr.org/timeline/us-relations-china.
54. Council on Foreign Relations.
55. US Treasury Department, "Major Holders of Treasury Securities," January 2021, https://ticdata.treasury.gov/Publish/mfh.txt.
56. Aaron Wininger, "China Makes Significant Commitments to Improve Intellectual Property Protection in Phase 1 Trade Deal," *National Law Review*, January 15, 2020, www.natlawreview.com/article/china-makes-significant-commitments-to-improve-intellectual-property-protection.
57. Andrew Eversden, "Here's Why the State Department May Need a New Cyber Office," Fifth Domain, March 4, 2020, www.fifthdomain.com/congress/capitol-hill/2020/03/04/heres-why-the-state-department-may-need-a-new-cyber-office/.
58. Julian E. Barnes, "Russia Continues to Meddle in US Elections to Help Trump, US Intelligence Says," *New York Times*, August 8, 2020, www.nytimes.com/2020/08/07/us/politics/russia-china-trump-biden-election-interference.html.
59. Jason Healey and Erik Korn, "Defense Support to the Private Sector," *Cyber Defense Review Special Edition 2019*, https://cyberdefensereview.army.mil/Portals/6/Session%205%20Number%201%20CDR-Special%20Edition-2019.pdf.
60. Jim Garamone, "Esper Describes DOD's Increased Cyber Offensive Strategy," Department of Defense, September 20, 2019, www.defense.gov/Explore/News/Article/Article/1966758/esper-describes-dods-increased-cyber-offensive-strategy/.
61. Jordan Smith, "Nakasone Says Federal Cyber Defenders Need Better Visibility within the U.S.," Meritalk, March 25, 2021, www.meritalk.com/articles/nakasone-says-federal-cyber-defenders-need-better-visibility-within-u-s/.
62. Healey and Korn, "Defense Support," 229.
63. Healey and Korn.

64. Healey and Korn.
65. Cyberspace Solarium Commission, March 2020 Report, www.solarium.gov/report.
66. Joseph Marks, "Only 6 Non-Federal Groups Share Cyber Threat Info with Homeland Security," Nextgov, June 27, 2018, www.nextgov.com/cybersecurity/2018/06/only-6 -non-federal-groups-share-cyber-threat-info-homeland-security/149343/.
67. Jaikumar Vijayan, "What Is an ISAC or ISAO? How These Cyber Threat Information Sharing Organizations Improve Security," CSO Online, July 9, 2019, www.csoonline.com /article/3406505/what-is-an-isac-or-isao-how-these-cyber-threat-information-sharing -organizations-improve-security.html.
68. House Resolution 3359—Cybersecurity and Infrastructure Security Agency Act of 2018, www.congress.gov/bill/115th-congress/house-bill/3359[[Page132STAT. 4169]].
69. David S. Turetsky, Brian H. Nussbaum, and Unal Tatar, "Success Stories in Cybersecurity Information Sharing," College of Emergency Preparedness, University of Albany, October 23, 2018, www.albany.edu/sscis.
70. Vijayan, "What Is an ISAC or ISAO?"
71. Andrew Eversden, "How Good Is the Government at Threat Information Sharing?," C4ISRNET, December 30, 2019, https://www.c4isrnet.com/dod/2019/12/30/how -good-is-the-government-at-threat-information-sharing/.
72. Eversden.
73. Eversden.
74. Marks, "Only 6 Non-Federal Groups."
75. Vijayan, "What Is an ISAC or ISAO?"

CHAPTER 5. REINVENTING CYBERSECURITY

1. House Republican Cybersecurity Task Force, "Recommendations of the House Republican Cybersecurity Task Force," 2006, www.hsdl.org/?view&did=736294; White House, "Cyberspace Policy Review: Assuring a Trusted and Resilient Information and Communications Infrastructure," 2009, www.cisa.gov/publication/2009-cyberspace-policy -review; President Barack Obama, "Executive Order—Improving Critical Infrastructure Cybersecurity," February 12, 2013, https://obamawhitehouse.archives.gov/the-press -office/2013/02/12/executive-order-improving-critical-infrastructure-cybersecurity; Department of Homeland Security, Information Technology Sector Coordinating Council & Information Technology Government Coordinating Council, "Collective Defense: A Collaborative Perspective from the IT Sector," 2019, www.it-scc.org/uploads /4/7/2/3/47232717/the_collective_defense_white_paper_12.19.pdf; Cyberspace Solarium Commission, "Report of the Cyberspace Solarium Commission," March 11, 2020, www.solarium.gov; House Homeland Security Committee & House Transportation and Infrastructure Committee, "Letter to National Security Advisor Jake Sullivan," May 11, 2021, https://transportation.house.gov/news/press-releases/homeland-security -transportation-and-infrastructure-leaders-write-white-house-national-security-advisor -sullivan-on-colonial-pipeline-ransomware-attack.
2. Richard A. Clarke and Robert K. Knake, The Fifth Domain: Defending Our Country, Our Companies, and Ourselves in the Age of Cyber Threats (New York: Penguin, 2019), 91.

3. "High-Risk Series: Substantial Efforts Needed to Achieve Greater Progress on High-Risk Areas," GAO, Washington, DC, March 6, 2019, 179, https://www.gao.gov/products/gao-19-157sp.

4. Jason Healey and Erik Korn, "Defense Support to the Private Sector," *Cyber Defense Review*, Special Edition, 2019, https://cyberdefensereview.army.mil/Portals/6/Session%205%20Number%201%20CDR-Special%20Edition-2019.pdf.

5. Cyberspace Solarium Commission Report, March 2020, www.solarium.gov/report.

6. Larry Clinton, "Best Practices for Operating Government-Industry Partnerships in Cyber Security," *Journal of Strategic Security* 8, no. 4 (2015), https://scholarcommons.usf.edu/jss/vol8/iss4/4/.

7. Wouter Aghina, Karin Ahlback, Aaron De Smet, Gerald Lackey, Michael Lurie, Monica Murarka, and Christopher Handscomb, "The Five Trademarks of Agile Organizations," McKinsey, January 22, 2018, www.mckinsey.com/business-functions/organization/our-insights/the-five-trademarks-of-agile-organizations.

8. IT SCC, "Collective Defense: A Collaborative Perspective from the IT Sector," *Homeland Security*, 3, December 19, 2018, www.it-scc.org/uploads/4/7/2/3/47232717/the_collective_defense_white_paper_12.19.pdf.

9. Internet Security Alliance (ISA) and National Association of Corporate Directors (NACD), Cyber-Risk Oversight 2020, http://isalliance.org/wp-content/uploads/2020/02/RD-3-2020_NACD_Cyber_Handbook__WEB_022020.pdf.

10. Pricewaterhouse Coopers, "Turnaround and Transformation in Cybersecurity: Key Findings from The Global State of Information Security® Survey," 2016, www.pwc.com/sg/en/publications/assets/pwc-global-state-of-information-security-survey-2016.pdf.

11. ISA and NACD, Cyber-Risk Oversight 2020.

12. ISA and NACD.

13. IT Sector Coordinating Council and the Department of Homeland Security, "Collective Defense: A Collaborative Perspective from the IT Sector," May 2020, 2, www.it-scc.org/uploads/4/7/2/3/47232717/the_collective_defense_white_paper_12.19.pdf.

14. Department of Homeland Security (DHS), National Infrastructure Protection Plan, 2013, www.cisa.gov/national-infrastructure-protection-plan.

15. IT Sector Coordinating Council, "Collective Defense."

16. IT Sector Coordinating Council.

17. Sean Atkins and Chappell Lawson, "Regulation or Integration? Cybersecurity for Critical Infrastructure and Its Implication for Business-Government Relations," Massachusetts Institute of Technology, December 2020.

18. Information Technology Sector Coordinating Council and Government Coordinating Council, "Collective Defense: A Collaborative Perspective from the IT Sector," Department of Homeland Security, December 19, 2020, 8, https://www.it-scc.org/uploads/4/7/2/3/47232717/the_collective_defense_white_paper_12.19pdf.

19. US GAO, "DOD Needs to Clarify Its Roles and Responsibilities for Defense Support of Civil Authorities during Cyber Incidents," April 4, 2016, hwww.gao.gov/products/GAO-16-332.

20. Gareth Morgan, *Images of Organization* (Thousand Oaks, CA: Sage, 2006), 12–13.

21. Aghina et al., "Five Trademarks."

22. National Association of Corporate Directors and Internet Security Alliance, "Cyber Risk Oversight 2020: Key Principles and Practical Guidance for Corporate Directors,"

National Association of Corporate Directors, 2020, 26, https://www.nacdonline.org/insights/publications.cfm?ItemNumber=67298.

23. Aghina et al.
24. Clinton, "Best Practices."
25. Shameen Prashantham and Jonathan Woetzel, "Three Lessons from Chinese Firms on Effective Digital Collaboration," *Harvard Business Review*, August 10, 2020, https://hbr.org/2020/08/3-lessons-from-chinese-firms-on-effective-digital-collaboration.
26. Larry Clinton, "Best Practices."
27. Aghina et al., "Five Trademarks."
28. Internet Security Alliance, "The Cyber Security Social Contract Policy Recommendations for the Obama Administration and 111th Congress," 2008, 9, https://obamawhitehouse.archives.gov/files/documents/cyber/ISA%20-%20The%20Cyber%20Security%20Social%20Contract.pdf.
29. IT Sector Coordinating Council, "Collective Defense."
30. USTelecom, "USTelecom 2021 Cybersecurity Survey: Critical Infrastructure Small and Medium-Sized Businesses (SMBs)," 2021, https://issuu.com/ustelecom/docs/smb-cyber-report_final-issuu.
31. ESI ThoughtLab, "Driving Cybersecurity Performance," 2020, https://econsultsolutions.com/esi-thoughtlab/driving-cybersecurity-performance/.
32. IT Sector Coordinating Council.
33. For other examples of innovative cyber programs in need of systematic assessment, see chaps. 8 and 10.

CHAPTER 6. THE CYBERSECURITY POLICY WE NEED

1. Department of Justice, "FY 2022 FBI Budget Request at a Glance," June 7, 2021, www.justice.gov/jmd/page/file/1399031/download.
2. William Dixon, "Fighting Cybercrime: What Happens to the Law When the Law Cannot Be Enforced?," World Economic Forum, February 19, 2019, www.weforum.org/agenda/2019/02/fighting-cybercrime-what-happens-to-the-law-when-the-law-cannot-be-enforced/.
3. James Lewis, "Section 301 Investigation: China's Acts, Policies and Practices Related to Technology Transfer, Intellectual Property, and Innovation," Center for Strategic and International Studies, April 2020, https://csis-website-prod.s3.amazonaws.com/s3fs-public/publication/200422_Lewis_Investigation_v4.pdf?vRNUKyco1phYotvBNqET9kuz2GjKNAsL.
4. Remington Toner and Ellis Talton, "A Lack of Cybersecurity Funding and Expertise Threatens U.S. Infrastructure," *Forbes*, April 23, 2018, www.forbes.com/sites/ellistalton/2018/04/23/the-u-s-governments-lack-of-cybersecurity-expertise-threatens-our-infrastructure/#7ff4f36e49e0.
5. US Government Printing Office (GPO), "A Budget for a Better America," 2021, www.govinfo.gov/content/pkg/BUDGET-2021-PER/pdf/BUDGET-2021-PER-6-6.pdf.
6. US GPO.
7. Office of Management and Budget, "Summary of the President's Discretionary Funding Request," April 9, 2021, www.whitehouse.gov/wp-content/uploads/2021/04/FY2022-Discretionary-Request.pdf.

8. Grace Dille, "Federal Civilian Cyber Spending Jumps 14% in FY2022 Budget, to $9.8 Billion," MeriTalk, May 28, 2021, www.meritalk.com/articles/federal-civilian-cyber-spending-jumps-14-in-fy2022-budget-to-9-8b/.

9. Liza Lin, "China's Trillion-Dollar Campaign Fuels a Tech Race with the U.S.," *Wall Street Journal*, June 11, 2020, www.wsj.com/articles/chinas-trillion-dollar-campaign-fuels-a-tech-race-with-the-u-s-11591892854.

10. Dille, "Federal Civilian Cyber Spending."

11. "China to Lead Global Cybersecurity Market Growth in Next 5 Years," Xinhua Net, September 9, 2019, http://www.xinhuanet.com/english/2019-09/09/c_138377152.

12. Department of Homeland Security Science and Technology Directorate Budget Overview, FY 2021, www.dhs.gov/sites/default/files/publications/science_and_technology_directorate.pdf.

13. National Institute of Standards and Technology, FY 2021 Budget Request, www.nist.gov/system/files/documents/2020/02/11/FY2021-NIST-Budget-Book.pdf.

14. Department of Homeland Security, "FY 2022 Budget in Brief," 2021, www.dhs.gov/sites/default/files/publications/dhs_bib_web_version_final_508.pdf; American Institute of Physics, "FY22 Budget Outlook: National Institute of Standards and Technology," November 2, 2021, www.aip.org/fyi/2021/fy22-budget-outlook-national-institute-standards-and-technology.

15. Mike Cherney, "Can Businesses Keep Up with New Cyber Threats?," *Wall Street Journal*, October 6, 2020, www.wsj.com/articles/can-businesses-keep-up-with-new-cyber-threats-11601996485.

16. "Forecast: Information Security and Risk Management, Worldwide, 2018-2024, 2Q20 Update," Gartner, www.gartner.com/en/documents/3988093/forecast-information-security-and-risk-management-worldw.

17. Steve Tengler, "The Top Twenty Unspoken Automotive Cybersecurity Questions and Their Risks," *Forbes*, September 1, 2020, https://www.forbes.com/sites/stevetengler/2020/09/01/the-top-twenty-unspoken-automotive-cybersecurity-questions-and-their-risks/?sh=7e39bcb0457d.

18. IT-SCC, "Collective Defense: A Collaborative Perspective from the IT Sector," 2019, www.it-scc.org/uploads/4/7/2/3/47232717/the_collective_defense_white_paper_12.19.pdf.

19. American Institute of Physics, "Final FY21 Appropriations: STEM Education," February 26, 2021, www.aip.org/fyi/2021/final-fy21-appropriations-stem-education.

20. State Council for the People's Republic of China, "China's Government Spending on Education Above 4% of GDP for 7 Consecutive Years," October 17, 2019, http://english.www.gov.cn/statecouncil/ministries/201910/17/content_WS5da82aa2c6d0bcf8c4c1549c.html.

21. OECD.Stat Database, Organization for Economic Development and Cooperation, https://stats.oecd.org/Index.aspx?DataSetCode=MSTI_PUB.

22. Congressional Research Service, "Global Research and Development Expenditures: Fact Sheet (2020)," April 20, 2020, 1, https://fas.org/sgp/crs/misc/R44283.pdf.

23. Congressional Research Service.

24. Congressional Research Service.

25. Stimpson Study Group, "Counterterrorism Spending: Protecting America While Promoting Efficiencies and Accountability," May 2018, www.stimson.org/wp-content/files/file-attachments/CT_Spending_Report_0.pdf.

26. US Telecom, "2021 Cybersecurity Survey: Critical Infrastructure Small and Medium-Sized Businesses," www.ustelecom.org/research/2021-cybersecurity-survey-critical-infrastructure-small-and-medium-sized-businesses/.

27. US Telecom, 8.

28. Burt Braverman, Maria T. Browne, and Jonathan Mark, "Let Her Rip! FCC Adopts Remove-and-Replace Rules," January 15, 2021, www.dwt.com/insights/2021/01/fcc-huawei-zte-rip-and-replace-rules; Charlie Mitchell, "Sen. King, a Solarium Commission Leader, Sees Incident Reporting Mandate as Key Element in Deterrence Policy," Inside Cybersecurity, June 30, 2021, https://insidecybersecurity.com/daily-news/sen-king-solarium-commission-leader-sees-incident-reporting-mandate-key-element; Charlie Mitchell, "Sen. Manchin Kicks Off Process to Move Energy Bill with Grid Security Elements; Industry Backs Cyber Incentives," Inside Cybersecurity, June 24, 2021, https://insidecybersecurity.com/daily-news/sen-manchin-kicks-process-move-energy-bill-grid-security-elements-industry-backs-cyber; Charlie Mitchell, "DHS, DOJ Pull Together Tools on Ransomware, State Dept. Offers Reward for Tips on Threats to Critical Infrastructure," Inside Cybersecurity, July 15, 2021, https://insidecybersecurity.com/daily-news/dhs-doj-pull-together-tools-ransomware-state-dept-offers-reward-tips-threats-critical.

29. Douglas Hubbard, How to Measure Anything in Cybersecurity (Hoboken, NJ: Wiley & Sons, 2016), 85; ESI Thoughtlab, "Driving Cybersecurity Performance," 2020, https://econsultsolutions.com/esi-thoughtlab/driving-cybersecurity-performance/.

30. White House, "Executive Order on Improving the Nation's Cybersecurity," May 12, 2021, www.whitehouse.gov/briefing-room/presidential-actions/2021/05/12/executive-order-on-improving-the-nations-cybersecurity/.

31. Lindsey O'Donnell-Welch, "Biden Memo Orders Cybersecurity Mandates for National Security Systems," Decipher, January 19, 2022, https://duo.com/decipher/biden-memo-orders-cybersecurity-mandates-for-national-security-systems.

32. Council of Europe, "Convention on Cybercrime," 2001, https://rm.coe.int/1680081561.

33. David E. Sanger, Clifford Krauss, and Nicole Perloth, "Cyberattack Forces a Shutdown of a Top U.S. Pipeline," New York Times, May 8, 2021, www.nytimes.com/2021/05/08/us/politics/cyberattack-colonial-pipeline.html.

34. Department of Justice, "Department of Justice Seizes $2.3 Million in Cryptocurrency Paid to the Ransomware Extortionists Darkside," June 7, 2021, www.justice.gov/opa/pr/department-justice-seizes-23-million-cryptocurrency-paid-ransomware-extortionists-darkside.

35. "Meat Giant JBS Pays $11 million in Ransom to Resolve Cyberattack," BBC News, June 10, 2021, www.bbc.com/news/business-57423008.

36. Matt Stieb, "What's Driving the Surge in Ransomware Attacks?," New York Magazine, June 11, 2021, https://nymag.com/intelligencer/article/ransomware-attacks-2021.html.

37. David Braue, "Global Ransomware Damage Costs Predicted to Exceed $265 Billion in 2031," Cybercrime Magazine, June 3, 2021, https://cybersecurityventures.com/global-ransomware-damage-costs-predicted-to-reach-250-billion-usd-by-2031/.

38. "Ransomware as Service (RaaS) Explained," Crowdstrike, January 28, 2021, www.crowdstrike.com/cybersecurity-101/ransomware/ransomware-as-a-service-raas/.

39. McKinsey & Company, "Financial Crime and Fraud in the Age of Cybersecurity," October 2019, www.mckinsey.com/~/media/McKinsey/Business%20Functions/Risk/Our%20Insights/Financial%20crime%20and%20fraud%20in%20the%20age%20of%20cybersecurity/Financial-crime-and-fraud-in-the-age-of-cybersecurity.pdf.

40. McKinsey & Company.

41. Daniel Gonzales, Sarah Harting, Mary Kate Adgie, Julia Brackup, Lindsey Polley, and Karlyn D. Stanley, "A Defense Industrial Base Cyber Protection Program for Unclassified Defense Networks," RAND Corporation, 2020, www.rand.org/pubs/research_reports /RR4227.html.

42. IT-Sector Coordinating Council and Department of Homeland Security, "Collective Defense: A Collaborative Perspective from the IT Sector," May 2020, www.it-scc.org /uploads/4/7/2/3/47232717/the_collective_defense_white_paper_12.19.pdf.

43. IT-Sector Coordinating Council and Department of Homeland Security.

44. Cybersecurity Supply/Demand Heat Map, CyberSeek, accessed April 26, 2021, www .cyberseek.org/heatmap.html.

45. "Occupational Outlook Handbook: Information Security Analysts," U.S. Bureau of Labor Statistics, accessed April 26, 2021, www.bls.gov/ooh/computer-and-information -technology/information-security-analysts.htm.

46. US Government Accountability Office (GAO), "High-Risk Series: Substantial Efforts Needed to Achieve Greater Progress on High-Risk Areas," March 2019, 179, www.gao .gov/assets/700/697245.pdf.

47. United States GAO, "High-Risk Series: Dedicated Leaderships Needed to Address Limited Progress in Most High-Risk Areas," March 2021, www.gao.gov/assets/gao-21-119sp.pdf.

48. Internet Security Alliance (ISA), "The Cybersecurity Social Contract," October 2016, 142.

49. ISA.

50. Cybersecurity Talent Initiative, "About," April 27, 2021, https://cybertalentinitiative.org /about/.

51. Dave Nyczepir, "11 Federal Agencies Help Start Cybersecurity Talent Initiative," FedScoop, April 9, 2019, https://www.fedscoop.com/federal-cybersecurity-talent-initiative/.

52. "NASCIO Releases 2021 Federal Advocacy Priorities: Continues Call for Harmonized Cyber Regulations," January 14, 2021, www.nascio.org/press-releases/nascio-releases -2021-federal-advocacy-priorities-continues-call-for-harmonized-cyber-regulations/.

53. US GAO, "Cybersecurity Selected Federal Agencies Need to Coordinate on Requirements and Assessments of States," Report, May 2020, https://www.gao.gov/assets/710 /707178.pdf.

54. US GAO.

55. Cyberspace Solarium Commission Report, March 2020, 7, www.solarium.gov/report.

CHAPTER 7. HEALTH

1. Jessica Davis, "Data Breaches Will Cost Health Care $4B in 2019, Threats Outpace Tech," Health IT Security, November 5, 2019, https://healthitsecurity.com/news/data -breaches-will-cost-healthcare-4b-in-2019-threats-outpace-tech.

2. Guy Martin et al., "Cybersecurity and Health Care: How Safe Are We?," BMJ 358, j3179 (July 6, 2017), http://doi.org/10.1136/bmj.j3179.

3. Scott Ikeda, "Health Care Cyber Attacks Rise by 55%, over 26 Million in the U.S. Impacted," CPO Magazine, February 26, 2021, www.cpomagazine.com/cyber-security /healthcare-cyber-attacks-rise-by-55-over-26-million-in-the-u-s-impacted/.

4. Kat Jercich, "The Biggest Health Care Data Breaches of 2021," Healthcare IT News, November 16, 2021, www.healthcareitnews.com/news/biggest-health care-data-breaches-2021.

5. James Rundle, "Hospitals Suffer New Wave of Hacking Attempts," *Wall Street Journal*, February 2, 2021, /www.wsj.com/articles/hospitals-suffer-new-wave-of-hacking-attempts-11612261802.

6. Davis, "Data Breaches."

7 Chloe Kent, "Cyber Attacks Targeting Health Sector Surge amid Covid-19 Crisis," Medical Device Network, March 16, 2020, www.medicaldevice-network.com/news/coronavirus-cybersecurity.

8. "Hospitals Targeted in Rising Wave of Ryuk Ransomware Attacks," *Check Point Software LTD* (Blog), October 29, 2020, https://blog.checkpoint.com/2020/10/29/hospitals-targeted-in-rising-wave-of-ryuk-ransomware-attacks/.

9. Anuja Vaidya, "Report: Health Care Data Breaches Spiked 55% in 2020," MedCity News, February 17, 2021, https://medcitynews.com/2021/02/report-healthcare-data-breaches-spiked-55-in-2020/.

10. US Centers for Disease Control and Prevention (CDC), "Using Telehealth to Expand Access to Essential Health Services during the COVID-19 Pandemic," updated June 10, 2020, www.cdc.gov/coronavirus/2019-ncov/hcp/telehealth.html.

11. Martin et al., "Cybersecurity and Health Care."

12. Lynne Coventry and Dawn Branley, "Cybersecurity in Health Care: A Narrative Review of Trends, Threats and Ways Forward," *Maturitas* 113 (2018): 48–52.

13. Coventry and Branley, 50.

14. US CDC, "COVID-19-Related Phone Scam and Phishing Attacks," April 3, 2020, www.cdc.gov/media/phishing.html.

15. Cybersecurity Watch, "Why Connected Medical Device Security Matters," Crowe, July 20, 2021, www.crowe.com/cybersecurity-watch/why-connected-medical-device-security-matters.

16. Coventry and Branley, "Cybersecurity in Health Care," 50.

17. US CDC, "Using Telehealth."

18. Peter Jaret, "Exposing Vulnerabilities: How Hackers Could Target Your Medical Devices," Association of American Medical Colleges, November 12, 2018, www.aamc.org/news-insights/exposing-vulnerabilities-how-hackers-could-target-your-medical-devices.

19. US Cybersecurity & Infrastructure Security Agency (CISA), *ICS Medical Advisory (ICSMA-19-080-01) Medtronic Conexus Radio Frequency Telemetry Protocol (Update B)*, updated June 4, 2020, https://us-cert.cisa.gov/ics/advisories/ICSMA-19-080-01.

20. Jessica Davis, "Flaws in GE Radiology Medical Device Authentication Pose Patient Data Risk," Health IT Security, December 9, 2020, https://healthitsecurity.com/news/flaws-in-ge-radiology-medical-device-authentication-pose-patient-data-risk.

21. Jaret, "Exposing Vulnerabilities."

22. Coventry and Branley, "Cybersecurity in Health Care," 50.

23. Coventry and Branley.

24. University of California, San Diego, "How Unsecured Medical Record Systems and Medical Devices Put Patient Lives at Risk," ScienceDaily, August 29, 2018, www.sciencedaily.com/releases/2018/08/180829115554.htm.

25. Robert Lord and Dillon Roseen, "Chapter 3: Culture," Do No Harm 2.0, NewAmerica.org, updated October 17, 2019, https://www.newamerica.org/cybersecurity-initiative/reports/do-no-harm-20/chapter-3-culture.

26. Aloha McBride, "How COVID-19 Has Triggered a Sprint toward Smarter Health Care," EY, December 9, 2021, www.ey.com/en_us/health/how-covid-19-has-triggered-a-sprint-toward-smarter-health-care.

27. EY, "What Connections Will Move Health from Reimagining to Reality?," August 8, 2019, https://assets.ey.com/content/dam/ey-sites/ey-com/en_gl/topics/health/ey-new-horizons-2019.pdf.

28. US Department of Health and Human Services (HHS), "HHS Issues New Report Highlighting Dramatic Trends in Medicare Beneficiary Telehealth Utilization amid COVID-19," July 28, 2020, www.hhs.gov/about/news/2020/07/28/hhs-issues-new-report-highlighting-dramatic-trends-in-medicare-beneficiary-telehealth-utilization-amid-covid-19.html.

29. E. Snell, "Healthcare Cyberattack Reported by 81% of Execs, Says Survey," Health IT Security, August 27, 2015, https://healthitsecurity.com/news/healthcare-cyberattack-reported-by-81-of-execs-says-survey.

30. Darrell M. West and Emily Skahill, "Hospitals and Health Care Face Increasing Cybersecurity Risks," August 23, 2021, www.brinknews.com/the-evolving-cybersecurity-risks-in-hospitals-and-the-health-care-industry/.

31. IBM, "Cost of a Data Breach Report 2021," www.ibm.com/downloads/cas/OJDVQGRY.

32. US Department of Health and Human Services, "HHS Issues New Report."

33. Jessica Davis, "Data Breaches Cost Health Care $6.5M, or $429 Per Patient Record," Health IT Security, July 23, 2019, https://healthitsecurity.com/news/data-breaches-cost-healthcare-6.5m-or-429-per-patient-record.

34. "Opinion: What Are Health Care Organizations Lacking in Terms of Cybersecurity? Proper Leadership Structure," Becker's Health IT, July 22, 2014, www.beckershospitalreview.com/healthcare-information-technology/opinion-what-are-healthcare-organizations-lacking-in-terms-of-cybersecurity-proper-leadership-structure.html.

35. US HHS, *Report on Improving Cybersecurity in the Health Care Industry*, Health Care Industry Cybersecurity Task Force, 2017, https://www.phe.gov/Preparedness/planning/CyberTF/Documents/report2017.pdf.

36. Darrell M. West and Emily Skahill, "Hospitals and Health Care Face Increasing Cybersecurity Risks," August 23, 2021, www.brinknews.com/the-evolving-cybersecurity-risks-in-hospitals-and-the-health-care-industry/.

37. US HHS, *Report on Improving Cybersecurity*.

38. Martin et al., "Cybersecurity and Health Care."

39. US HHS, *Report on Improving Cybersecurity*; Hailey Mensik, "Operating Margins Plummet at US Hospitals, Kaufman Hall Says," Healthcare Dive, April 22, 2020, www.healthcaredive.com/news/Kaufman-hospitals-operating-margin-Decline/576491/; Lord and Roseen, "Chapter 3: Culture."

40. IBM, "Cost of a Data Breach Report 2021."

41. Ponemon Institute, "2017 Cost of a Data Breach Study," *Security Intelligence*, June 13, 2017, www.ncsl.org/documents/taskforces/IBM_Ponemon2017CostofDataBreachStudy.pdf.

42. Susan Morse, "Health Care's Number One Financial Issue Is Cybersecurity," Healthcare Finance News, June 30, 2019, www.healthcarefinancenews.com/news/healthcares-number-one-financial-issue-cybersecurity.

43. Jessica Davis, "Data Breaches Cost Health Care $6.5M, or $429 Per Patient Record," Health IT Security, July 23, 2019, https://healthitsecurity.com/news/data-breaches-cost-health care-6.5m-or-429-per-patient-record.

44. "Opinion: What Are Health Care Organizations Lacking in Terms of Cybersecurity? Proper Leadership Structure," Becker's Health IT, July 22, 2014, www.beckershospitalreview.com /healthcare-information-technology/opinion-what-are-healthcare-organizations-lacking -in-terms-of-cybersecurity-proper-leadership-structure.html.

45. "Opinion: What Are Health Care Organizations Lacking?"

46. US HHS, *Report on Improving Cybersecurity*.

47. US HHS.

48. Martin et al., "Cybersecurity and Health Care."

49. "Nielsen Survey Shows Gaps in How Patients Are Experiencing Accountable Care," Council of Accountable Physician Practices, June 15, 2016, https://accountablecaredoctors .org/integratedcoordinated-care/nielsen-survey-shows-gaps-patients-experiencing -accountable-care.

50. US HHS, *Report on Improving Cybersecurity*.

51. Hailey Mensik, "Operating Margins Plummet at US Hospitals, Kaufman Hall Says," Healthcare Dive, April 22, 2020, www.healthcaredive.com/news/Kaufman-hospitals -operating-margin-Decline/576491.

52. Lord and Roseen, "Chapter 3: Culture."

53. American Medical Association (AMA), "Meaningful Use: Electronic Health Record (EHR) incentive programs," January 27, 2020, www.ama-assn.org/practice-management /medicare-medicaid/meaningful-use-electronic-health-record-ehr-incentive.

54. AMA.

55. AMA.

56. AMA.

57. Paul Bischoff, "Ransomware Attacks on US Health Care Organizations Cost $20.8bn in 2020," *Comparitech*, March 10, 2021, www.comparitech.com/blog/information-security /ransomware-attacks-hospitals-data/.

58. American Bar Association, "Loan Repayment Assistance Programs," www.americanbar .org/groups/center-pro-bono/resources/directory_of_law_school_public_interest _pro_bono_programs/definitions/pi_lrap/.

CHAPTER 8. DEFENSE

1. US HHS, "Defense Industrial Base Sector-Specific Plan 2010," 105, May, 2010, www.cisa .gov/sites/default/files/publications/nipp-ssp-defense-industrial-base-2010-508.pdf.

2. National Defense Industrial Association, "Vital Signs 2020: The Health and Readiness of the Defense Industrial Base," 2020, www.ndia.org/-/media/vital-signs/vital-signs _screen_v3.ashx?la=en.

3. "Vital-Signs_2021_digital.Pdf," 9, accessed April 25, 2021, https://content.ndia.org /-/media/vital-signs/2021/vital-signs_2021_digital.ashx.

4. "History of NDISAC," 2019, https://ndisac.org/resource-library/history-of-ndisac/.

5. US General Services Admininistration, Federal Advisory Committee Act, February 26, 2019, www.gsa.gov/policy-regulations/policy/federal-advisory-committee-management /legislation-and-regulations/the-federal-advisory-committee-act.

6. "Defense Federal Acquisition Regulation," accessed April 26, 2021, www.acquisition.gov /sites/default/files/current/dfars/pdf/DFARS.pdf.

7. To its great credit and contrary to the fears of most DIB companies, DCMA has implemented a fair and professional assessment process. It is hard to see, however, where that level of scrutiny could scale up to enough suppliers to make a difference.

8. Daniel Gonzales, Sarah Harting, Mary Kate Adgie, Julia Brackup, Lindsey Polley, and Karlyn D. Stanley, "Unclassified and Secure: A Defense Industrial Base Cyber Protection Program for Unclassified Defense Networks," RAND Corporation, 2020, www.rand.org/pubs/research_reports/RR4227.html.

CHAPTER 9. FINANCIAL SERVICES

The authors' views expressed in this chapter are their own; Kenneth Huh and Tarun Krishnakumar collaborated on this chapter when they were researchers at the Internet Security Alliance (ISA) in 2020.

1. Anna Zakrzewski et al., "Global Wealth 2019: Reigniting Radical Growth," Boston Consulting Group, accessed June 20, 2019, https://web-assets.bcg.com/img-src/BCG-Reigniting-Radical-Growth-June-2019_tcm9-222638.pdf.

2. James Coker, "Two-Thirds of Financial Services Firms Suffered Cyber-Attacks in the Past Year," *InfoSecurity*, November 5, 2020, www.infosecurity-magazine.com/news/two-thirds-financial-services/.

3. "2020 Data Breach Investigations Report," Verizon, accessed July 19, 2020, https://enterprise.verizon.com/resources/reports/2020-data-breach-investigations-report.pdf.

4. "The Cost of Cybercrime: Ninth Annual Cost of Cybercrime Study," Accenture, July 15, 2019, www.accenture.com/_acnmedia/PDF-96/Accenture-2019-Cost-of-Cybercrime-Study-Final.pdf.

5. LexisNexis Risk Solutions, "2020 True Cost of Fraud Study: Financial Services and Lending Report," accessed May 6, 2021, https://risk.lexisnexis.com/insights-resources/research/true-cost-of-fraud-study-financial-services-and-lending-edition.

6. Eugene Becker, "What Are Your Odds of Getting Your Identity Stolen?," Identity Force, April 15, 2021, www.identityforce.com/blog/identity-theft-odds-identity-theft-statistics.

7. Federal Trade Commission, "New Data Shows FTC Received 2.2 Million Fraud Reports from Consumers in 2020," February 4, 2021, www.ftc.gov/news-events/press-releases/2021/02/new-data-shows-ftc-received-2-2-million-fraud-reports-consumers.

8. Insurance Information Institute, "Facts + Statistics: Identity Theft and Cybercrime," accessed May 12, 2021, www.iii.org/fact-statistic/facts-statistics-identity-theft-and-cybercrime.

9. Jenifer Kuadi, "15 Insane Identity Theft Statistics to Keep in Mind in 2020," Legal Job Site, January 6, 2021, https://legaljobsite.net/identity-theft-statistics/.

10. *Javelin*, "IDF Scam Graphic," accessed May 12, 2021, www.javelinstrategy.com/sites/default/files/2021%20IDF%20Scam%20Graphic.pdf?_hsfp=4186699840&_hssc=251652889.2.1620317484678&_hstc=251652889.9cc52f5c639f7b016b56f1675204ea7c.1620317484677.1620317484677.1620317484677.1.

11. Kuadi, "15 Insane Identity Theft Statistics."

12. Glenn Larson, "Synthetic Identity Fraud Is the Fastest Growing Financial Crime—What Can Banks Do to Fight It?," *Forbes*, October 8, 2019, www.forbes.com/sites/forbes

techcouncil/2019/10/08/synthetic-identity-fraud-is-the-fastest-growing-financial
-crime-what-can-banks-do-to-fight-it/#6df547d17ecb.

13. Bryan Richardson and Derek Waldron, "Fighting Back against Synthetic Identity Fraud,"
McKinsey & Co., January 2, 2019, https://www.mckinsey.com/business-functions/risk
/our-insights/fighting-back-against-synthetic-identity-fraud#; and Larson, "Synthetic
Identity Fraud."

14. Jeremy Grant et al., "Identifiers & Verification in a Post-Breach World," Federal Identity Forum and Expo, September 26, 2018, https://events.afcea.org/FedID18/Public
/SessionDetails.aspx?FromPage=Sessions.aspx&SessionID=6580&SessionDateID=510.

15. Orla McCaffrey, "People Aren't Visiting Branches; Banks Are Wondering How Many
They Actually Need," Wall Street Journal, June 7, 2020, https://ww.wsj.com/articles
/people-arent-visiting-branches-banks-are-wondering-how-many-they-actually-need
-11591531200.

16. "Survey: Pandemic Drove Increase in Mobile Banking, Decline in Branch Traffic,"
ABA Banking Journal, June 9, 2021, https://bankingjournal.aba.com/2021/06/survey
-pandemic-drove-increase-in-mobile-banking-decline-in-branch-traffic/.

17. Jeremy Grant, "The Future of Identity in Financial Services: Threats, Challenges, and
Opportunities," Testimony to U.S. House Financial Services Committee, September 12,
2019, https://financialservices.house.gov/uploadedfiles/hhrg-116-ba00-wstate-grantj
-20190912.pdf.

18. Better Identity Coalition, "Better Identity in America: A Blueprint for Policymakers," July
2018, https://docs.house.gov/meetings/BA/BA00/20190912/109912/HHRG-116
-BA00-Wstate-GrantJ-20190912-SD001.pdf.

19. Elizabeth Renieris, "The Role of Identity in Europe's Digital Future," Good ID, March 26,
2020, https://www.good-id.org/en/articles/role-identity-europes-digital-future/.

20. US Government Accountability Office, "Financial Regulation: Complex and Fragmented
Structure Could be Streamlined to Improve Effectiveness," February 2016, www.gao.gov
/assets/680/675400.pdf.

21. US Government Accountability Office.

22. Financial Services Sector Coordinating Council, "Financial Services Sector Cybersecurity Profile," October 25, 2018, https://fsscc.org/published-documents/.

23. Financial Stability Board, "Stocktake of Publicly Released Cybersecurity Regulations,
Guidance and Supervisory Practices," October 13, 2017, www.fsb.org/wp-content
/uploads/P131017-2.pdf.

24. Financial Services Sector Coordinating Council, "Financial Services Sector Cybersecurity Profile."

25. Financial Services Sector Coordinating Council.

26. Commission on Enhancing National Cybersecurity, "Report on Securing and Growing
the Digital Economy," December 1, 2016, https://iapp.org/media/pdf/resource_center
/2016-cybersecurity-commission-report-final.pdf.

27. Accenture, "The Cost of Cybercrime: Ninth Annual Cost of Cybercrime Study," accessed
July 19, 2020, www.accenture.com/us-en/insights/financial-services/cost-cybercrime
-study-financial-services.

28. Edith M. Lederer, "Top UN Official Warns Malicious Emails on Rise in Pandemic,"
Associated Press, May 23, 2020, https://apnews.com/article/c7e7fc7e582351f8f55293
d0bf21d7fb.

29. Ransomware Threat Report, Unit 41 by Palo Alto Networks, 2021, www.paloaltonetworks
.com/content/dam/pan/en_US/assets/pdf/reports/Unit_42/unit42-ransomware-threat
-report-2021.pdf?utm_source=marketo&utm_medium=email&utm_campaign=2021-05
-10%2009:29:00-Global-DA-EN-21-03-05-7014u000001ZIEtAAO-P3-Cortex-unit-42
-ransomware-threat-report.

30. Shannon Vavra, "Ransomware Demands up by 43% so far in 2021, Coveware Says,"
CyberScoop, April 27, 2021, www.cyberscoop.com/ransomware-extortion-demands
-increasing-coveware/.

31. Dark Reading Staff, "Malware Campaign Hides in Resumes and Medical Leave Forms,"
Dark Reading, June 5, 2020, www.darkreading.com/vulnerabilities-threats/malware
-campaign-hides-in-resumes-and-medical-leave-forms.

32. iomart, "Dangerous Data: How to Protect Your Business from Costly Data Breaches,"
May 6, 2020, https://blog.iomart.com/dangerous-data-how-to-protect-your-business
-from-costly-data-breaches/.

33. FBI National Press Office, "FBI Releases the Internet Crime Complaint Center *2020
Internet Crime Report*, including COVID-19 Scam Statistics," FBI, March 17, 2021, www
.fbi.gov/news/pressrel/press-releases/fbi-releases-the-internet-crime-complaint-center
-2020-internet-crime-report-including-covid-19-scam-statistics.

34. Jurgen Stock, Michael Daniel, and Tal Goldstein, "Partnerships Are Our Best Weapon in
the Fight against Cybercrime; Here's Why," World Economic Forum, January 21, 2020,
www.weforum.org/agenda/2020/01/partnerships-are-our-best-weapon-in-the-fight
-against-cybercrime-heres-why/.

35. Stock, Daniel, and Goldstein.

36. Stock, Daniel, and Goldstein.

37. Joyce Hakmeh, "Building a Stronger International Legal Framework on Cybercrime,"
Chatham House, June 6, 2017, www.chathamhouse.org/expert/comment/building
-stronger-international-legal-framework-cybercrime.

38. Laurens Cerulus, "Europe Nears Tipping Point on Russian Hacking," Politico, June 3,
2020, www.politico.com/news/2020/06/03/europe-russian-hackers-sanctions-300124.

CHAPTER 10. ENERGY

1. "Utility of the Future," Massachusetts Institute of Technology, December 2016, http://
energy.mit.edu/wp-content/uploads/2016/12/Utility-of-the-Future-Full-Report.pdf.

2. Don C. Smith, "Enhancing Cybersecurity in the Energy Sector: A Critical Priority," *Journal of Energy & Natural Resources Law* 36, no. 4 (September 24, 2018): 373–80, DOI:
10.1080/02646811.2018.1516362.

3. Smith.

4. James McBride, "How Does the U.S. Power Grid Work?," Council on Foreign Relations,
updated May 14, 2021, www.cfr.org/backgrounder/modernizing-us-energy-grid.

5. US Department of Energy, Office of Electricity, accessed September 1, 2020, www
.smartgrid.gov/the_smart_grid/smart_grid.html.

6. "Maximizing Economic Value and Consumer Equity," January 2017, 2020, www
.energy.gov/sites/prod/files/2017/02/f34/Chapter%20II--Maximizing%20Economic
%20Value%20and%20Consumer%20Equity.pdf.

7. "Maximizing Economic Value."

8. International Energy Agency, "Digitalisation and Energy,"November 2017, www.iea.org /reports/digitalisation-and-energy#a-new-era-in-energy.

9. "How Electricity Choice Allows Consumers to Choose Clean Energy at Home," Clean Technica, December 9, 2018, https://cleantechnica.com/2018/12/09/how-electricity -choice-allows-consumers-to-choose-clean-energy-at-home/.

10. Carey W. King, "Consumers Express Community Values with Their Electricity Choices," *IEEE Spectrum*, May 11, 2017, https://spectrum.ieee.org/energywise/energy/policy /consumers-express-community-values-with-their-electricity-choices.

11. *International Journal of Renewable Energy and Smart Grid* (*IJRESG*) 1, no. 1 (September 2012), www.ijsgce.com/index.php?m=content&c=index&a=lists&catid=27.

12. *IJRESG*.

13. Robert Walton, "NERC Finding 25% of Utilities Exposed to SolarWinds Hack Indicates Growing ICS Vulnerabilities, Analysts Say," *Utility Dive*, April 15, 2021, www.utilitydive .com/news/nerc-finding-25-of-utilities-exposed-to-solarwinds-hack-indicates-growing /598449/.

14. Cybersecurity and Infrastructure Security Agency, "Understanding and Mitigating Russian State-Sponsored Cyber Threats to U.S. Critical Infrastructure," January 11, 2022, www.cisa.gov/uscert/ncas/alerts/aa22-011a.

15. FBI, "Cyber threats are always growing. Join @FBILosAngeles Assistant Director in Charge Kristi Johnson and @SCE's Brian Barrios as they discuss the importance of ongoing, productive partnerships in protecting the energy sector," January 27, 2022, 1:19 p.m. https://twitter.com/FBI/status/1486765877961838598?s=20&t=31sRMM85NA -gXtz7KY13Pg.

16. Dan Goodin, "Breached Water Plant Employees Used the Same TeamViewer Password and No Firewall," *Ars Technica*, February 10, 2021, https://arstechnica.com/information -technology/2021/02/breached-water-plant-employees-used-the-same-teamviewer -password-and-no-firewall/.

17. Massachusetts Department of Environmental Protection, "Cybersecurity Advisory for Public Water Suppliers," accessed April 17, 2021, www.mass.gov/service-details/cyber security-advisory-for-public-water-suppliers.

18. Robert Walton, "Electric Sector Can Learn from the Florida Water Utility Hack, Say Experts," *Utility Dive*, February 11, 2021, www.utilitydive.com/news/electric-sector-can -learn-from-the-florida-water-utility-hack-say-experts/594914/.

19. Cyberspace Solarium Commission, March 2020 Report, www.solarium.gov/report.

20. Eric Geller, "White House Will Ask Water Utilities to Deploy Network Monitoring Tools, Report Cyber Threats," POLITICO Pro, January 27, 2022, https://subscriber .politicopro.com/article/2022/01/white-house-will-ask-water-utilities-to-deploy -network-monitoring-tools-report-cyber-threats-00002599.

21. *IJRESG*.

22. Adam Cooper and Mike Shuster, "Electric Company Smart Meter Deployments: Foundation for a Smart Grid (2021 Update)," April 2021, https://www.edisonfoundation.net /-/media/Files/IEI/publications/IEI_Smart_Meter_Report_April_2021.ashx.

23. NISTIR 7628, "Guidelines for Smart Grid Cyber Security: Vol. 2, Privacy and the Smart Grid," August 2010, 13–14.

24. NISTIR 7628.

25. Robert K. Knake, "A Cyberattack on the U.S. Power Grid," Council on Foreign Relations, April 3, 2017, www.cfr.org/report/cyberattack-us-power-grid.

26. International Energy Agency, "Digitalisation and Energy."

27. Cyril W. Draffen Jr., "Cybersecurity White Paper," Massachusetts Institute of Technology, January 2, 2017, https://energy.mit.edu/wp-content/uploads/2017/07/Cybersecurity-White-Paper.pdf.

28. Draffen.

29. Smith, "Enhancing Cybersecurity."

30. Knake, "A Cyberattack."

31. Knake.

32. Blake Sobczak, "Report Reveals Play-by-Play of First U.S. Grid Cyberattack," E&E News, September 5, 2019, www.eenews.net/stories/1061111289.

33. Sobczak.

34. Kim Zetter, "Inside the Cunning, Unprecedented Hack of Ukraine's Power Grid," Wired, March 3, 2016, www.wired.com/2016/03/inside-cunning-unprecedented-hack-ukraines-power-grid/.

35. Zetter, "Inside the Cunning."

36. Draffen, "Cybersecurity White Paper."

37. David Sanger and Nicole Pelroth, "U.S. Escalates Online Attacks on Russia's Power Grid," New York Times, June 15, 2019, www.nytimes.com/2019/06/15/us/politics/trump-cyber-russia-grid.html.

38. Chuck Brooks, "Public Private Partnerships and the Cybersecurity Challenge of Protecting Critical Infrastructure," Forbes, May 6, 2019, www.forbes.com/sites/cognitiveworld/2019/05/06/public-private-partnerships-and-the-cybersecurity-challenge-of-protecting-critical-infrastructure/#5c33ca905a57.

39. Sanger and Pelroth, "U.S. Escalates."

40. Megan Brown, "Cyber Imperative: Preserve and Strengthen Public-Private Partnerships," National Security Institute, October 2018, http://nationalsecurity.gmu.edu/wp-content/uploads/2018/10/Cyber-Imperative-Final-Web.pdf.

41. DHS, "Information Sharing and Analysis Organizations (ISAOS)," accessed September 1, 2020, /www.cisa.gov/information-sharing-and-analysis-organizations-isaos.

42. Brown, "Cyber Imperative."

43. National Council of Information Sharing and Analysis Centers (ISACs), "About ISACs," 2020, www.nationalisacs.org/about-isacs.

44. Chris Bing, "Inside 'Project Indigo,' the Quiet Info-Sharing Program between Banks and U.S. Cyber Command," Cyberscoop, May 21, 2018, www.cyberscoop.com/project-indigo-fs-isac-cyber-command-information-sharing-dhs/.

45. Bing.

46. Cyberspace Solarium Commission, March 2020 Report.

47. "U.S. Department of Energy, U.S. Department of Homeland Security, and U.S. Department of Defense Announce Pathfinder Initiative to Protect U.S. Energy Critical Infrastructure," February 3, 2020, www.energy.gov/articles/us-department-energy-us-department-homeland-security-and-us-department-defense-announce.

48. David Vergun, "Cyber Strategy Protects Critical U.S. Infrastructure," US Department of Defense, September 6, 2019, www.defense.gov/Explore/News/Article/Article/1954009/cyber-strategy-protects-critical-us-infrastructure/.

49. Cyberspace Solarium Commission, March 2020 Report.
50. Cyberspace Solarium Commission.
51. Cyberspace Solarium Commission.
52. Taylor Armerding, "Security Experts: Cyber Sharing Isn't Enough," *Computer World*, September 22, 2015, www.computerworld.com/article/2985399/security-experts-cyber-sharing-isnt-enough.html.
53. Robert Watson, "Small, Regional Utilities Located Near Critical Infrastructure Targeted in Cyberattack: *WSJ*," *Utility Dive*, November 26, 2019, www.utilitydive.com/news/small-regional-utilities-located-near-critical-infrastructure-targeted-in/568074/.
54. Watson.
55. Watson.

CHAPTER 11. RETAIL

1. Alison Deutsch, "The 5 Industries Driving the U.S. Economy," Investopedia, updated October 24, 2021, www.investopedia.com/articles/investing/042915/5-industries-driving-us-economy.asp.
2. Danielle Inman, "Retail Sales to Now Exceed $4.44 Trillion in 2021, as NRF Revises Annual Forecast," National Retail Federation, June 9, 2021, https://nrf.com/media-center/press-releases/retail-sales-now-exceed-444-trillion-2021-nrf-revises-annual-forecast.
3. Mark Matthews, "Retail Store Numbers Continue to Grow," National Retail Federation, August 12, 2019, https://nrf.com/blog/retail-store-numbers-continue-grow.
4. Jessica Young, "US Ecommerce Sales Grow 14.9% in 2019," Digital Commerce 360, February 19, 2020, www.digitalcommerce360.com/article/us-ecommerce-sales/.
5. Fareeha Ali and Jessica Young, "US Ecommerce Grows 32.4% in 2020," Digital Commerce 360, January 29, 2021, www.digitalcommerce360.com/article/us-ecommerce-sales/.
6. "2018 Credential Spill Report," Shape Security, https://em360tech.com/index.php/continuity/white-papers/shape-security-2018-credential-spill-report.
7. Verizon, "2020 Data Breach Investigations Report—Retail," https://enterprise.verizon.com/resources/reports/dbir/2020/data-breach-statistics-by-industry/retail-data-breaches-security/.
8. IBM Security, "Cost of a Data Breach Report," 2019, www.ibm.com/downloads/cas/ZBZLY7KL?_ga=2.16346678.100177559.1594732455-885564525.1594732455.
9. Jason Thompson, "IntSights Finds Organized Retail Crime Costs Retailers $30 Billion Each Year," IntSights, November 14, 2019, https://intsights.com/press-releases/intsights-finds-organized-retail-crime-costs-retailers-30-billion-each-year.
10. Verizon, "2020 Data Breach."
11. Verizon.
12. Verizon.
13. IBM Security, "Cost of a Data Breach Report," 2020, www.ibm.com/downloads/cas/RZAX14GX.
14. IBM Security.
15. IBM Security.
16. Roman Cuprina and Olena Kovalenko, "Artificial Intelligence for Retail in 2020," SPD Group, December 20, 2019, https://spd.group/artificial-intelligence/ai-for-retail/.

17. Cuprina and Kovalenko.
18. Dan Pitman, "Cyber Security Risk in Retail and How to Handle It," *Forbes*, February 12, 2019, www.forbes.com/sites/danpitman1/2019/02/12/cyber-security-risk-in-retail -and-how-to-handle-it/#7043a62949a0.
19. IBM Security, "Cost of a Data Breach," 2020.
20. IBM Security.
21. "Driving Cybersecurity Performance: ESI ThoughtLab," https://econsultsolutions.com /esi-thoughtlab/driving-cybersecurity-performance/.
22. IBM Security, "Cost of a Data Breach," 2020.
23. "M-Trends 2021 Special Report," FireEye Mandiant Services, https://content.fireeye .com/m-trends/rpt-m-trends-2021.
24. Mark Jones, "The Retail Giants at Serious Risk of Cyber-Attacks," TechHQ, November 10, 2020, https://techhq.com/2020/11/the-retail-giants-at-significant-risk-of-cyber -attacks/.
25. McKinsey Statista, "Share of Consumers in the United States Using Online Shopping for Selected Product Categories before and after COVID-19 as of August 2020," www-statista -com.proxyau.wrlc.org/statistics/1134709/consumers-us-online-purchase-before-after -covid-categories/.
26. Ali and Young, "US Ecommerce."
27. Verizon, "2020 Data Breach."
28. IBM Security, "Cost of a Data Breach," 2020.
29. Tatiana Walk-Morris, "Beyond the Data Breach: How Retail Is Addressing Cybersecurity," Retail Dive, June 6, 2019, www.retaildive.com/news/beyond-the-data-breach-how -retail-is-addressing-cybersecurity/555563/.
30. "Cyber(attack) Monday: Hackers Target the Retail Industry as E-Commerce Thrives," IntSights, www.intsights.com/rs/071-ZWD-900/images/Cyber%20Attack%20Monday .pdf.
31. Kevin McCoy, "Target to Pay $18.5M for 2013 Data Breach That Affected 41 Million Consumers," *USA Today*, May 23, 2017, www.usatoday.com/story/money/2017/05/23 /target-pay-185m-2013-data-breach-affected-consumers/102063932/.
32. "The Cost of Data Security: Are Cybersecurity Investments Worth It?," *CloudMask,* January 28, 2022, www.cloudmask.com/blog/the-cost-of-data-security-are-cybersecurity -investments-worth-it; and Kim Crawley, "Cybersecurity Budgets Explained: How Much Do Companies Spend on Cybersecurity?," *AT&T Business*, May 5, 2020, https://cybersecurity .att.com/blogs/security-essentials/how-to-justify-your-cybersecurity-budget.
33. David Turetsky, Brian Nussbaum, and Unal Tatar, "Cybersecurity Sharing Success Stories," *Lawfare*, July 15, 2020, www.lawfareblog.com/cybersecurity-information-sharing -success-stories.
34. Walk-Morris, "Beyond the Data Breach."
35. Marianne Wilson, "Many Retailers Still Lack Response Plans for Cyberattacks," Chain Store Age, November 15, 2019, https://chainstoreage.com/many-retailers-still-lack -response-plans-cyberattacks.
36. Maddie Shepherd, "28 Surprising Working from Home Statistics," Fundera, April 7, 2020, www.fundera.com/resources/working-from-home-statistics.
37. "Remote Work Study: How Cyber Habits at Home Threaten Corporate Network Security," CyberArk, June 3, 2020, www.cyberark.com/press/remote-work-study-how-cyber -habits-at-home-threaten-corporate-network-security/.

38. Ponemon Institute, "Measuring & Managing the Cyber Risks to Business Operations," December, 2018, https://static.tenable.com/marketing/research-reports/Research-Report -Ponemon-Institute-Measuring_and_Managing_the_Cyber_Risks_to_Business _Operations.pdf.

39. Jai Vijayan, "Third-Party Breaches—and the Number of Records Exposed—Increased Sharply in 2019," Dark Reading, February 12, 2020, www.darkreading.com/attacks -breaches/third-party-breaches-and-the-number-of-records-exposed-increased-sharply -in-2019.

40. Blake Morgan, "50 Stats Showing Why Companies Need to Prioritize Consumer Privacy," *Forbes*, June 22, 2020, www.forbes.com/sites/blakemorgan/2020/06/22/50-stats -showing-why-companies-need-to-prioritize-consumer-privacy/#45e747a037f6.

41. Louise Matsakis, "The *Wired* Guide to Your Personal Data (and Who Is Using It)," *Wired*, February 15, 2019, www.wired.com/story/wired-guide-personal-data-collection/.

42. Verizon, "Data Breach Investigations Report," accessed January 25, 2022, www.verizon .com/business/resources/reports/2021/2021-data-breach-investigations-report.pdf.

43. Matsakis, "The *Wired* Guide."

44. Emily Tabatabai, "States Continue to Expand Definition of 'Personal Information,'" International Association of Privacy Professionals, February 27, 2017, https://iapp.org/news /a/states-continue-to-expand-definition-of-personal-information/.

45. Brian Dean, "Privacy v. Security," Secureworks, March 23, 2017, www.secureworks.com /blog/privacy-vs-security.

46. Dean.

47. Dean.

48. David Uberti, "Tech Firms Filing to Go Public Warn Investors of Shifts in Privacy Rules," *Wall Street Journal Cybersecurity Pro*, August 28, 2020, www.wsj.com/articles/tech-firms -filing-to-go-public-warn-investors-of-shifts-in-privacy-rules-11598607001.

49. Rob Sides, Matt Marsh, Rob Goldberg, and Michael Mangold, "Consumer Privacy in Retail: The Next Regulatory and Competitive Frontier," Deloitte, 2019, www2.deloitte .com/content/dam/Deloitte/us/Documents/consumer-business/us-retail-privacy -survey-2019.pdf.

50. Morgan, "50 Stats Showing Why Companies Need to Prioritize Consumer Privacy."

51. "California Consumer Privacy Act," State of California Department of Justice, Office of the Attorney Genera, https://oag.ca.gov/privacy/ccpa#:~:text=This%20landmark%20 law%20secures%20new%20privacy%20rights%20for%20California%20consumers%2C %20including%3A&text=The%20right%20to%20delete%20personal,for%20exercising %20their%20CCPA%20rights.

52. Berkeley Economic Advising and Research, LLC, "Standardized Regulatory Impact Assessment: California Consumer Privacy Act of 2018 Regulations," State of California Department of Justice, Office of the Attorney General, August 2019, www.dof.ca.gov /Forecasting/Economics/Major_Regulations/Major_Regulations_Table/documents /CCPA_Regulations-SRIA-DOF.pdf.

53. Nuala O'Connor, "Reforming the U.S. Approach to Data Protection and Privacy," Council on Foreign Relations, January 30, 2018, www.cfr.org/report/reforming-us-approach -data-protection.

54. Tabatabai, "States Continue to Expand Definition of 'Personal Information."

55. White House, President Barack Obama, Office of the Press Secretary, "We Can't Wait: Obama Administration Unveils Blueprint for a 'Privacy Bill of Rights' to Protect Consumers

Online," February 23, 2012, https://obamawhitehouse.archives.gov/the-press-office /2012/02/23/we-can-t-wait-obama-administration-unveils-blueprint-privacy-bill-rights.

56. O'Connor, "Reforming the U.S. Approach."

57. US Department of Homeland Security, "Collective Defense: A Collaborative Perspective from the IT Sector," Department of Homeland Security and Information Technology Sector Coordinating Council, p. 4, www.it-scc.org/uploads/4/7/2/3/47232717/the _collective_defense_white_paper_12.19.pdf.

58. Department of Homeland Security, 5.

59. Department of Homeland Security, 5.

60. Kristina Stewart, "3 Cyber Threats and 4 Ways to Protect Against Them," National Retail Federation, June 28, 2019, https://nrf.com/blog/3-cyber-threats-and-4-ways-protect -against-them.

CHAPTER 12. TELECOMMUNICATIONS

1. GDPR, "GDPR Fines & Data Breach Penalties," July 29, 2020, www.gdpreu.org /compliance/fines-and-penalties/.

2. "What If COVID Had Happened in 1990 Instead of 2020 or 2030?," Internet Security Alliance, https://isalliance.org/what-if-covid-had-happened-in-1990-instead-of-2020-or -2030/.

3. Skye Lan, "Huawei and ZTE Secure Nearly Half of the Global 5G Equipment Market," EqualOcean, July 8, 2020, https://equalocean.com/news/2020070814197.

4. Stuart Lau, "EU Slams China's 'Authoritarian Shift' and Broken Economic Promises," Politico, April 25, 2021, www.politico.eu/article/eu-china-biden-economy-climate -europe/.

5. Nokia, "Open RAN Explained," October 16, 2020, www.nokia.com/about-us/newsroom /articles/open-ran-explained/.

CHAPTER 13. INFORMATION TECHNOLOGY

The authors' views expressed in this chapter are their own. Tarun Krishnakumar collaborated on this chapter when he was a researcher at the Internet Security Alliance (ISA) in 2020.

1. Hannah Shaban and David Lynch, "U.S. Stocks Hit Record High, Ending Shortest Bear Market in History," *Washington Post*, August 18, 2020, www.washingtonpost.com /business/2020/08/18/stocks-record-high-sp-500/.

2. Monica Anderson, "Most Americans Say Social Media Companies Have Too Much Power, Influence in Politics," Pew Research Center, July 22, 2020, www.pewresearch.org /fact-tank/2020/07/22/most-americans-say-social-media-companies-have-too-much -power-influence-in-politics/.

3. Ted Van Green, "Few Americans Are Confident in Tech Companies to Prevent Mis-use of Their Platforms in the 2020 Election," Pew Research Center, September 9, 2020, www.pewresearch.org/fact-tank/2020/02/24/few-americans-are-confident-in-tech -companies-to-prevent-misuse-of-their-platforms-in-the-2020-election/.

4. Brooke Auxier et al., "Americans and Privacy: Concerned, Confused and Feeling Lack of Control over Their Personal Information," Pew Research Center, November 15, 2019, www

.pewresearch.org/internet/2019/11/15/americans-and-privacy-concerned-confused-and
-feeling-lack-of-control-over-their-personal-information/.

5. Billy Perrigo, "European Union Announces New Big Tech Regulations," *Time*, December 16, 2020, https://time.com/5921760/europe-digital-services-act-big-tech/.

6. Jonathan Zittrain, Matthew Olsen, David O'Brien, and Bruce Schneier, "Don't Panic: Making Progress on the 'Going Dark' Debate," Berkman Center Research, Publication 2016-1, February 1, 2016, https://dash.harvard.edu/bitstream/handle/1/28552576/Dont_Panic _Making_Progress_on_Going_Dark_Debate.pdf?sequence=1&isAllowed=y.

7. Zittrain et al.

8. US DOJ, "Lawful Access," October 30, 2020, www.justice.gov/olp/lawful-access.

9. Jennifer Valentino-DeVries, "Tracking Phones, Google Is a Dragnet for the Police," *New York Times*, April 13, 2019, www.nytimes.com/interactive/2019/04/13/us/google -location-tracking-police.html.

10. Laura Hautala, "COVID-19 Contact Tracing Apps Create Privacy Pitfalls around the World," CNET, August 8, 2020, www.cnet.com/news/covid-contact-tracing-apps-bring -privacy-pitfalls-around-the-world/.

11. Arthur Coviello Jr., "RSA Conference 2014 Keynote," February 14, 2014, https://web .archive.org/web/20140714192650/.

12. Internet Security Alliance, The Cybersecurity Social Contract (2016), 119.

13. Zittrain et al., "Don't Panic."

14. "Jeffrey A. Rosen Delivers Remarks at Justice Department's Lawful Access Summit," October 4, 2019, www.justice.gov/opa/speech/deputy-attorney-general-jeffrey-rosen -delivers-remarks-justice-departments-lawful-access.

15. White House, "Executive Order on Preventing Online Censorship," Presidential Executive Order, May 28, 2020, https://trumpwhitehouse.archives.gov/presidential-actions /executive-order-preventing-online-censorship/.

16. Protection for Private Blocking and Screening of Offensive Material, 47 U.S.C. §230(c)(1), accessed September 1, 2020, https://uscode.house.gov/view.xhtml?req=(title:47%20section: 230%20edition:prelim).

17. Susan Benkelman, "The Law That Made the Internet What It Is Today," *Washington Post*, April 26, 2019, www.washingtonpost.com/outlook/the-law-that-made-the-internet-what -it-is-today/2019/04/26/aa637f9c-57c5-11e9-9136-f8e636f1f6df_story.html.

18. Jeff Kosseff, "Testimony of Jeff Kosseff," Written Testimony on the PACT Act and Section 230: The Impact of the Law That Helped Create the Internet and an Examination of Proposed Reforms for Today's Online World, United States Naval Academy, July 28, 2020, www.commerce.senate.gov/services/files/444EFF87-84E3-46DB-B8DB -24DC9A424869.

19. Zeran v. America Online, 129 F.3d 327, 332 (4th Cir. 1997).

20. Kosseff, "Testimony."

21. Kosseff.

22. Anshu Siripurapu, "Trump's Executive Order: What to Know about Section 230," Council on Foreign Relations, December 2, 2020, www.cfr.org/in-brief/trumps-executive -order-what-know-about-section-230.

23. US DOJ, "Section 230—Nurturing Innovation or Fostering Unaccountability? Key Takeaways and Recommendations," June 2020, www.justice.gov/file/1286331/download.

24. Kosseff, "Testimony."

25. "Schatz, Thune Introduce New Legislation to Update Section 230, Strengthen Rules, Transparency on Online Content Moderation, Hold Internet Companies Accountable for Moderation Practices," Schatz.Senate.gov, June 24, 2020, /www.schatz.senate .gov/press-releases/schatz-thune-introduce-new-legislation-to-update-section-230 -strengthen-rules-transparency-on-online-content-moderation-hold-internet-companies -accountable-for-moderation-practices.

INDEX

ABOUT THE CONTRIBUTORS

RYAN BOULAIS is Chief Information Security Officer at AES. Previously, Boulais was vice president of Shared Security Services for Thomson Reuters globally. His areas of focus were identity and access management, security platforms, data loss prevention, and compliance/vendor risk management. He was with GE for over five years, culminating in becoming vice president of global security operations, in charge of all cybersecurity incidents across the company's nine businesses, over three hundred thousand employees, and infrastructure both on the premises and in Cloud environments.

JEFFREY C. BROWN was formerly Vice President and Chief Information Security Officer at Raytheon Technologies. Previously, he held numerous operational and staff positions within the air force. He holds a degree in computer science from the US Air Force Academy, a master's degree in computer science from the University of California, Berkeley, and a master's degree in national security strategy from the National Defense University. He is a contributing author to the ISA's Cybersecurity Social Contract Handbook (2016).

LARRY CLINTON is President of the Internet Security Alliance. He advises industry and government on cyber policy. He has briefed NATO, the OAS, the G20, and the US Congress. He has twice been named to the Corporate 100 list of the most influential individuals in corporate governance. He has written cybersecurity best practices books that are used in the United States, Europe, Latin America, and Asia.

LOU DESORBO is Senior Vice President and Chief Security and Risk Officer for Centene Corporation. Previously, he served in a variety of leadership roles with Deloitte, Booz Allen Hamilton, the Joint Task Force–Global Network Operations (now US Cyber Command), and Northrop Grumman after separating from the US Air Force. He holds an MBA from Colorado

State University and a BS in electronics management from Southern Illinois University.

JAMISON GARDNER is a member the *Georgetown Journal of Law and Public Policy* and the First-Generation Student Union. He has a JD degree from Georgetown Law.

MICHAEL GORDON is Chief Information Security Officer for Lockheed Martin Corporation. He is serving his tenth year on the Board of Directors of the National Defense Information Sharing and Analysis Center (ND-ISAC) and its predecessor, the Defense Security Information Exchange (DSIE). Gordon also serves as chairman of the Defense Industrial Base Sector Coordinating Council (DIB SCC), which supports the security and resilience of the DIB as one of the nation's designated permanent sixteen critical infrastructure sectors. He holds an undergraduate degree in engineering physics and a master's degree in technical management from Embry-Riddle Aeronautical University, as well an MBA and master of information assurance degree from the University of Dallas.

ALEXANDER T. GREEN received a JD degree from the Georgetown University Law Center in 2022. While at Georgetown Law, he served as a staff editor on the *Georgetown Journal of Law & Public Policy* and was vice president of the Corporate & Financial Law Organization. Before law school, he competed as a Division 1 student-athlete on the Men's Golf Team at the University of Alabama, from which he graduated in 2019 after studying finance with a specialization in economics.

JOSH HIGGINS is Senior Director of Policy and Communications at the Internet Security Alliance. Previously, he was a journalist for Inside Cybersecurity. He holds a bachelor's degree in communication and political science from Virginia Tech.

MICHAEL HIGGINS is Vice President of Information Security and Chief Information Security Officer for L3Harris Technologies. He holds a bachelor's degree in electrical engineering from the State University of New York at Stony Brook and is involved in various industry committees.

KENNETH HUH is manager of the complete life cycle of cybersecurity risks for BNY Mellon. Prior to joining BNY Mellon, Huh was an adviser on information security strategies to *Fortune* 500 companies, the top five US banks, and the US government. He holds a bachelor's degree in business administration from James Madison University.

ANDY KIRKLAND is Chief Information Security Officer for Starbucks Coffee Company. He has twenty years of experience working in information security and FDA regulatory environments. He holds a bachelor's degree in business and mathematics from Adrian College.

TARUN KRISHNAKUMAR is an attorney licensed to practice law in the United States (California) and abroad. He has experience working on emerging issues in technology law and policy, including privacy, cybersecurity, intellectual property, e-commerce, and content regulation. He has worked in both litigation and advisory capacities. He received his law degree from India's top law school, the National Law School of India, Bangalore, and also holds a graduate degree from Georgetown Law.

GARY MCALUM is Senior Vice President and Chief Security Officer at USAA. Previously, he served in the US Air Force for twenty-five years in a variety of staff and leadership positions in the information technology field, including telecommunications, deployable and satellite communications, network operations, and information security, and in the front line of cyberspace operations for the Department of Defense. He holds a bachelor's degree in mathematics from the Citadel, a master's degree in management information systems from the University of Arizona, and a master's degree in national resource strategy from the Industrial College of the Armed Forces. In addition, he is a Certified Information Systems Security Professional (CISSP) and a Certified Fraud Examiner (CFE).

GREG MONTANA is Corporate Executive Vice President and Chief Risk Officer for FIS Global. Previously, he worked at Bank of America as senior vice president and senior operational risk executive; PayPal, as senior director of global risk operations; and Lloyds Banking Group, as director of operational, credit, and compliance risk. Montana holds a master's degree in business administration from the Wharton School of the University of Pennsylvania and received a bachelor's degree from Boston College. He was an adjunct professor of risk management at Flagler College in St. Augustine, Florida, for seven fall semesters (2013–19) and received the Risk Management Association's Special Service Award in October 2012, the same year he joined FIS. He has also published four articles in the *RMA Journal*.

ANTHONY SHAPELLA is Head of Analytics for AIG's Global Cyber Insurance business. Previously, he served as chief risk officer for AIG's Liability and Financial Lines Insurance businesses, which account for over $5 billion of annual premium. Shapella joined AIG from Towers Watson, where he helped companies design, implement, and improve Enterprise Risk Management frameworks and practices. He has a master's degree in strategic management from the Fox School of Business at Temple University and a bachelor's degree in business administration and finance from Mount St. Mary's University.

RICHARD SPEARMAN is Corporate Security Director for Vodafone Group. He joined Vodafone in 2015 after twenty-five years in the United Kingdom's Foreign and Commonwealth Office, including postings to Istanbul, Paris, and Washington. Prior to this, he had worked for five years for Save the Children Fund UK with postings to Pakistan and the Gambia.

KIERSTEN E. TODT is Chief of Staff at the Cybersecurity and Infrastructure Security Agency (CISA), responsible for the planning, allocation of resources, and development of long-range objectives in support of the department's goals and milestones, ensuring that the CISA's director is prepared to interdict or respond to threats to the homeland. In addition to holding a number of high-level positions in the private sector and in the federal government, Todt cofounded and served as managing director of the Cyber Readiness Institute (CRI), a nonprofit initiative that convenes senior executives of global companies to develop free cybersecurity tools and resources for small businesses, worldwide. She was a member of the team supporting the National Institute of Standards and Technology (NIST) in the development of the Voluntary Cybersecurity Framework called for in President Obama's 2013 Executive Order 13636 on cybersecurity and in 2016 served as executive director of President Obama's independent, bipartisan Commission on Enhancing National Cybersecurity. She graduated from Princeton University with a degree in public policy from the School of Public and International Affairs and a certificate in African-American Studies and holds a master's degree in public policy and a certificate in negotiation and conflict resolution from the John F. Kennedy School of Government at Harvard University. Todt's commentary on cybersecurity, homeland security, and sport security issues has been featured in national television and print media outlets.

J. R. WILLIAMSON is Senior Vice President and Chief Information Security Officer for Leidos. Previously, he held positions at Northrop Grumman, serving as the corporate CIO, deputy chief information security officer, chief engineer, chief technologist, director of the Enterprise OneNGC Program Office, and executive director of IT Infrastructure and Enterprise Services Operations. Before joining Northrop Grumman, Williamson served a four-year stint as a civilian working for Headquarters, US Marine Corps in the Special Services unit. He holds a bachelor's degree in decision sciences and information management from George Mason University and a master's degree in information systems from Virginia Tech.

CARTER (YINGZHOU) ZHENG is a research assistant at Internet Security Alliance. He has a master's degree in global security from the New York University Center for Global Affairs.